This Hallowed Ground: Guides to Civil War Battlefields

SERIES EDITORS

Brooks D. Simpson
Arizona State University

Mark Grimsley
The Ohio State University

Steven E. Woodworth
Texas Christian University

WILSON'S CREEK, PEA RIDGE, AND PRAIRIE GROVE

A BATTLEFIELD GUIDE, WITH A SECTION ON WIRE ROAD

EARL J. HESS, RICHARD W. HATCHER III,
WILLIAM GARRETT PISTON, AND WILLIAM L. SHEA

Cartography by Christopher L. Brest

•

University of Nebraska Press

Lincoln and London

Library of Congress Cataloging-in-Publication Data
Wilson's Creek, Pea Ridge, and Prairie Grove : a battlefield guide,
with a section on Wire Road / Earl J. Hess . . . [et. al.] ;
cartography by Christopher L. Brest
    p.   cm. – (This hallowed ground)
Includes bibliographical references.
ISBN-13: 978-0-8032-7366-5 (pbk. : alk. paper)
ISBN-10: 0-8032-7366-5 (pbk. : alk. paper)
1. Wilson's Creek National Battlefield (Mo.)—Guidebooks.
2. Wilson's Creek, Battle of, Mo., 1861.
3. Pea Ridge National Military Park (Ark.)—Guidebooks.
4. Pea Ridge, Battle of, Ark., 1862.
5. Prairie Grove, Battle of, Ark., 1862.
6. Missouri—History—Civil War, 1861–1865—Battlefields—Guidebooks.
7. Arkansas—History—Civil War, 861–1865—Battlefields—Guidebooks.
8. United States—History—Civil War, 1861–1865—Battlefields—Guidebooks.
9. Battlefields—United States—Guidebooks.
I. Hess, Earl J.   II. Brest, Christopher Lawrence, 1950–   III. Series
E472.23W58   2006   973.7'309767—dc22   2006014327

Contents

Acknowledgments

We wish to thank Dr. Tom and Karen
Sweeney, proprietors of General
Sweeny's Museum in Republic,
Missouri, for permission to use
photographs from the museum's collection, as well as the dedicated, hard-
working staff of the Wilson's Creek
National Battlefield for many favors
large and small.

Thanks also to the late Douglas
Keller and Robert L. Still of the Pea
Ridge National Military Park, and
our appreciation to the editors of the
series, *This Hallowed Ground: Guides to
Civil War Battlefields.*

An affair of outposts. BLCW 1:126

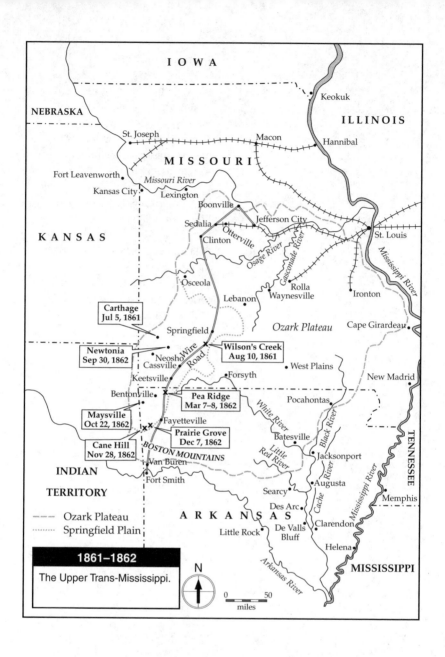

IOWA

Keokuk

NEBRASKA

ILLINOIS

St. Joseph · Macon · Hannibal

MISSOURI

Fort Leavenworth · *Missouri River*

Kansas City · Lexington

Boonville

KANSAS

Sedalia · Jefferson City · St. Louis

Clinton · Otterville

Osage River · *Gasconade River* · *Mississippi River*

Osceola

Rolla · Ironton

Lebanon · Waynesville

**Carthage
Jul 5, 1861**

Springfield · *Ozark Plateau* · Cape Girardeau

**Newtonia
Sep 30, 1862**

Neosho · Cassville · *Wire Road* · **Wilson's Creek
Aug 10, 1861**

Keetsville · Forsyth · West Plains

New Madrid

Bentonville · **Pea Ridge
Mar 7–8, 1862**

Pocahontas

White River

**Maysville
Oct 22, 1862**

Fayetteville · **Prairie Grove
Dec 7, 1862**

Batesville

Black River

TENNESSEE

**Cane Hill
Nov 28, 1862**

BOSTON MOUNTAINS · *Little Red River*

Jacksonport

Van Buren

Fort Smith

INDIAN

TERRITORY

Searcy · Augusta

Cache River · *Mississippi River*

Des Arc

Memphis

– – – Ozark Plateau

ARKANSAS

········· Springfield Plain

Little Rock · De Valls Bluff · Clarendon

Helena

1861–1862

The Upper Trans-Mississippi.

MISSISSIPPI

Arkansas River

N

0   50
miles

Introduction

The battles of Wilson's Creek, Pea Ridge, and Prairie Grove were three of the most significant engagements of the Civil War west of the Mississippi River. They influenced the course of the first half of the war in that region and helped shape Union military efforts to control the Trans-Mississippi while significantly contributing to Confederate defeat. It was essential that the Federals dominate Missouri and northern Arkansas in order to support their major effort to control the Mississippi Valley. While the Yankees never completely defeated Rebel forces in Missouri and Arkansas, they were able to deny the Confederates an opportunity to dominate this vital region and use its resources for the Southern war effort. The campaigns that led to Wilson's Creek and Pea Ridge progressively drove Confederate forces out of Missouri during the first year of the war, and the Prairie Grove campaign kept them in central Arkansas during the middle part of the conflict. Although these campaigns garnered less attention in the public mind than more-famous battles in the East, they were absolutely vital in maintaining the relentless Union pressure in the western theater that resulted in spectacular victories such as Maj. Gen. Ulysses S. Grant's capture of Vicksburg in July 1863.

Two of the three battlefields covered by this book are protected by the U.S. National Park Service. Pea Ridge National Military Park encompasses nearly all the land that saw any action, while Wilson's Creek National Battlefield encloses about 70 percent of the contested ground. This is far more than is typical for the larger engagements east of the Mississippi River. While the same has not been true of the Prairie Grove battlefield, dedicated park personnel and local supporters are protecting more acres every year. As a result, Prairie Grove Battlefield State Park will not only preserve more historic ground over time but also present a more complete vision of the battle to visitors.

There are no major tour guides in print for any of the three battlefields except for those published in *Blue and Gray*, a magazine providing self-guided tours for a variety of Civil War sites. This book is an effort to provide much more than is possible in a magazine article. It will offer the reader a complete guide to the ground, information to understand the larger strategic and grand tactical background of the military action, and vignettes to appreciate the personal experience of participants. The format is generally that provided by the other books in this successful series, *This Hallowed Ground:*

Guides to Civil War Battlefields. We have altered that format a bit to include driving tours for the sites associated with the campaigns that led up to Pea Ridge and Prairie Grove so the reader may understand how the road system and topography of the Trans-Mississippi affected Civil War campaigning. Also, Wire Road itself, which made these campaigns possible, is treated with a driving tour that traverses 150 miles of Ozark terrain.

The authors have collaborated by writing sections of this guide that match their special knowledge of these three related battles. William Garrett Piston and Richard W. Hatcher III wrote the tour of Wilson's Creek, Earl J. Hess the tour of Pea Ridge, and William L. Shea the tour of Prairie Grove. Hess also wrote the guide to Wire Road, with help from his colleagues—Piston contributed the segment from Springfield to Madry, Missouri (and test drove the entire route), while Shea revised the section dealing with the area from Dripping Springs to Van Buren, Arkansas.

More than just a tour guide, this book also provides minihistories of Wilson's Creek, Pea Ridge, and Prairie Grove. With coverage of the associated campaigns, it also provides a history of Civil War operations in the Ozark region of southwestern Missouri and northwestern Arkansas during the first eighteen months of the war. This area was the center of conflict in the upper Trans Mississippi during 1861 and 1862 and witnessed events that not only changed the region but also affected the entire course of the Civil War.

How to Use This Guide

This book is somewhat unusual for the series in that it provides touring information for your visits to not one but three significant battlefields. The guide format, however, is the same for all three.

The sections devoted to each battle begin with an overview setting out the history of the campaign and battle, including an analysis of their significance, so that you have a solid introduction to the context of the action before you begin your visit. Each battlefield tour is then divided into logical sections that coordinate the flow of combat with the route you will take. Optional excursions take you on side trips of interest.

Two unique aspects of this guide are worthy of note. First, in addition to taking you on a detailed tour of each battlefield, it also provides you with wide-ranging driving tours of sites associated with the Pea Ridge and Prairie Grove campaigns. Both of these operations involved troops marching long distances to reach the battleground, and there are many interesting sites within an easy drive of the respective battlefield park that help explain the campaign. It was not possible to do this with the Wilson's Creek campaign because the Federals marched only a short distance outside Springfield to attack the Southerners, who had been settled in their encampments for some time.

The other distinctive feature of this guide is the tour of Wire Road. Battlefields were like the tip of a spear, the dangerous ground where the results of long marches across hundreds of miles of countryside were decided. But across what kind of landscape did the armies have to move? And for the visitor, how does the modern road system correlate to the Civil War–era network? The Wire Road tour helps answer these questions by taking you across 150 miles of the Ozark landscape of southwestern Missouri and northwestern Arkansas. The battlefield tours examine a constricted landscape, whereas the road tour covers a vast, expansive landscape involving climate, transportation arteries, and sprawling terrain features.

Throughout this guide to three battles, two campaigns, and one road, some of the main stops are divided into two or more substops. Substops seldom ask you to do much additional walking. They are simply designed to develop the action at each point in a clear, organized fashion. In the guidebook, each stop has a section of text "married" to a map. This technique enables you to visualize the troop dispositions and movements at each stop without having to flip around the guide looking for maps.

The stops and substops follow a standard format: **Directions, Orientation, What Happened, Analysis, and/or Vignette.**

The **Directions** tell you how to get from one stop to the next (and sometimes from one substop to another). They not only give you driving instructions but also ask you, once you have reached a given stop, to walk to a precise spot on the battlefield. When driving, keep an eye on your odometer; many distances are given to the nearest tenth of a mile. Important note: The directions often suggest points of interest en route from one stop to another. We have found that it works best to give the directions to a given stop first and then mention the points of interest. These are always introduced by the words *en route.*

Orientation. Once you have reached a stop, this section describes the area around you so that you can quickly pick out the key terrain and get your bearings.

Often these descriptions use the following directions relative to your facing:

straight ahead

left front   *right front*

left   *right*

left rear   *right rear*

behind/directly to the rear

Often, after the relative directions (left, right, etc.), we add the compass directions (north, south, etc.) in parentheses. The maps can also help you get your bearings.

What Happened. This is the heart of each stop. It explains the action succinctly without becoming simplistic, and whenever possible it also explains how the terrain affected the fighting.

Many stops have a section called **Analysis,** which explains why a particular decision was made, why a given attack met with success or failure, and so on. The purpose is to give you additional insight into the battle.

Others have a section called **Vignette,** whose purpose is to enhance your emotional understanding of the battle by offering a short eyewitness account or a particularly vivid anecdote.

A few conventions are used in the guidebook to keep confusion to a minimum. We have tried not to burden the text with a proliferation of names and unit designations. These are used as sparingly as a solid understanding of the battle permits. Names of Confederate leaders and field units are in italics. The full name and rank of each individual is usually given only the first time he is mentioned in a tour; the Order of Battle in the back of the book can remind you of each man's level of command when needed.

It is important to drive safely, take your time, get out of your car, and think about the place where you stand and the moment you inhabit. Then think about the moment those thousands of Union and Confederate soldiers inhabited in 1861 or 1862. Understand their emotions, and let yourself be swept along with the tide of history for a while. These battlefields are among the most precious cultural artifacts of our society, and the United States is comparatively blessed with well-protected sites associated with our past wars. It is important that we appreciate this blessing, understand the significance of this hallowed ground—and have fun as well.

Earl J. Hess

Mark Grimsley,
Brooks D. Simpson, &
Steven E. Woodworth
SERIES EDITORS

On the skirmish line. BLCW 3:31

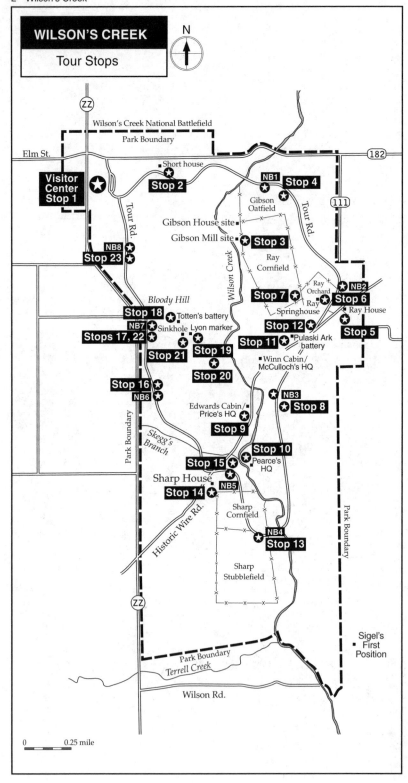

WILSON'S CREEK
Tour Stops

N

Wilson's Creek National Battlefield
Park Boundary

Elm St.

ZZ

182

111

Visitor Center Stop 1

Short house

Stop 2

NB1 Stop 4

Gibson Oatfield

Tour Rd.

Tour Rd.

Gibson House site

Gibson Mill site

Stop 3

Ray Cornfield

NB8 Stop 23

Wilson Creek

Ray Orchard

Stop 7

NB2 Stop 6

Ray Springhouse

Ray House

Bloody Hill

Stop 18

Totten's battery

Stop 12

Stop 5

NB7 Sinkhole Lyon marker

Stops 17, 22

Stop 11

Pulaski Ark battery

Stop 21

Stop 19

Winn Cabin/ McCulloch's HQ

Stop 20

Stop 16

NB6

NB3 Stop 8

Edwards Cabin/ Price's HQ

Skegg's Branch

Stop 9

Park Boundary

Stop 10

Stop 15

Pearce's HQ

Sharp House

Park Boundary

Stop 14

NB5

Historic Wire Rd.

Sharp Cornfield

NB4 Stop 13

ZZ

Sharp Stubblefield

Sigel's First Position

Park Boundary

Terrell Creek

Wilson Rd.

0   0.25 mile

Overview

The battle of Wilson's Creek on August 10, 1861, was the culmination of a campaign that started the previous June, though its roots stretched back to "Bleeding Kansas," the struggle that began in 1854 to determine whether Missouri's western neighbor would be a free or slave state. Six years of intermittent violence along the border preceded the fateful presidential election of 1860. Most Missourians hoped to avoid a secession crisis. Their state was western by its geographic location but largely Southern in heritage. A small planter class exported slave-produced hemp and tobacco down the Missouri and Mississippi rivers. Yet a tremendous influx of immigrants (mostly Germans, who settled in and around St. Louis), and a growing railway system that connected the state via Illinois to the North's free-labor economy, pointed toward a different future. Stephen Douglas, the compromise Northern Democrat, won Missouri's electoral vote in 1860. Although seven Southern states left the Union to form the Confederacy by February 1861, Missouri delegates meeting in convention the following March rejected secession.

Although most Missourians desired neutrality, Gov. Claiborne Fox *Jackson* favored the South. When Fort Sumter fell to Confederate attack in April and Pres. Abraham Lincoln called on state governors for 75,000 militia troops to restore the Union, *Jackson* refused to comply. Instead, he allowed several pro-secessionist volunteer militia companies to encamp just outside St. Louis, hoping they could seize the Federal arsenal located in the city. As the governor negotiated secretly with Confederate authorities, many of the militia brazenly displayed Southern flags.

Capt. Nathaniel Lyon, a West Point graduate passionately committed to defending his post, the St. Louis Arsenal, and maintaining the authority of the national government, foiled the governor's plans. With a small force of U.S. Army Regulars and a large contingent of volunteers (mostly German Americans), he seized the initiative by capturing "Camp Jackson," the encampment of the Missouri militia, on May 10. But when Lyon followed this bloodless coup by marching his captives through the city streets, a riot ensued. His troops fired on the crowd, killing or wounding over one hundred civilians, including women and children.

The "Camp Jackson Massacre" polarized Missouri. To defend the state, the previously pro-Union legislature created the Missouri State Guard, a county-based militia divided into nine geographic divisions, each headed by a brigadier general. *Jackson* named Sterling *Price*, a Mexican War hero and former governor, as major general to command the State Guard forces in the field. As Missouri's white male population between the ages of eighteen and forty-five numbered almost 100,000, the military potential of the State Guard was enormous.

Lyon, who had been promoted to brigadier general, realized that time favored the secessionist cause in Missouri. Therefore in mid-June he launched a preemptive campaign that drove the legislature from the state capital, Jefferson City, and quickly secured Missouri's key river and railway communications network. After receiving reinforcements from Kansas, he pushed south and west in three columns, forcing State Guard units to withdraw deep into the Ozarks before they could be properly organized, trained, and equipped. Lyon united his forces at Springfield in late July. Styled the Army of the West, they numbered almost 7,000 men. Lyon longed for a decisive battle to punish those who defied Federal authority. But Maj. Gen. John C. Frémont had different plans. As the newly appointed Union commander for Missouri, he urged Lyon to retire northeast to Rolla, the nearest railhead, where he could be resupplied more easily and be in position to support the primary Federal objective in the West, opening the Mississippi River. Lyon refused. In early August he defiantly marched southwest, hoping to battle the Missouri State Guard before *Price* could receive assistance from the Confederacy.

But *Price* already had help. While some 7,000 state guardsmen rallied at Cowskin Prairie in the extreme southwestern corner of the state, the Missouri general contacted Brig. Gen. Benjamin *McCulloch*, who commanded Confederate forces in northwestern Arkansas. *McCulloch* was a former Texas Ranger and hero of the Mexican War. He and *Price* disliked each other instantly for reasons that have never been clear. *McCulloch* agreed, however, that they faced a common enemy in Lyon. After securing permission from Richmond, he advanced into Missouri, a state that had not passed an ordinance of secession, in July. His force, more than 5,000 strong, consisted of a brigade of Confederate troops under his direct command and a brigade of Arkansas State Troops, militiamen led by Brig. Gen. Nicholas Bartlett *Pearce*. By mutual agreement, *McCulloch* commanded the composite Southern force, called the Western Army, which assembled at Cassville on July 29. Command of *McCulloch's* Confederate brigade passed unofficially to Col. James M. *McIntosh*. Although *McCulloch* was initially enthusiastic about the prospects of defeating Lyon, he was dismayed by the condition of the Missouri State Guard. Only a small portion of the men had uniforms or modern military

arms. Most wore civilian clothing and carried either outdated
muskets from state arsenals or hunting weapons brought
from home. Two thousand Missourians had no arms at all,
and ammunition for those who did was in critically short
supply. As the Western Army moved northeast along Wire
Road, *Price's* lax standards of discipline alarmed *McCulloch*.

On August 2 and 3 the leading elements of the Northern
and Southern forces clashed briefly at Dug Springs. *McCulloch*
believed the Missouri State Guard performed poorly, and he
followed cautiously when Lyon retired toward Springfield on
August 4. The Federals reached Springfield the next day. On
August 6 *McCulloch* halted his pursuit nine miles southwest
of the town, where Wire Road crossed Wilson Creek. (Wilson
Creek was mislabeled "Wilson's Creek" by the soldiers. Here
"Wilson Creek" refers to the stream and "Wilson's Creek" refers to the battle.)

For three days the Texan scouted the approaches to Springfield while *Price* fumed at his passivity. Under pressure from
the Missourian, *McCulloch* ordered a night march on August
9, planning to attack Springfield at dawn. But when rain
showers threatened, he decided to delay the movement until
morning in hopes of better weather. The Western Army had
an average of only twenty-five rounds of ammunition per
man, and many in the Missouri State Guard lacked the car-
tridge boxes they needed to keep their powder dry. When the
soldiers settled down to rest, *McCulloch* failed to repost the
pickets who normally guarded the camp at night. As darkness fell, the valley of Wilson Creek sheltered just over 12,000
soldiers, together with an unknown number of women, children, and slaves who accompanied the Southern army. Some
100 civilians lived on the farms in and around the camp.

From August 6 to August 9, Lyon became increasingly dis-
traught. Frémont refused to send reinforcements, and hundreds of Lyon's volunteers departed daily as their short-term
enlistments expired. In a matter of days he would have only
a few hundred Regulars under his command. Prudence dic-
tated a withdrawal, but Lyon knew the Southerners outnumbered him, particularly in cavalry. He feared that during a
retreat they might slip past him and block his route, forcing
him to fight on ground not of his choosing. Retreat would
also mean abandoning Missouri Unionists, who were numerous in the Springfield vicinity, to possible reprisals. Most of
all he was loath to turn back without hurting his enemies,
whose opposition to the Federal government enraged him to
the point that his objectivity was compromised.

After several conferences with his subordinates, Lyon decided to move out of Springfield on the night of August 9 to

attack the Southerners in their camps at dawn the following day. The plan was to surprise and stun the enemy, giving the Federals time to retreat safely. At nearly the last minute, however, Lyon accepted a proposal from Col. Franz Sigel, commander of the 3rd Missouri Infantry. Sigel was a native of Baden, educated in prestigious German military schools, with combat experience from Germany's revolutions of 1848. He recommended dividing the small Federal army into two columns, one under Lyon's command and one under his own, in order to strike the Southerners simultaneously from two directions. Lyon agreed, apparently believing Sigel's daring plan held the possibility of defeating *McCulloch* decisively. Instead of attacking along Wire Road, where the enemy might be prepared, Lyon decided to move west out of Springfield, then turn due south to strike the northern end of *McCulloch's* camps. Sigel would move south and then west to reach high ground near the southern end of the enemy's position.

Nineteen days earlier at Bull Run, near Manassas Junction, Virginia, a Federal army had suffered an embarrassing defeat. Now the war's second major battle was about to begin. Although both Lyon and *McCulloch* reportedly employed civilian spies, including women, neither was aware of the other's intended movements. Neither had commanded an army in battle, and both men were mentally and physically fatigued by their responsibilities. While the forces they led were hardly mobs, they did lack training and experience. The Federals possessed the advantage of surprise, while Southerners had an almost two-to-one advantage in numbers.

Despite being out of communication and beyond supporting distance of each other, Lyon and Sigel achieved their difficult objective of attacking simultaneously at dawn, catching the Southerners completely off guard. The fortunes of the two Federal columns, however, differed greatly.

Lyon ran into unexpected resistance from the Missouri State Guard on the northern spur and main crest of the broad rise later christened Bloody Hill. This largely negated his advantage from surprise. *Price* was able to get his Missourians out of their camps in the valley of Wilson Creek, defend his position, and seize the initiative, forcing Lyon onto the defensive. The Southern forces launched four assaults, during the second of which Lyon was killed and command of the Federals passed to Maj. Samuel Sturgis. *McCulloch* led elements of his Confederate brigade and *Pearce's* Arkansas State Troops into the fray. A shortage of ammunition combined with inexperience to rob the Southerners of their numerical advantage. With his own ammunition growing short and with no word from Sigel, Sturgis withdrew from the battle-field around noon. The Southerners were too exhausted to pursue.

Sigel's initial attack on the southern end of the enemy's camps was a complete success. Placing his artillery on high ground, his dawn bombardment drove some 1,500 Southerners away in a panic, allowing the Federals to move to a position astride Wire Road. This placed them in the rear of *McCulloch's* army, astride its vulnerable line of communication—a brilliant achievement. Sigel lost the advantages he had gained, however, by poorly positioning his troops, neglecting basic security, and making no attempt to communicate with Lyon. *McCulloch* turned defeat into victory by leading a counterattack that drove Sigel's column from the field in disarray, capturing almost all of its artillery. Because fighting was still in progress at Bloody Hill, *McCulloch* authorized only a minimal pursuit, and the majority of the Federals returned to Springfield without further incident.

In the hours immediately following the battle, both sides believed they had achieved a victory. Despite Sigel's debacle, the Federals who fought under Lyon and Sturgis on Bloody Hill thrice fended off assaults from superior numbers and left the field of their own accord, leaving their enemies too stunned to pursue. While surprised by the initial Federal assaults, the Southerners crushed Sigel's column and they believed that they had forced Lyon's column off Bloody Hill as well. The news of Lyon's death made the victory even sweeter.

After regrouping in Springfield, the Army of the West began its withdrawal from southwestern Missouri on the morning of August 11, leaving all but a handful of its wounded either on the field or in Springfield. It reached Rolla safely on August 19. Although Sturgis and most of the officers who had been in Lyon's column criticized Sigel in letters to the War Department, the Lincoln administration needed ethnic heroes. Sigel was promoted to major general and fought again during the Pea Ridge campaign.

The Western Army entered Springfield later in the day on August 11. *Price* argued for an advance to the Missouri River, for the slaveholding population there were the strongest supporters of secession. *McCulloch* demurred. He believed *Price* could recruit soldiers in the wake of their victory, but sustaining them would be another matter. Besides, Missouri had not left the Union. Caution seemed the wisest course, so within days *McCulloch's* Confederates and *Pearce's* Arkansas State Troops returned south of the Missouri border.

McCulloch proved to be an accurate prophet. *Price* advanced to Lexington and captured a Federal garrison there on September 20 following a substantial battle. Within days recruits swelled the Missouri State Guard to more than 20,000 men. Many lacked weapons, however, and *Price* had no logistical system of any kind. When the Federals advanced from their secure base in St. Louis, *Price* retreated, and his army shrank with every mile he moved south. He was back in the southwestern corner of the state, with only 8,000 men, by October. There was one bright spot for the Southern cause as fall moved toward its close. In October a rump session of the state legislature, meeting in Neosho, passed an ordinance of secession. The Confederate Congress admitted the state the following month, and for the remainder of the war, Confederate flags bore a star for Missouri. The state's ultimate status, Union or Confederate, was not determined until the following March, some 100 miles south of Wilson Creek at a place where Wire Road climbed up to the Pea Ridge plateau and ran past a roadside inn called Elkhorn Tavern. Both *McCulloch* and *Price* would be there.

Brigadier-General Nathaniel Lyon.
From a photograph. BLCW 3:31

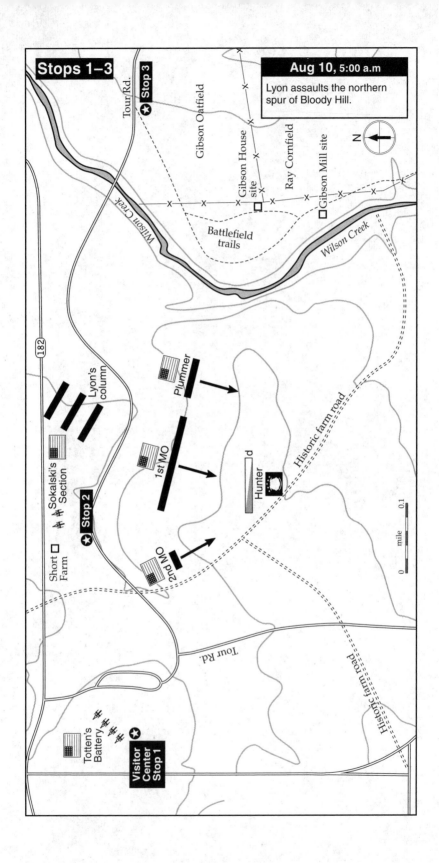

Stops 1–3

Aug 10, 5:00 a.m

Lyon assaults the northern spur of Bloody Hill.

N

Tour Rd.

Stop 3

Gibson Oatfield

Gibson House site

Ray Cornfield

Gibson Mill site

Battlefield trails

Wilson Creek

Wilson Creek

182

Lyon's column

Sokalski's Section

Short Farm

Stop 2

Plummer

1st MO

2nd MO

Hunter

Historic farm road

Tour Rd.

Historic farm road

Totten's Battery

Visitor Center Stop 1

0   mile   0.1

STOP 1   Visitor Center

The Visitor Center provides an excellent introduction to the battlefield. Begin at the auditorium, where a brief film summarizes the complex political events leading up to the battle, outlines the course of the fighting, and discusses its consequences for the Civil War in Missouri. Next, view the electronic map adjacent to the auditorium, where a program of colored lights demonstrates the battle's major troop movements. The electronic map is particularly important for its depiction of the ground cover that existed on the battlefield in 1861. Several features of the electronic map merit close attention: the breadth of Bloody Hill and the distance Lyon had to cover from his entrance on the battlefield to its crest; the Ray House and Ray Cornfield; the *Pulaski Battery* position; and Sigel's final position at the Sharp farm.

The Visitor Center features a rotating series of displays concerning various aspects of the battle and an excellent bookstore. It also houses the John K. Hulston Library, the largest collection of Civil War books in the National Park Service and an invaluable resource in studying the war in the Trans-Mississippi. The library is open to everyone, though material may not be checked out. Be sure to utilize the facilities in the Visitor Center before you begin your tour, for neither water nor restrooms are available elsewhere.

At the conclusion of your tour, visit General Sweeny's Museum, recently acquired by the National Park Service. It is located opposite the entrance to the Wilson's Creek National Battlefield, just across FARM ROAD 182, with a parking lot off of County Road ZZ. The entrance fee to the park covers admission to the museum. General Sweeny's houses the nation's largest collection of artifacts, photographs, and documents relating to the Civil War in the Trans-Mississippi.

As you leave the Visitor Center, *turn right* and face south. The Visitor Center sits on the high ground where four guns of Capt. James Totten's Company F, 2nd U.S. Artillery were positioned to support Lyon's assault on the northern spur of Bloody Hill. These events are discussed at Stop 2.

The National Park Service (NB) TOUR ROAD circles clockwise, with eight marked stops that provide interpretation of the battle. Additional interpretative sites are accessible via a series of interior trails, open only to persons walking or riding horseback.

This guide uses an independent numbering system for recommended stops but includes references to the battlefield tour stops in parentheses. For example, "Stop 3. Gibson Mill (NB1)," is the third stop in this guide but the first stop on the battlefield TOUR ROAD. Also, please note that several of the battlefield tour stops will encompass multiple stops mentioned in this guide. For example, Stops 5, 6, and 7 are all located at (NB2).

Because the TOUR ROAD does not allow the visitor to view the battle sites in chronological order, and because some important events occurred simultaneously, it is helpful to think of the battle in terms of several distinct phases.

Phase One occurred when Lyon and Sigel, commanding separate columns of the Army of the West, attacked the northern and southern ends of the camps occupied by McCulloch's Western Army. Lyon's entry onto the field at the E. B. Short farm and his assault of the unnamed northern spur of Bloody Hill are interpreted at Stops 2, 3, and 22. Sigel's simultaneous, successful bombardment of the Southern cavalry at the Joseph Sharp farm is discussed at Stop 13.

Phase Two occurred when Lyon pushed on to the top of the main portion of Bloody Hill and Sigel reached Sharp Farm, taking a position across Wire Road. Visitors view the crest of Bloody Hill at Stop 17. Sigel's movements and final position are interpreted at Stop 14.

Phase Three involved Lyon's attempt to protect his left flank by sending Joseph Plummer across Wilson Creek toward Wire Road. Plummer was defeated and retreated back to Bloody Hill, leaving McCulloch free to concentrate on other threats. Interpretation of these events occurs at Stops 3–7.

Phase Four concerned the actions of McCulloch and Price to save the Western Army. Price brought the Missouri State Guard out of its camps to face Lyon on Bloody Hill. After taking actions to deal with Plummer, McCulloch used his own Confederate brigade and Pearce's Arkansas State Troops to secure his position. He also took steps to meet Sigel's threat to the south. These events concern Stops 8–12.

Phase Five occurred when McCulloch drove Sigel from his position at the Sharp Farm. This is interpreted at Stop 15.

Phase Six involved the fight for Bloody Hill, Lyon's death, and the Union withdrawal. Price initially faced Lyon alone, but over time men from both McCulloch's and Pearce's brigades joined the struggle. The Southerners made three major assaults up Bloody Hill, all of which ended in failure. These are discussed at Stops 16–21.

The final phase occurred when the Federals, now commanded by Sturgis, withdrew from the field. This is interpreted at Stop 22.

STOP 2   Elias B. Short Farm, 4:45–5:30 A.M.

Directions   *Pass through* the gate that marks the beginning of the TOUR
                            ROAD, *proceed* 0.1 mile, and *halt.*

Orientation   The Elias B. Short farm sat on the high ground to your left.
                            The northern spur of Bloody Hill is to your right.

What Happened   (The events interpreted here relate to Phase One of the bat-
                            tle.) Lyon's column left Springfield around 6:00 P.M. on the
                            evening of August 9. It consisted of 4,300 men (3,800 infan-
                            try, 350 mounted men, and 150 cannoneers with ten guns)
                            organized into three brigades under Maj. Samuel Sturgis, Lt.
                            Col. George L. Andrews, and Col. George W. Deitzler (see "Or-
                            der of Battle"). Instead of using Wire Road, which the enemy
                            might anticipate, Lyon marched due west from Springfield
                            along farm roads for several miles, then turned south, mov-
                            ing cross country to strike the northern end of *McCulloch's*
                            camps. Shortly after midnight the Union forces rested about
                            two miles northeast of the Short farm. Although the Federals
                            heard thunder, they were not rained upon.

                            Lyon resumed the march around 4:00 A.M. After encoun-
                            tering and brushing aside a group of Southerners presumed
                            to be pickets, he formed his leading units into line of battle
                            and pushed on cautiously. As the Federals entered the Short
                            farm around 4:45 A.M., they noticed a Southern unit on the
                            sparsely wooded ridge to their front—the northern spur of
                            Bloody Hill. Col. DeWitt C. *Hunter* led these men, 300 strong.
                            Col. James *Cawthorn* had dispatched them to investigate a
                            report that enemy troops were approaching. The alarm had
                            come from the men Lyon first encountered, who were not
                            pickets but unauthorized foragers.

                            The Battle of Wilson's Creek began when *Hunter* dismounted
                            his men to resist Lyon's advance (see "Order of Battle" for the
                            organization of the Missouri State Guard). In response Lyon
                            sent four guns from Totten's Battery to high ground west of
                            the Short farmhouse to provide supporting fire (their posi-
                            tion was near the Visitor Center). The two remaining guns
                            opened fire from the farmyard itself, while the 1st Missouri,
                            2nd Missouri, and Plummer's battalion of Regulars pushed
                            forward. The remainder of Lyon's force waited in column. It
                            was dawn, a few minutes before 5:00 A.M., when the crash
                            of artillery broke the morning silence. The Federals took no
                            more than thirty minutes to drive *Hunter* from the northern
                            spur, but this gave *Cawthorn* time to get the remainder of his
                            men out of their camps and into line facing north on the

main crest of Bloody Hill. It is likely that fewer than a dozen men were killed or wounded in this phase of the battle.

Analysis

Lyon timed his approach to begin at dawn, simultaneous with Sigel's attack on the southern end of *McCulloch's* camps. He could not communicate with Sigel, however, and needed to move as quickly as possible across Bloody Hill so that his small force could disrupt the numerically superior Southerners in their camps along Wilson Creek. *Cawthorn's* actions negated much of the Federal advantage from surprise and compensated for the Southerners' failure to post pickets. By dispatching *Hunter* and moving the rest of his horsemen to the main portion of Bloody Hill, *Cawthorn* bought time. He apparently acted on his own initiative without waiting for orders from his superior, Brig. Gen. James S. *Rains*. At some point (when is unclear) *Rains* sent word to *McCulloch* that enemy activity had been spotted near the Short farm.

Vignette

The Short farmhouse was a small white structure with green shutters. Elias B. Short and his wife, Rebecca, had six children, boys and girls ranging in age from four to sixteen. A Union sympathizer, Elias had moved most of his horses and cattle to a safe location when the Western Army arrived in the vicinity on August 6. The Southerners posted guards to protect the Short property, which included fifty beehives. These guards were withdrawn on August 9 in anticipation of the Southern attack on Springfield slated for the next day. The Shorts were eating breakfast when the head of Lyon's column reached their backyard. Nine-year-old John Short was as partisan as his father. Years later he recalled his thrill at the sight of General Lyon riding past on a dapple-gray horse. The Union commander was not ordinarily an imposing figure. He stood only five feet, five inches tall, with sandy red hair and a frizzled beard. Despite Lyon's recent promotion to brigadier general, on the day of the battle he dressed in his worn prewar captain's coat and sported a plain white felt hat. Yet his blue-gray eyes could flash with a determination equal to none. Seeing Lyon, John Short realized that a battle was imminent, and he felt confident that *McCulloch's* men "would be wiped off the earth." [1]

STOP 3   Gibson Mill, 5:30–6:30 A.M. (NB1)

Directions   *Proceed* along the TOUR ROAD. At a bridge 0.6 mile from the Visitor Center, the road crosses an unnamed tributary of Wilson Creek. Note the low valley of this stream off to your left. Lyon's column approached by marching south parallel to the stream (toward you), turning west (back the way you came) to reach the Short farm at about 5:00 A.M. As you *continue* on the TOUR ROAD and *cross* the bridge over Wilson Creek, you can see along its banks traces of the millrace built in conjunction with the Gibson Mill. After 0.2 mile beyond the bridge, *turn right* into the parking lot for the Gibson Mill. From there *walk* 0.4 mile along the trail to a sign marking the mill site.

From the Gibson Mill site you may also *walk south* along the interior access trail, which terminates at Wire Road near the *Pulaski Light Battery* position (Stop 12).

Orientation   As you stand facing Wilson Creek, you are at the location of John Gibson's mill; nothing of the structure remains. Directly across the creek is the northern spur of Bloody Hill. About 0.1 mile downstream (to your left), a farm road crossed the creek at a ford. On the west bank (across the creek from you), this road ran into a ravine between the northern spur and main portion of Bloody Hill. Curving north, it ran over the northern spur to the Short farm.

Rains, commanding the *Eighth Division* of the Missouri State Guard, made his headquarters at the Gibson Mill. Although the division's infantry and artillery were camped over a mile to the south, most of its 1,210 horsemen, combined under *Cawthorn*, were camped across the creek in the ravine. Like the rest of the Western Army, these men had prepared to march on Springfield during the night of August 9. When rain caused *McCulloch* to order a delay until the following morning, they slept undisturbed, without posting pickets.

Leaving the creek, the trail loops back to the parking lot and past the ruins of the foundation of the Gibson home. In 1861 most of the eighty fenced acres surrounding it were sewn in oats, which had been harvested prior to the battle.

What Happened   (The events interpreted here relate to Phase Three of the battle.) Once Lyon reached the crest of the northern spur of Bloody Hill, he had a clear view of Wire Road and the Ray farm across Wilson Creek to the southeast. Due south, in the direction he intended to advance, he could see *Cawthorn's* camp in the ravine and Southern horsemen rushing to defend the main portion of Bloody Hill. The hill itself was covered in waist-high prairie grass and dotted with scrub oaks and occasional thickets. Because the hill was broad and undulating, Lyon could not see the Southern camps near Wire Road's ford of Wilson Creek. Trusting that Sigel's attack on the far end of the enemy's position had occurred at dawn as planned, he decided to push forward immediately to the main crest of Bloody Hill. In order to protect his left flank, he detached a force under Capt. Joseph Plummer to cross Wilson Creek and take a position astride Wire Road near the Ray House (Stop 5). Plummer commanded a battalion of 300 men who had been recruited for the Regular Army but were not yet assigned to any unit. He took these infantrymen, and about 300 mounted Home Guards from Springfield, back down the northern spur and across Wilson Creek just north of Gibson Mill. This took them through heavily wooded terrain and into deep water, for Gibson had dammed the creek to ensure an adequate flow for his mill. Plummer's men had quite a struggle before they emerged into Gibson's oat field and turned south, crossing the fences into the northern end of the Ray Cornfield. The ground rose as they proceeded south. Sewn broadcast rather than in rows, the moderately high corn did not block their view. As the Federals reached the center of the field, Plummer observed an enemy battery to their front, firing obliquely upon Lyon's troops on Bloody Hill. To meet this threat Plummer continued moving due south rather than angling southeast to secure Wire Road at the Ray House as originally planned.

Analysis

Lyon's decision to order Plummer across Wilson Creek amid the rugged terrain north of Gibson Mill rather than south of it, where there was a ford, had significant consequences. The captain's unavoidable delay gave *McCulloch* time to respond (see Stops 5 and 7). Yet Lyon's decision was rational. He knew the Federals would be under fire as they moved down through the ravine and up the slopes of the main portion of Bloody Hill. Ignorant of the terrain Plumber would encounter, he probably assumed it would be safer and almost as quick for Plummer to cross above the mill rather than downstream at the ford.

Vignette

John Gibson and his wife, Martha, were in their fifties at the time of the battle. Twenty-two-year-old Nancy Gibson was the only one of their seven children still living with them. In addition to the mill and oat field, Gibson owned several horses and a number of cattle, bringing the total value of his holding to $3,000—a substantial sum in those days. His resources, and those of the other civilians living within a five-mile radius of his mill, were fully exploited by the Western Army camped along Wilson Creek. *McCulloch's* men and horses consumed more than 96,000 pounds of food and fodder daily. Although the mill was not damaged during the battle, Gibson's livestock and stored grain were probably requisitioned without compensation. His neighbors suffered equally.

Major-General Benjamin McCulloch, C.S.A., killed in the Battle of Pea Ridge, March 7, 1862. From a photograph. BLCW 1:300

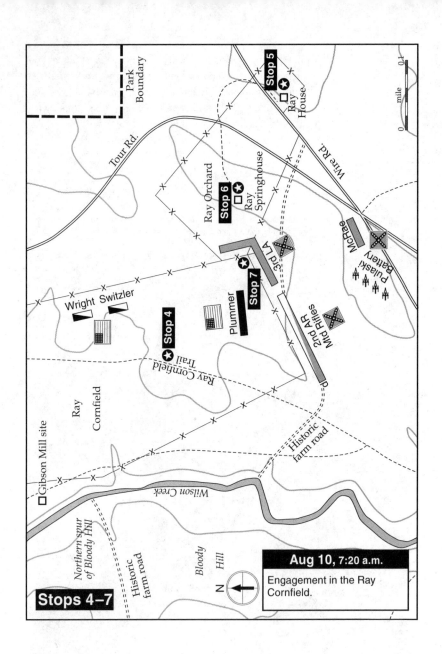

Aug 10, 7:20 a.m.

Engagement in the Ray Cornfield.

Stops 4–7

Stop 5

Ray House

Stop 6

Ray Orchard

Ray Springhouse

Wire Rd.

McRae

Pulaski Battery

3rd LA

Stop 7

Plummer

Wright   Switzler

Stop 4

Ray Cornfield Trail

2nd AR Mtd Rifles

Tour Rd.

Park Boundary

Gibson Mill site

Ray Cornfield

Historic farm road

Wilson Creek

Northern spur of Bloody Hill

Historic farm road

Bloody Hill

N

0   mile   0.1

STOP 4   Ray Cornfield Trail, North Access

Directions   *Proceed* 0.1 mile along the TOUR ROAD to the interior access
                             trail that crosses the road at this point. To the left (north) the
                             trail leads 0.05 mile to the Edgar Cemetery, a post Civil War
                             graveyard not connected with the battle. To the right (south)
                             the trail leads through the Ray Cornfield. To view the area
                             of the cornfield fight, *proceed* south along the trail approxi-
                             mately 0.4 mile, *halting* just after crossing a small ravine. Af-
                             ter viewing this area you may *continue* along the trail, which
                             leads to Wire Road near its ford of Wilson Creek, or *return* to
                             the Gibson Mill site and follow the road to Stop 5.

Orientation   As you face right (west) from the trail, you can view the main
                             body of Bloody Hill as well as its northern spur. In 1861 none
                             of this terrain was heavily forested (as it currently is). If you
                             turn back to face down the trail and look to your front left,
                             you will see the ground Plummer crossed, moving away from
                             you, as he marched toward the Ray House.

What Happened   The fight in the Ray Cornfield is covered at Stop 7.

Capt. Reuben Kay, Slack's 4th
Division, Missouri State Guard,
wounded at Wilson's Creek.
Courtesy National Park Service,
Wilson's Creek National Battlefield.

Sgt. George W. Hutt,
1st Kansas Infantry.
Courtesy National Park
Service, Wilson's Creek
National Battlefield

STOP 5   Ray House, 7:00 A.M. (NB2)

Directions   *Proceed* from the Gibson Mill site 0.6 mile along the TOUR
                      ROAD to the parking lot of the Ray House. A pathway leads to
                      the house itself.

Orientation   The Ray House, home to John and Roxanna Ray, is the only
                      original structure extant on the battlefield. Restored to its
                      1861 appearance, it is open for visitation only on a limited
                      schedule. The Ray holdings included a barn and chicken
                      coop, both located near the house. Standing with your back
                      to the front porch, you will see Wire Road immediately in
                      front of the house. Also known as the Telegraph Road from
                      the lines erected along its length in 1860, it linked Jefferson
                      City, Missouri, via Springfield, with Fayetteville, Arkansas.
                      Across Wire Road (and the TOUR ROAD), the ground slopes
                      steeply into a ravine, at the bottom of which is the Ray
                      Springhouse (Stop 6). The area around it was planted as an
                      orchard. A split-rail fence on the high ground beyond the ra-
                      vine delineates its limits. Just beyond the fence, out of sight,
                      is the southern end of the Ray Cornfield (Stop 7). The ridge
                      on the horizon is the northern spur of Bloody Hill. To your
                      left, out of sight, Wire Road leads past the *Pulaski Light Battery*
                      (Stop 12), *McCulloch's* headquarters (Stop 11), and the Edwards
                      Cabin (Stop 9).

What Happened   (Events interpreted here relate to Phase Three of the battle.)
                      According to family tradition, John Ray sat on his front porch
                      throughout the morning of August 10, observing the fighting
                      and its consequences. The troop movements Ray witnessed
                      began elsewhere. When *McCulloch* learned that the Western
                      Army was under attack and that Plummer had crossed Wil-
                      son Creek, entering the Ray Cornfield, he moved to protect
                      the Western Army's right flank. Turning to his own brigade
                      of Confederates, *McCulloch* ordered Col. James M. *McIntosh* to
                      take his own unit, the *2nd Arkansas Mounted Rifles*, Col. Louis
                      Hébert's 3rd Louisiana Infantry, and Col. Dandridge *McRae's*
                      undesignated battalion of Arkansas infantry up Wire Road
                      to meet the threat (see "Order of Battle" for the Western
                      Army). As they passed the *Pulaski Light Battery*, *McIntosh* de-
                      tached *McRae's* battalion to support the artillerists. *McIntosh*,
                      therefore, had some 900 men when his column came into
                      John Ray's view sometime after 7:00 A.M. As the Southern-
                      ers neared the house, they turned north, following a farm
                      road that ran past the Ray Springhouse. Ray could not see
                      the details of the fight amid his corn, but after about an hour
                      he saw many of the men *McIntosh* had led forward retreating

in great haste. Shells from Federal artillery atop Bloody Hill began exploding only yards from his home after a portion of the *3rd Louisiana* halted to rally behind it. None struck the house, but one did damage the adjacent chicken coop. After Southern doctors raised a yellow flag to indicate that they were using the house as a hospital, the shelling ceased.

Analysis

The Ray House was the most important of several medical facilities established during and after the battle. Although individual regiments had attached surgeons, neither army at Wilson's Creek had a medical director or any centralized plan to treat casualties. Left to improvise, the physicians on the field performed heroically. By best estimate the battle produced 1,818 casualties: 873 from Lyon's Army of the West and 945 from *McCulloch's* Western Army. The Federals collected their wounded in *Cawthorn's* old camp in the ravine between the main portion of Bloody Hill and its northern spur. Because they brought only two ambulances, they evacuated only a small number of them to Springfield on August 10. Many Federal doctors remained on the field after the battle. Following contemporary custom, they were not made prisoners but eventually returned to their respective regiments. The doctors in *McCulloch's* army established several treatment stations along the banks of Wilson Creek, where shade and water were abundant. There are no records to indicate how many men were treated at the Ray House itself, but it must have been hundreds. The worst cases remained there for more than six weeks. The majority of the patients were moved to Springfield as soon as possible, which devastated the small town of 3,000. Almost all suitable structures, including private homes, were crammed with injured soldiers. Dr. William *Cantrell*, surgeon of the *1st Arkansas Mounted Rifles*, described Springfield as "a vast hospital" and estimated that "a hundred doctors could be employed constantly." Women living adjacent to the battlefield and in Springfield itself stepped forward to meet the crisis. In the weeks following the battle, male and female volunteer nurses came to Springfield from Arkansas, Kansas, and throughout Missouri. Like the military surgeons, they treated patients without regard to political affiliation.

Vignette

The Ray House was the center of the small rural community in the vicinity of Wilson Creek. John was the local postmaster and his home was a mail stop on the Butterfield Overland Stage route, which ran west to New Mexico. Owning 440 acres, he was quite prosperous. John and Roxanna lived with their nine children and a farmhand, Julius Short. Although

Unionists, they were also slaveholders, owning a woman named Rhoda and her three children. Roxanna and the rest of the household took shelter in a cellar during the battle. While the house and barn were spared by the fighting, the Rays lost all of their livestock and stored food to the Southern army, and their lives were turned upside down by the requisition of their home for use as a hospital.

An incident of August 10 reveals the strength of military honor and customs even amid a bitter civil war. When the Union forces retreated, they accidentally left Lyon's body on the field. Southern soldiers brought it to the Ray House. Despite the medical crisis, the deceased general's enemies placed him in a bed, leaving their own wounded on the hard floorboards—rank had it privileges, even in death. That evening, John Ray accompanied a military escort from the Missouri State Guard, which returned Lyon's body to Union forces in Springfield. Ironically the Federals forgot Lyon's remains once again when they evacuated the town on August 11. Mary Phelps, wife of Rep. John Phelps, a prominent local Unionist, buried Lyon at their farm, which is now the Phelps Grove Park in Springfield. The general's relatives later moved the body to his hometown in Connecticut.

STOP 6   Ray Springhouse

Directions   *Return* to the parking lot, *walk across* the road, and *follow* the
                             trail fifty yards down the ravine to the springhouse.

Orientation   Using a farm road that ran not far from the springhouse,
                             McIntosh's column crossed the ravine in which you are stand-
                             ing, climbing the hill behind the springhouse to battle
                             Plummer in the cornfield beyond. The current structure is
                             a reconstruction of the 1861 springhouse, built on the origi-
                             nal foundations. On August 10 the slopes of the ravine were
                             planted in fruit trees and fenced in as an orchard (see Map 5).

Vignette   Food resources and abundant spring water such as that at the
                             Ray farm were the reason *McCulloch* selected a campsite for
                             the Western Army along Wilson Creek. Men would have been
                             detailed daily to draw water from this spring as well as others
                             nearby. After the battle Roxanna Ray and her children (and,
                             in all probability, the slave Rhoda and her children) carried
                             buckets of water up to the house to relieve the sufferings of
                             the wounded and dying soldiers. One can only imagine the
                             psychological effect of the battle and its aftermath on the
                             children.

A modern view of the
restored Ray House,
with Wire Road in the
foreground. Courtesy
National Park Service,
Wilson's Creek National
Battlefield.

STOP 7   Ray Cornfield, 6:45–8:40 A.M.

Directions   *Follow* the trail to the left of the springhouse, *climb* the hill, and *walk* fifty yards to the junction of the fences delineating the junction of the orchard and the Ray Cornfield.

Orientation   As you stand along the fence marking the eastern boundary of the Ray Cornfield, you are looking from the orchard across into the cornfield. The vista to your front provides an excellent view of Bloody Hill. Note that it is extremely broad, though not very high. Modern forestation tends to conceal its many undulations, but you can clearly see both the main body of the hill and its northern spur. Note also, to your right front, that the cornfield itself is very uneven. Plummer's men crossed it from right to left, aiming toward the *Pulaski Light Battery*. Although modern forestation conceals the specific positions, to your left front is the ridge on which the *Pulaski Light Battery* (Stop 12) and *McCulloch's* headquarters at the Larkin Winn home (Stop 11) were located. During the cornfield fight, *McIntosh's* men occupied an angled line that encompassed portions of both the southern and eastern fences of the field. Companies of the *3rd Louisiana* were deployed where you stand.

What Happened   (The fight in the Ray Cornfield marked the end of Phase Three of the battle.) Plummer's mission was to reach Wire Road, thereby securing the left flank of Lyon's attack. Already slowed by a difficult crossing of Wilson Creek, Plummer halted about 6:45 A.M., somewhere near the center of the Ray Cornfield, when his column was fired upon from the east. The shots probably came from stray members of *Cawthorn's Cavalry* of *Rains's* division of the Missouri State Guard, who had fled their camps in the vicinity of Gibson Mill when the Federals first approached. Plummer's men returned fire, driving off the Missourians without suffering any casualties. When he resumed his march southeast, Plummer caught sight of the *Pulaski Light Battery*, which was trading shots with the Union guns atop Bloody Hill. Leaving his Missouri Home Guard troops to the rear as protection from a reappearance of the Southern cavalry, Plummer deployed his own battalion of Regular Army recruits into line of battle and marched south, determined to capture the enemy battery. As the Federals approached the southern boundary of the Ray Cornfield, they came under fire from both the front and the left flank. Although they suspected an ambush, they were actually victims of coincidence; Northern and Southern soldiers had simply collided at the Ray Cornfield.

Plummer's delays gave *McIntosh's* command time to reach the scene and deal with the threat to the Southern right. The *3rd Louisiana* led this column as it reached the top of the hill behind the Ray Springhouse. It was about 7:20 A.M. Colonel *Hébert* directed his men to the right. They marched east, parallel to the southern boundary fence, then turned left (north) along the eastern boundary to give the rest of the column room to spread out. Only two of *Hébert's* companies had fully deployed when Plummer's men pushed into view through the standing corn, but they were in an excellent position to fire on the Union front and left flank. Both sides claimed the other fired first, and participants estimated the range to be as close as a stone's throw. As soon as the fighting began, Plummer ordered his men to kneel or lie down for protection. Although the corn offered concealment, it also hindered their view of the enemy, whose fire grew more intense as the remainder of the Louisianans and the *2nd Arkansas Mounted Rifles* moved up to the southern boundary fences. The split-rail fence was so choked with weeds that even when Plummer's men stood up to fire, they could not get a clear view of the Southerners, most of whom knelt behind the cover.

Plummer's 300 men faced 900 under *McIntosh*, but the disparity in numbers was negated by the fact that much of the firing was blind—weeds, rails, or cornstalks blocked almost everyone's view. After perhaps half an hour, the clouds of white smoke from discharged weapons became so thick that a spontaneous lull developed, and taunts replaced bullets. *McIntosh* ended the stalemate by ordering a charge. This drove Plummer's battalion and the Union Home Guards back across the cornfield in great haste and disorder. They recrossed Wilson Creek at the Gibson Mill and remained in a supporting position for the remainder of the battle. The Southern pursuit reached the vicinity of the mill, potentially threatening the Union lines on Bloody Hill. But at this juncture alert Union artillerists changed position on the hill's crest (see Stop 17). Rapid fire from Lt. John V. Du Bois's battery drove the Southerners back the way they came. A portion of the *3rd Louisiana* fled toward the Ray House, rallying in the backyard. The remainder, along with the *2nd Arkansas*, reformed in the low ground near Wire Road's ford of Wilson Creek. The fighting ended about 8:40 A.M. Plummer lost 19 men killed, 52 wounded, and 9 missing. *McIntosh* probably suffered fewer than 75 casualties.

Analysis   Although this fighting produced no immediate advantage for either side, *McIntosh's* repulse of Plummer ended the threat to the Southern right and freed troops that *McCulloch* later used to defeat Sigel. Analysis of the action in and around the Ray Cornfield is fraught with "ifs." Had Plummer captured the *Pulaski Light Battery* or driven it from its commanding position, Lyon's advance on Bloody Hill would certainly have fared better. The general's caution in his assault, however, came from the this battery's initial fire (discussed in relation to Stop 12), which Plummer could not have prevented under any circumstances. The Federal left flank and rear would certainly have been vulnerable had *McIntosh* been able to cross Wilson Creek at the Gibson Mill, and the Federal artillery fire that stopped him merits discussion. Du Bois's Battery drove 900 Southerners away in near panic, even though the unit's fire was inaccurate and probably inflicted fewer than a dozen casualties. Civil War artillery shells burst in the air, and coming under such fire could be psychologically devastating. In the Ray Cornfield fight and elsewhere (see Stops 13 and 16), artillery had an influence disproportionate to its lethality.

Vignette

Although the clash in the Ray Cornfield did not last long, those who participated in it keenly remembered its ferocity and the confused conditions under which they fought. "We were guided mainly by the sound of musketry and the voices of men," one Federal soldier remembered, while another recalled seeing four comrades killed by his side, even as they hugged the ground. "Nevertheless, the men stood steadily and squarely up to their work," Plummer boasted. On the opposite side of the field, Sgt. Willie *Tunnard* of the 3rd Louisiana recalled: "Men were dropping all along the line; it was becoming uncomfortably hot." For another Louisianan, Sgt. William *Watson*, noise was the dominant sensation. "The sergeant-major came up to me to deliver some order," he noted, "but I could not hear it for the firing; he was coming closer to repeat it when he fell shot dead."[2]

A modern view of the Ray Cornfield, looking west toward Bloody Hill. Courtesy National Park Service, Wilson's Creek National Battlefield.

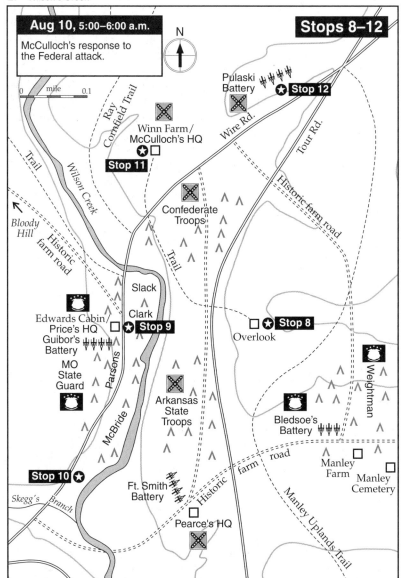

Aug 10, 5:00–6:00 a.m.

McCulloch's response to the Federal attack.

N

Stops 8–12

0   mile   0.1

Ray Cornfield Trail

Pulaski Battery

★ Stop 12

Winn Farm/ McCulloch's HQ

Wire Rd.

★ □

Stop 11

Tour Rd.

Trail

Wilson Creek

Historic farm road

Bloody Hill

Historic farm road

Confederate Troops

Trail

Slack

Clark

Edwards Cabin/ Price's HQ

□ ★ **Stop 9**

□ ★ **Stop 8**

Overlook

Guibor's Battery

MO State Guard

Parsons

Weightman

Arkansas State Troops

Bledsoe's Battery

McBride

Stop 10 ★

Ft. Smith Battery

Historic farm road

Manley Farm

Manley Cemetery

Skegg's Branch

Pearce's HQ

Manley Uplands Trail

STOP 8   East Battlefield Overlook (NB3)

Directions   *Return* to the Ray House parking lot, then *proceed* along the
                    TOUR ROAD 0.5 mile to the parking lot for the East Battlefield
                    Overlook. There are interpretative signs adjacent to the lot,
                    but for most seasons of the year, modern forestation blocks
                    the view of the valley of Wilson Creek. The 0.4-mile trail
                    climbing to the overlook begins with a set of wooden steps
                    across (east of) the road (behind you, if you are facing the

interpretative signs at the parking lot). Returning from the overlook, you will see to your left a junction with the Manley Uplands Trail, which is discussed below.

Orientation

As you face west, in the direction of the park's interpretative sign for the East Overlook, Bloody Hill lies to your right front. The Edwards Cabin site is in the creek valley to your front, visible through the trees only in winter. To your left front you can see Wire Road entering woods on a hilltop, and just to the left of that, the fences marking the fields of the Sharp Farm. Sigel's final position (Stop 14) is hidden by trees.

What Happened

(The events that took place in the valley of Wilson Creek below concern Phase Four, the actions of *McCulloch* and *Price* to save the Western Army, and are described under Stops 9–12).

STOP 9   Edwards Cabin / *Price's* HQ, 5:00–6:00 A.M.

Directions   *Walk* along the access trail that begins at the East Battlefield
                      Overlook parking lot down to Wire Road, approximately 0.25
                      mile. *Turn left* and *proceed* approximately 0.25 mile south-
                      west along Wire Road, crossing Wilson Creek at the modern
                      bridge, to the marker on the right designating the location
                      of *Price's* headquarters at the Edwards Cabin.

                      En route, as you cross the modern bridge, you can see to
                      your left the shallow ford where Wire Road originally crossed
                      Wilson Creek. The stream has not changed significantly since
                      the time of the battle. Looking upstream and downstream,
                      note that while the creek could be crossed on foot at almost
                      any location, steep banks restricted wheeled vehicles to the
                      ford itself.

Orientation   As you face the Edwards Cabin, Bloody Hill is to your right
                      front. The hill encompasses the high area to your far right,
                      now crowned with trees not present in 1861, as well as the
                      long slopes stretching to your front left, where the mixed
                      grass and thickets resemble the type of vegetation that cov-
                      ered the entire hill at the time of the battle.

                      When the Western Army reached Wilson Creek on August
                      6, most of the infantry of the Missouri State Guard camped
                      on the unfenced flat land west of the creek farmed by Wil-
                      liam B. Edwards. *Price* made the cabin his headquarters.

What Happened   The response of the Southern forces to the Federal attack was
                      affected by timing, terrain, and acoustics. *McCulloch* was at his
                      headquarters (Stop 11) when, shortly after dawn, he received
                      word concerning enemy activity to the north near the Short
                      farm. The general discounted this news because it came from
                      Rains, who had panicked during a skirmish on August 2. As a
                      precaution, however, he dispatched orders for Col. Elkanah
                      Greer's South Kansas–Texas Cavalry and Capt. Charles A. *Carroll's*
                      undesignated company of Arkansas cavalry to leave their
                      camps at Sharp Farm and assemble at the ford. *McCulloch* in-
                      tended to send them to the Short farm to investigate but ob-
                      viously believed there was no need for haste. He and *McIntosh*
                      then rode to *Price's* headquarters at the Edwards Cabin to dis-
                      cuss the intended march on Springfield. They arrived shortly
                      after 5:00 A.M. Since *Greer* and *Carroll* would have to pass the
                      Edwards farm, *McCulloch* was in a position to give them oral
                      instructions about investigating *Rains's* report.

                      As *McCulloch* and *Price* ate breakfast in the farmyard, they
                      failed to hear either the fighting on the northern spur of
                      Bloody Hill or Sigel's opening guns to the south (see Stop

13). They were victims of a phenomenon called "acoustic shadow." This occurs when terrain, air density, and wind direction combine to prevent noises ordinarily audible at long distances (such as artillery fire) from being heard in certain locations, even though close by. About 5:20 A.M. a breathless rider galloped up to the Edwards Cabin announcing that *Rains* was under attack by "twenty thousand men and 100 pieces of artillery." *McCulloch* dismissed this wild report as additional evidence of *Rains's* incompetence. But when a second rider arrived ten minutes later with a coherent account, *McCulloch* and *Price* recognized the danger and took immediate action.

McCulloch and *McIntosh* returned to the army commander's headquarters, leaving *Price* to rouse the Missouri State Guard from its camps. This took an uncommon amount of time. *Price* commanded a total of 7,171 men, including 2,000 unarmed, unattached recruits, whose location on the field when the battle opened is not known. The infantry of *Slack's*, *Clark's*, *Parsons's*, and *McBride's* divisions were, in that order, spread across both sides of Wire Road from the ford of Wilson Creek almost to Skegg's Branch. While a few slept in tents pitched in neat rows, others lay on the open ground or sheltered themselves in the thickets adjacent to the creek. *Guibor's Battery* of *Parsons's* division, which constituted half of the State Guard artillery, was located near the Edward's Cabin. But *Bledsoe's Battery* and *Weightman's Infantry*, both of *Rains's* division, were camped almost a mile away at the Caleb B. Manley farm (a site accessible via the Manley Uplands Trail), on the high ground east of Wilson Creek. The mounted units of the State Guard divisions were split. *Rains's* horsemen were already under attack to the north, while the rest of the Missouri cavalry was consolidated in the fields south of the Sharp farmhouse. Most of the soldiers were either still asleep or cooking breakfast, and it took time for them to grab their weapons and assemble by companies. A few of them panicked as Federal artillery shells, fired blindly and at long range, exploded above the camps.

Price intended to stop Lyon on the northern spur of Bloody Hill. He therefore ordered the State Guard units to follow a farm road that ran from the Edwards Cabin up the slopes of the main portion of Bloody Hill. Chaos ensued as thousands of men attempted to form up along this narrow track and the one-lane Wire Road adjacent to it. It was well after 6:00 A.M. before anyone was ready to move. By that time *Price* was forced to change his plans. When he rode forward for a personal reconnaissance, he witnessed the Federals driving *Cawthorn's* men from the crest of Bloody Hill. Returning to the valley, the Missouri commander began forming a line of infantry to challenge Lyon for possession of what would obviously be the key terrain, Bloody Hill. He placed the infantry from *Slack's* division as an anchor near the creek and then began extending his battle line to the left, stretching the men across the long, undulating lower slopes of the hill west of the Edwards Cabin. But before *Price* could launch an attack, his men encountered elements of Lyon's column probing down the slopes. (The subsequent fight is discussed in relation to Stop 16, below.)

Analysis

McCulloch's shortcomings during Phase Four of the battle were significant. His failure to repost pickets on the evening of August 9, after calling off the night march on Springfield, left the Western Army unguarded the following morning. *Cawthorn's* delaying action on the northern spur of Bloody Hill provided compensation, though *McCulloch* negated this slightly by ignoring the first messenger from *Rains*. Moreover, the Southerners were caught completely off guard by Sigel's column to the south (see Stop 13). Once convinced of the danger, however, *McCulloch* performed well, and he made a sensible decision to direct *Price* and the Missouri State Guard against Bloody Hill. The greatest damage to the Southern cause came from acoustic shadow, which not only concealed the noise of Lyon's initial assault but also of Sigel's simultaneous opening guns. Acoustic shadow was also reported at the later battles of Seven Pines, Gaines's Mill, Perryville, and Chancellorsville.

Price deserves credit for his response to the crisis. Most of the Missouri State Guard was camped on a roughly north-south axis parallel to Wilson Creek. *Price's* task was to move his men out of their division camps and into a line of battle, facing north, anchored on the creek at the northern end of the camps. This sounds simple, but amid the confusion caused by the surprise attack, it was neither easy nor rapid. Once the Federals reached the crest of the main portion of Bloody Hill, the acoustic shadow evaporated. The steady roar of artillery unnerved the Southern men and panicked their horses. As the 2,000 unarmed guardsmen fled for safety, a large number of their comrades who did possess weapons joined them. The ignominious flight of these armed men reduced the Missourians' combat effectiveness and compromised unit cohesion. Under the circumstances *Price* was wise to form his battle line in the simplest possible manner, even though it may not have been the quickest. Although organized into "divisions," the State Guard had little practice maneuvering above the level of individual companies.

Since *Slack's* division was closest, *Price* formed its companies into line first, then turned to the next closest division, *Clark's*. While this meant that *McBride's* division, farthest south, probably waited for more than an hour to move into position, each unit that went into line did so with solid support to its right. Although some intermingling of units occurred, it was minimal. *Price* also wanted to control his men as tightly as possible, for since they possessed so little ammunition, the consequences of wasting it could be disastrous.

Although William B. Edwards lived on a very small farm, he had prospered in recent years, purchasing an additional forty acres of land. The cabin was also home to his wife, Mary, and their nineteen-year-old son, James. No information has survived concerning the effect of the battle on their lives.

Cpl. Alonzo H. *Shelton* of *Slack's* division recalled how startled his comrades were by an enemy artillery shell that "whistled along down the road close to where we were eating." The surprise attack caused pandemonium, but while some men ran away, others showed uncommon courage. He remembered how a handful of unarmed men stayed with the command to replace casualties. They "watched their chance to get a gun, and then went into the fight."[3]

The men of the Missouri State Guard varied greatly in training, experience, clothing, and equipment. Some companies, such as Col. Joseph M. *Kelly's Washington Blues* of St. Louis, were prewar militia units possessing fancy uniforms and modern rifles when the war began. Others, such as the *Warsaw Grays*, were hastily uniformed through the efforts and nimble fingers of loved ones in their hometowns. The colors blue and gray had no political significance in 1861. The majority of the State Guard wore ordinary civilian clothing, most of it probably the drab brown known as butternut. Arms included outdated smoothbore muskets taken from local arsenals and hunting weapons brought from home. Since campaigning was hard on clothing, the Missourians supplemented their initial attire, whether plain or imposing, with civilian items purchased from country stores. They also made clothing from bulk cloth issued to them by quartermasters. A favorite item was the overshirt, a simple garment made of any available material and rendered "military" by the addition of enough fancy trim to suit the wearer's taste.

STOP 10   *Fort Smith Light Battery | Pearce's* HQ, 5:00–8:00 A.M.

Directions   *Walk* southwest from the Edwards Cabin along Wire Road for
                       0.6 mile to the ford of Skegg's Branch (dry for much of the
                       year). *Turn around* and *proceed back* the way you came for 150
                       yards. *Turn right* to face Wilson Creek.

Orientation   The high ground to your front was the site of Capt. John *Reid's
                       Fort Smith Light Battery.* A farm road led up to the hill, fording
                       the creek at this point. Lightly wooded in 1861, it is now so
                       heavily forested that the position is difficult to see even in
                       winter. There is no public access to it. *Pearce* made his head-
                       quarters adjacent to the battery. Most of the 2,334 Arkansas
                       State Troops he commanded camped on the high ground
                       above the creek in a line stretching left to a position opposite
                       the Edwards Cabin (see "Order of Battle" for organization).
                       The road that ran up to the battery continued east to the
                       Manley farm, where *Bledsoe's Battery* and *Weightman's* infantry,
                       members of *Rains's* division of the Missouri State Guard, lay
                       camped. (You can view this general area via the Manley Up-
                       lands Trail, discussed below, but the State Guard's campsites
                       are not marked.) After passing the farm, the road connected
                       with north-south roads leading to Springfield.

What Happened   The same acoustic shadow that covered *McCulloch* and *Price*
                       at the Edwards Cabin initially prevented General *Pearce*
                       from hearing either Lyon's struggle for the northern spur of
                       Bloody Hill or Sigel's opening guns to the south. Ironically
                       Pearce first received a report concerning the enemy from un-
                       authorized foragers who encountered Federals well east of
                       the Manley farm (beyond the battlefield boundary). While
                       these Northerners were merely pickets Sigel had left to guard
                       his rear during his night march, their discovery convinced
                       Pearce that a threat existed in that direction, and he sent no-
                       tice to *McCulloch.* Soon, however, messengers brought word
                       of the fighting atop Bloody Hill and at Sharp Farm. When
                       McCulloch joined *Pearce* at his headquarters, they decided that
                       since *Bledsoe's Battery* and *Weightman's* infantry had left the
                       Manley farm to join the rest of *Price's* command, the Arkansas
                       State Troops should stay east of Wilson Creek to guard the
                       army's right flank. *Reid* deployed the four guns of his *Fort
                       Smith Light Battery* for action. *Pearce* placed the *4th* and *5th
                       Arkansas Infantry* nearby and sent the *3rd Arkansas Infantry* to
                       support the *Pulaski Light Battery.* His mounted units acted as
                       pickets.

Analysis

McCulloch believed that he was threatened simultaneously from the north, east, and south. While he acted logically to defend the Western Army from an attack coming from the direction of the Manley farm, his dispositions robbed the Southerners of strength that could have been used elsewhere. *Pearce* was apparently content to remain passive. The *Fort Smith Light Battery* stood silent until late in the battle, when it supported *McCulloch's* attack on Sigel (see Stop 15).

A modern view of the southern slopes of Bloody Hill. Courtesy National Park Service, Wilson's Creek National Battlefield.

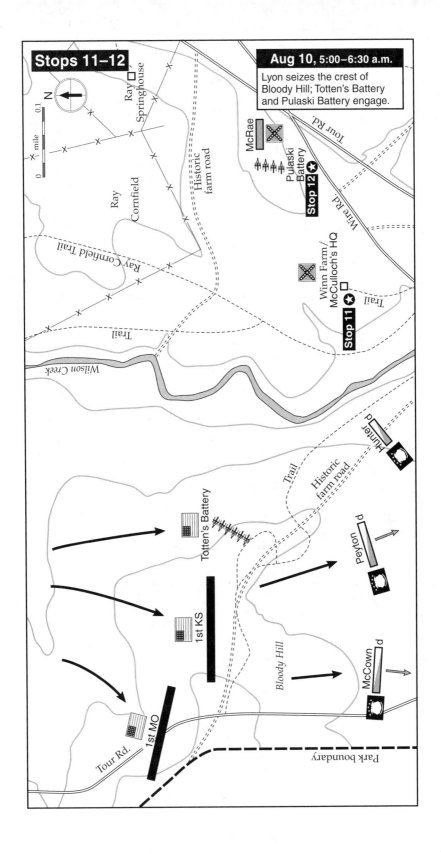

Stops 11–12

N

Ray Springhouse

Historic farm road

Ray Cornfield

Ray Cornfield Trail

Trail

Wilson Creek

Aug 10, 5:00–6:30 a.m.

Lyon seizes the crest of
Bloody Hill; Totten's Battery
and Pulaski Battery engage.

McRae

Pulaski Battery

Tour Rd.

Wire Rd.

Stop 12

Winn Farm/
McCulloch's HQ

Trail

Stop 11

Hunter d

Trail

Historic farm road

Totten's Battery

Peyton d

1st KS

Bloody Hill

McCown d

1st MO

Tour Rd.

Park boundary

STOP 11   Winn Farm / *McCulloch's* HQ, 4:45–5:00 A.M.

Directions   *Walk back* along Wire Road past the Edwards Cabin, crossing
                     Wilson Creek, until you reach the turn off to the right for the
                     trail leading back to the East Battlefield Overlook parking
                     lot. *Turn left* instead, following the short trail marked "Pu-
                     laski Battery" to the top of the hill.

Orientation   Stand facing the NB marker for the *Pulaski Light Battery*. This
                     identifies your position as the Guinn farm, location of the
                     Pulaski Light Battery and *McCulloch's* headquarters. While the
                     Texan did make his headquarters here, it was the Larkin
                     Winn farm, and the battery was nearby rather than at this
                     spot. Directly ahead to the west is Bloody Hill, with Wilson
                     Creek running past the base of its steep eastern slope. Mod-
                     ern vegetation blocks the view of the Ray Cornfield to the
                     northeast and the *Pulaski Light Battery's* position to the east.

What Happened   After canceling the Western Army's planned march on the
                     evening of August 9 because of rain, *McCulloch* returned to his
                     headquarters. Here, as noted above, he received word around
                     dawn the next morning concerning enemy movement near
                     the Short farm. Although not unduly concerned, he ordered
                     the *South Kansas–Texas Cavalry* and *Carroll's* Arkansas cavalry
                     company to assemble at the creek ford, intending to send
                     them to investigate. He then left for *Price's* headquarters at
                     the Edwards Cabin to organize the Southern forces for their
                     delayed movement on Springfield.

Vignette   Larkin D. Winn; his wife, Sofronia; and their eight children
                     had lived in a modest cabin, farming a small fenced-in area
                     atop the cleared hill as well as land just to the north. For
                     reasons not known, they left in 1860, and the site was un-
                     inhabited when *McCulloch* selected it for his headquarters.

STOP 12   *Pulaski Light Battery*, 5:30–6:30 A.M.

Directions   *Descend* the path from the Winn farm. *Turn left* at Wire Road
                       and *walk* 0.4 mile to the place on your left where the slope of
                       the ridge is no longer steep, offering easy access to the top for
                       wheeled vehicles. The small plateau above the road to your
                       front is the unmarked site of the *Pulaski Light Battery*. Lightly
                       wooded in 1861, it is now heavily forested and has no public
                       access.

Orientation   In 1861 this position provided an unobstructed view of the
                       Ray Cornfield, due north, and Bloody Hill, to the west. The
                       Ray House is 0.3 mile to your right.

What Happened   When the Western Army arrived at Wilson Creek, Capt. Wil-
                       liam E. *Woodruff* placed his *Pulaski Light Battery* near the Winn
                       farm to guard Wire Road running northeast to Springfield.
                       His men were preparing to march in that direction when
                       Lyon's movement to the crest of the main portion of Bloody
                       Hill attracted their attention (see Stop 17 for Lyon's actions).
                       Without waiting for orders, *Woodruff* deployed his guns and
                       opened fire, initiating a duel with Federal artillery that may
                       have lasted an hour. He also alerted *McCulloch* to Plummer's
                       movement in the Ray Cornfield, though the timing of events
                       suggests that *McCulloch* may have learned of this earlier from
                       a source not now known. During this time the general ap-
                       peared and approved of *Woodruff's* dispositions. Col. Dan-
                       dridge *McRae's* undesignated battalion of Arkansas infantry
                       arrived to guard the battery's right flank. Behind the guns
                       Wire Road teemed with activity as troops moved to and from
                       the fight in the Ray Cornfield. When the battery's ammuni-
                       tion ran low, *Woodruff* withdrew from the hill. After replen-
                       ishing his limbers, he moved to high ground south of Wire
                       Road (the precise location is unclear), firing to support *Price's*
                       assaults on Bloody Hill (see Stops 16 and 17).

Analysis   *Woodruff's* actions affected the battle dramatically. His fire
                       caught the Federal forces atop Bloody Hill on their left flank.
                       Although it caused few casualties, the shelling slowed Lyon's
                       movements and gave *Price* time to deploy the Missouri State
                       Guard. Thanks to the delay caused by *Hunter's* defense of
                       the northern spur of Bloody Hill and the further slowness
                       caused by *Woodruff's* guns, the initiative on this portion of
                       the battlefield gradually passed from the Northerners to the
                       Southerners.

Vignette

When organized as volunteer militia in 1860 in Little Rock, Pulaski County, Arkansas, *Woodruff's* unit was originally named the "Totten Light Battery." This honored Capt. James Totten, commander of the Federal arsenal located there. A popular figure with Southern sympathies, Totten helped train the artillerists. During the secession crisis, however, the captain withdrew with his men to St. Louis, where his force eventually became part of Lyon's Army of the West. Angered that Totten had not sided with the South, *Woodruff's* men took the name "Pulaski Light Battery" when they joined the Arkansas State Troops under *Pearce*.

During the battle *Woodruff* suspected correctly that the battery firing on him was Totten's reconstituted command. He was proud that his men, two of whom were only fifteen years old, successfully endured the fire of their former teacher. "My boys stood it like heroes—not a man flinched, although the balls came like hailstones," he recalled.[4] Actually the Federal fire was largely inaccurate, and *Woodruff* lost only three men. But one of these was Lt. Omer *Weaver*, scion of a prominent Little Rock family. Struck in the chest, his right arm mangled, *Weaver* lingered in great pain but without complaint, refusing the busy doctor's attention since he knew his wounds were mortal. After the battle *Woodruff* shipped *Weaver's* body back to Little Rock, where a large public funeral took place. The two enlisted men who died were buried on the field.

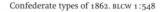

Confederate types of 1862. BLCW 1:548

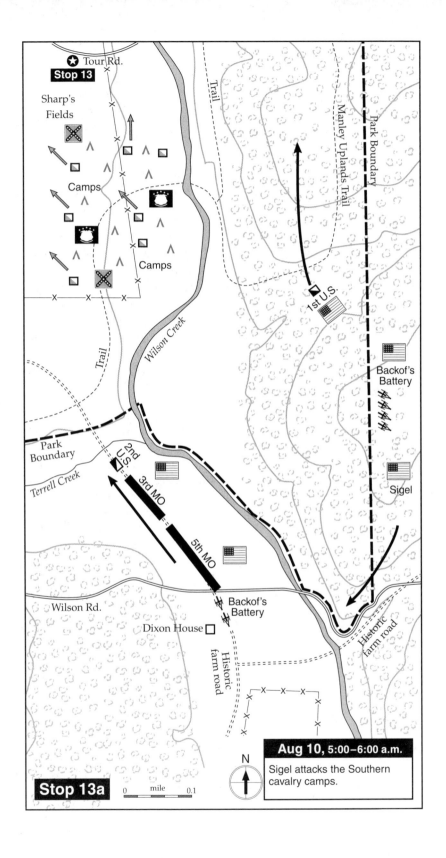

Tour Rd.
Stop 13

Sharp's
Fields

Camps

Camps

Wilson Creek

Trail

Trail

Manley Uplands Trail

Park Boundary

1st U.S.

Backof's
Battery

Sigel

Park
Boundary

Terrell Creek

2nd
U.S.

3rd MO

5th MO

Wilson Rd.

Dixon House

Backof's
Battery

Historic
farm road

Historic
farm road

Aug 10, 5:00–6:00 a.m.

Sigel attacks the Southern
cavalry camps.

N

Stop 13a

0   mile   0.1

Sigel's Attack and the Southern Response

STOP 13

Sigel's Second Position, 7:00–7:30 A.M. (NB4)

Because there is no public access to Sigel's first position (Phase One), events relating to both it and Sigel's second position (Phase Two) are discussed here.

Directions

Leaving the *Pulaski Light Battery* position, *walk back* the way you came on Wire Road, *turning left* onto the trail leading to the parking lot for the East Battlefield Overlook (Stop 8). *Proceed* along the TOUR ROAD for 0.7 mile to the parking area for Sigel's Second Position (NB4) on the south side of the road. Note two things *en route*. The straight stretch of road just after you leave Stop 8 lies atop an 1870 railway bed. The Arkansas State Troops were camped on the ground to your right. Shortly before the road curves right to cross Wilson Creek, there is parking on the left for access to the Manley Uplands Trail. This leads south toward Sigel's first position, but does not provide a view of it, before looping back north. It rejoins the road where it crosses Wire Road not far from the Ray House. This area was heavily wooded in 1861, as it is today. Hikers do not have a good view of the battlefield.

Orientation

You are in the northeast corner of Joseph Sharp's stubblefield, facing south. The Sharp Cornfield and Stop 14, the site of the Sharp farmhouse, are to your right rear. The fence in the distance to your front marks the southern boundary of Sharp's fields. About 0.2 mile beyond the fence (out of sight) lies Terrell Creek. (Access to this area is described in the Dixon Farm excursion below.) To your left Wilson Creek flows south, with a high ridge just beyond. Sigel's first position was in a clearing atop the ridge, at a point 0.8 mile to the southeast. Modern forestation conceals it from view. Sigel's second position was a line of battle in the middle of Sharp's stubblefield, facing northeast.

Some 1,500 men and horses from the Western Army camped randomly in the stubblefield and the adjacent ground to the east bordering Wilson Creek. They came from all three of the army's brigades: *McCulloch's* Confederates, *Pearce's* Arkansas State Troops, and *Price's* Missouri State Guard.

What Happened

To fulfill his role in Lyon's surprise attack, Sigel left Springfield at 6:30 P.M. on August 9, leading his column of 1,200 men south. His force contained the 3rd and 5th Missouri Infantry; Company I, 1st U.S. Cavalry; and Company C, 2nd U.S. Dragoons. Six guns of the Missouri Light Artillery lent

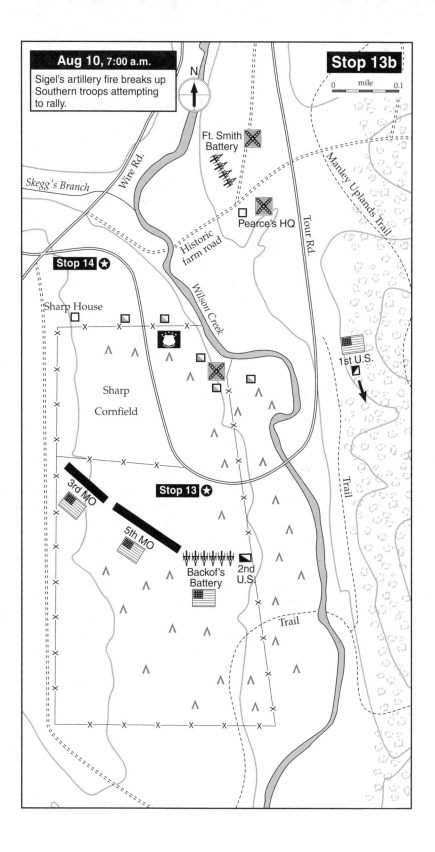

Aug 10, 7:00 a.m.

Sigel's artillery fire breaks up Southern troops attempting to rally.

N

Stop 13b

0   mile   0.1

Ft. Smith Battery

Skegg's Branch

Wire Rd.

Manley Uplands Trail

Historic farm road

Pearce's HQ

Tour Rd.

Stop 14 ★

Wilson Creek

Sharp House

1st U.S.

Sharp Cornfield

3rd MO

Stop 13 ★

5th MO

Trail

Backof's Battery

2nd U.S.

Trail

support. Raised by Maj. Franz Backof in St. Louis and usually called Backof's Battery, the artillerists were currently commanded by Capt. Gustavus A. Schaefer. Civilian guides led the Federals along farm roads through the darkness in complete secrecy. Just before dawn the column reached a clearing on the ridge east of Wilson Creek above Sharp's fields. At daylight Sigel established his first position on the battlefield by deploying four of the six guns from Backof's Battery to shell the Southern camp. Fortunately for Sigel, the acoustic shadow that blanketed the low ground around the Edwards Cabin did not prevent him from hearing the sound of Lyon's struggle for the northern spur of Bloody Hill. He opened fire about 5:00 A.M.

These opening rounds exploded among the Southern horsemen as they were preparing for their march on Springfield. Within minutes chaos reigned. Many Southerners fled north and east, toward the Sharp House and low ground along the creek. Others fled northwest into the woods west of the farm. At least half of these men took no further part in the battle. While the guns continued to fire, Sigel protected the battery's right flank by sending Capt. Eugene A. Carr's Company I, 1st U.S. Cavalry, north along the ridge. After the bombardment was well under way, Sigel advanced with the remaining two guns, the dragoons, and his infantry. Following farm roads, he crossed Wilson Creek at the Dixon farm and marched along the western edge of the stubblefield. The Federals found the field empty, for the artillery had driven away the entire enemy force.

About 6:30 A.M. Sigel halted in column along the northern edge of Sharp's stubblefield, sending messengers to order Carr's cavalrymen and the four guns on the hilltop to join him. This was a wise precaution, for Carr, moving farther north than Sigel had intended, spotted Southern forces rallying in the vicinity of the Sharp farmhouse and the low ground near the creek. Sigel saw them as well, and he took action once the arriving guns restored Backof's Battery to full strength. At about 7:00 A.M. he formed a line of battle in the stubblefield, facing northeast, and opened fire with canister. The Southerners, who probably numbered no more than 500 men, quickly scattered, leaving the Federals free to advance to the Sharp House and Wire Road.

Analysis

Sigel's successful march helped make the Federal assault at Wilson's Creek one of the most remarkable surprise attacks of the Civil War. Moreover, his bombardment was one of the most successful uses of artillery on the offensive during the entire conflict. Enemy casualties were light, for most of Sigel's gunners lacked experience and tended to overshoot their targets. But few of the Southern soldiers (or their horses) had ever been under artillery fire. The psychological effect of the bombardment outweighed its lethality.

Although Sigel could have saved time by regrouping his forces earlier, he continued to make excellent use of his artillery. His maneuvers placed him within striking distance of Wire Road, where he could be in the rear of the enemy, across their line of communications.

Vignette   Most of the men under Sigel's command were foreign born. A majority of the enlisted men in prewar units such as the 1st U.S. Cavalry and the 2nd U.S. Dragoons were either Irish or German immigrants. More than 90 percent of Sigel's volunteer infantrymen and artillerymen were St. Louis Germans, enlisted at his prompting during the secession crisis. Although the mounted forces wore regulation blue, the other units wore gray uniforms. The 3rd Missouri, which Sigel personally organized, sported red trim on their hats as well as on the shirts and trousers of their jeans uniforms.

OPTIONAL EXCURSION: Dixon Farm

The Dixon farm and the route Sigel followed to approach Sharp's stubblefield lie outside the battlefield's boundaries. Visitors have two options for viewing this area.

BY FOOT OR ON HORSEBACK

From Stop 14 *follow* Wire Road southwest 0.5 mile to the junction of the battlefield's Southwest Boundary Trail. This leads south for 0.5 mile before *turning east* to parallel Terrell Creek and the battlefield boundary. After another 0.5 mile the trail approaches Wilson Creek. *Turn right* to look across Terrell Creek, with Wilson Creek on your left. In 1861 the land to your front was the Dixon farm. The southern end of the stubblefield is on the plateau behind you.

From this point *retracing your steps* is the best option. If you continue to follow the Boundary Trail, you will reach a crossing of Wilson Creek suitable for horses only. Because of pollution, the creek's water is posted as a health hazard. Do not wade across the creek. If on horseback and you cross the creek, you will reach the Manley Uplands Trail.

BY AUTOMOBILE

From the Visitor Center *turn left* out of the parking lot and *follow* FARM ROAD 182 for 0.1 mile to COUNTY ZZ. *Turn left* onto COUNTY ZZ. *Proceed* south 2.6 miles, *turning left* onto WILSON

ROAD. *Go* 0.8 mile east to the ford of Wilson Creek. In 1861 John Dixon's farmhouse stood to the right of the road. There is no public access to this private property. As you *cross* Wilson Creek, look to your right. Sigel's column crossed some 100 yards downstream from the modern ford. After you cross Wilson Creek, the road immediately curves around a hill. Sigel's first position is on the high ground 0.25 mile to the northeast. There is no public access to this private property. To return to the park, you may either turn around and retrace your route or continue east 0.6 miles then *turn left* onto FARM ROAD 115 (which is also marked as HASELTINE ROAD). *Drive* north 2.5 miles to the junction of FARM ROAD 182. Here, looking straight ahead, note the large industrial smokestack in the distance. This marks the approximate location where Lyon's column halted during the early morning hours of August 10 on its approach to the battlefield. *Turn left* onto FARM ROAD 182. After going 0.6 mile you will see on the right a sign marking the battlefield boundary. As you pass this sign, *look* to your extreme right. Lyon approached the Short farm via this low ground. The entrance to the battlefield is 0.45 mile farther, on your left.

Major-General Franz Sigel.
From a photograph.
BLCW 1:286

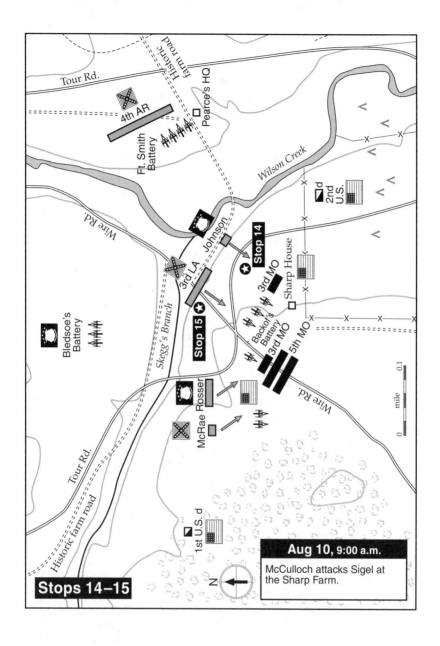

Tour Rd.

Historic farm road

Pearce's HQ

4th AR

Ft. Smith Battery

Wilson Creek

2nd U.S.

Johnson

Stop 14

3rd MO

Sharp House

3rd LA

Bledsoe's Battery

Wire Rd.

Skegg's Branch

Stop 15

Backof's Battery

3rd MO

5th MO

Wire Rd.

McRae Rosser

Tour Rd.

Historic farm road

1st U.S.

0   mile   0.1

Aug 10, 9:00 a.m.

McCulloch attacks Sigel at the Sharp Farm.

N

Stops 14–15

STOP 14   Sigel's Final Position (Sharp Farm), 8:00–8:30 A.M. (NB5)

Directions   *Proceed* 0.3 mile along the TOUR ROAD to Stop 14 (NB5). The en-
                     trance to the parking lot is on the left. *Park* your vehicle and
                     walk to the artillery pieces marking the position of Backof's
                     Battery.

Orientation   Face in the direction the guns point, northeast up Wire Road.
                     The TOUR ROAD crosses Wire Road to your front. Beyond this
                     the ground drops away into the valley of Wilson Creek. Ex-
                     cept in winter, modern forestation blocks your view of Bloody
                     Hill, which is to your left front. The rugged ground to your
                     left, however, was nearly as wooded in 1861 as it is today.
                     Behind you Wire Road, the Western Army's line of communi-
                     cation to Arkansas, climbs over a small rise. To your right and
                     right rear, rail fences mark John Sharp's fields. The northern-
                     most portion of this was a cornfield, apparently picked clean
                     or trampled flat by *McCulloch's* soldiers prior to the battle.
                     Sharp's large, white two-story home sat near the northwest
                     corner; a barn and other outbuildings stood nearby. A farm
                     road, no longer visible, ran along the western fence line, join-
                     ing Wire Road just behind you. Sigel's column approached
                     along this road, having followed it from the Dixon farm to
                     the south.

What Happened   (The events described here relate to Phase Two of the battle.)
                     After dispersing the Southerners attempting to rally, Sigel
                     reformed his column on the road bordering the stubblefield.
                     Carr's Company I, 1st U.S. Cavalry, arrived from the ridge
                     across Wilson Creek, and the Federals advanced to Wire Road.
                     Sigel immediately deployed Backof's Battery to the left of the
                     road, facing north. Rounds from the guns exploded on the
                     lower slopes of Bloody Hill, in the rear of the Southern troops
                     facing Lyon. Sigel protected his right flank by dispatching
                     Lt. Charles E. Farrand's Company C, 2nd U.S. Dragoons, into
                     the Sharp Cornfield, moving to the northeast corner before
                     dismounting behind the rails. To protect his opposite flank,
                     Sigel sent Carr's horsemen into the woods. Carr moved too
                     far to the northwest, however, leaving the main position vul-
                     nerable on the left. Sigel placed some 200 men of the 3rd
                     Missouri in line just to the right of the road, the rest of his
                     infantry remaining in column.

                     Around 8:30 A.M. the colonel ordered his guns to cease
                     firing at Bloody Hill, for fear of hitting Lyon's men by mis-
                     take. Neither Federals nor Southerners wore standard uni-
                     forms, and their identifying flags hung limp in the breeze-
                     less, humid air. Sigel believed he could see movement on the

far ridge near his first position, suggesting that Southerners were fleeing in that direction. Dozens of the enemy, fugitives from the artillery bombardments, came up to surrender, while the Federals had suffered no casualties at all. Sigel was convinced that victory was at hand. For safety, however, he re-adjusted his line, shifting four of his six guns to face up Wire Road. But he cautioned his men that since friendly troops should soon come down the road, they must not fire without orders. To prevent accidents, he sent a small number of men forward as lookouts.

Analysis

Despite Sigel's magnificent accomplishment in reaching Wire Road, his position was weak. As he did not place the 5th Missouri or the remainder of the 3rd Missouri in line, his guns were poorly supported, and some of his horsemen were out of contact. Because the ground dropped sharply to his front, creating a "dead zone" that his artillery could not cover, he should have dispatched a significant portion of his infantry into it as pickets. The tiny force he did send out was concerned only with preventing friendly fire casualties, not guarding against surprise. Yet Sigel made no attempt to contact Lyon via messenger. Overconfident, he surrendered the initiative to his enemy, who was quick to take advantage.

Vignette

Unlike their Unionist neighbors the Rays, Joseph D. Sharp and his wife, Mary, favored the Southern cause. Joseph owned three slaves and other property worth over $11,000, including 135 horses, hogs, sheep, and oxen. At age forty-nine he was by far the wealthiest man in the area. The Western Army had used his home as a hospital since its arrival on August 6. When Sigel's bombardment began at dawn on the tenth, John and Mary sought refuge in the cellar, along with their son Robert, daughters Mary and Margaret, and the slaves. The hospitalized Southern soldiers were apparently evacuated, though Sigel may have captured those too sick to move.

STOP 15   *McCulloch's* Attack, 8:30–9:00 A.M.

Directions   *Walk* 0.1 mile from the Backof Battery position northeast
                      along Wire Road, down into the valley of Skegg's Branch.
                      Do not cross the stream. Note the high ground to your right
                      front, the site of the *Fort Smith Light Battery*. The lower slopes
                      of Bloody Hill lie to your left front. *Turn around* and *proceed
                      back* the way you came for about twenty-five yards, facing in
                      the direction of the road. The relatively flat ground to your
                      front and sides is the "dead zone" that Sigel's artillery could
                      not cover, the area he failed to picket. *McCulloch* assembled
                      his forces here to attack the Federals. After reading the "What
                      Happened" section below, you may wish to return to the
                      Backof Battery before reading the "Analysis" and "Vignette"
                      sections. Your walk back follows the route of *McCulloch's* as-
                      sault. Note how the ground sheltered the Southerners until
                      they were right on top of the battery.

What Happened   (The attack occurred during Phase Four of the battle.) After
                      dispatching troops to meet Plummer's Federals in the Ray
                      Cornfield, and after checking with *Pearce*, *McCulloch* rode
                      south and observed Sigel's deployment in the Sharp farm-
                      yard. Realizing that a crisis was at hand, he returned to the
                      ford of Wire Road. There he found Lt. Col. Samuel M. *Hyams*
                      and some 300 of his gray-uniformed *3rd Louisiana Infantry*,
                      who had rallied after Federal artillery had driven them from
                      the cornfield (the other half, under *Hébert*, had fled to the
                      Ray House). Nearby were seventy members of the Missouri
                      State Guard under a captain named *Johnson*. *McCulloch* quickly
                      led both units down Wire Road and across Skegg's Branch.
                      When Sigel's lookouts saw them coming, they withdrew to
                      the Sharp House, erroneously informing the colonel that
                      Lyon's men were approaching. As some companies of the 1st
                      Iowa Infantry in Lyon's column wore gray, their mistake was
                      understandable. But their failure to make contact was a criti-
                      cal error, for it allowed *McCulloch* to deploy his men in the
                      "dead zone" without interference. Sigel finally sent a single
                      soldier from the 3rd Missouri forward to look for Lyon, but
                      McCulloch's men killed him before he could raise the alarm.

                      The Southern force numbered less than 400 when it
                      started up the steep slope toward Sharp Farm, but *McCulloch*
                      expected to strike the Federal battery on its right flank since
                      it had been facing north when he last observed it. Instead,
                      he faced four of its guns head on. Fortunately for the South-
                      ern cause, *McCulloch* received assistance. In response to Sigel's
                      earlier shelling of the Missouri State Guard on Bloody Hill,
                      Lt. Col. Thomas H. *Rosser* of *Rains's* division placed the three

guns of *Bledsoe's Battery* on high ground above the northern bank of Skegg's Branch and assembled perhaps 200 infantry to charge the enemy guns. The Missourians moved forward just as *McCulloch* did. A portion of *McRae's Arkansas Infantry*, free from its earlier task of guarding the *Pulaski Light Battery*, joined the assault at the last minute. The combined activity of *Rosser*, *McRae*, and *McCulloch* caught *Pearce's* attention, and he ordered the *Fort Smith Light Battery* to provide supporting fire. When the Louisianans reached the top of the hill, they found the Federal guns facing them less than twenty-five yards away. At that moment both *Bledsoe's Battery* and the *Fort Smith Light Battery* opened fire, to which at least two Federal guns responded. Then the Southern infantry opened with their muskets and charged.

Believing a tragic error had occurred, Sigel and his infantry commanders, Lt. Col. Anselm Albert of the 3rd Missouri and Col. Charles Salomon of the 5th Missouri, yelled in German and English for their men not to fire back. When they corrected themselves moments later, it was too late, and their men fled in panic. The two guns from Backof's Battery facing north managed to escape just before *Rosser's* men scrambled up the hill, but the other four were captured. Although Sigel courageously attempted to rally his men, there was no hope, and he soon joined them in flight. Most of the Federals ran down Wire Road. Farrand's dragoons and Carr's cavalrymen joined this mass, withdrawing from the flanks in good order. Sigel, one piece of artillery, and part of the 3rd Missouri sped toward the Dixon farm. *McCulloch* sent only a few mounted units in pursuit. The Federals escaping by Wire Road moved in several disorganized groups, turning north on the Little York Road to enter Springfield from the west. After reaching the Dixon farm, Sigel led his truncated column south by a circuitous route to a crossing of the James River. Carr joined them en route. Attacked by Southern pursuers as they crossed, the Federals scattered in panic, abandoning their artillery. They made their way north to Springfield individually (see "Sigel's Retreat" excursion below for more details).

McCulloch had decisively ended the threat to his rear and now was free to focus on the fighting at Bloody Hill. More than 20 percent of Sigel's force became casualties. On the Southern side only the Louisianans suffered heavily, losing by best estimate more than forty men, mostly wounded.

Analysis

Sigel neglected basic security and aligned his forces poorly. Few of his infantry fired a shot, while none of his horsemen did. In the center the Federals in column on the road fled before their officers could form them into line. On the left

Carr's cavalrymen had advanced so far north that *Rosser's* force passed behind them when they attacked the artillery. Although Farrand's dragoons on the right saw the enemy, the unguarded "dead zone" allowed *McCulloch* to close so quickly that the horsemen could not fire for fear of hitting friends.

Vignette

The lone soldier from the 3rd Missouri who Sigel sent to meet Lyon was Cpl. Charles Todt of Company K, a prewar physician serving in the ranks. As the *3rd Louisiana* approached, Todt realized that they were the enemy and aimed at *McCulloch*, who was leading them on horseback, dressed in the plain black velvet suit that he preferred to a uniform. Quick action by Cpl. Henry H. *Gentles* ended Todt's life. "That was a good shot," *McCulloch* observed as the Northern soldier fell. He turned to *Gentles's* company commander, John P. *Vigilini*, and said, "Captain, take your men up and give them hell." [5] The Southerners overran Sigel's position so quickly that shells from the *Fort Smith Light Battery* accidentally killed Capt. R. M. *Hinson* and Pvt. E. A. *Whetstone*, his brother-in-law. Several others were also wounded by friendly fire. The brief bombardment severely damaged the Sharp House, though the family remained safe in the cellar. Bodies lay in their yard for days following the battle, while their home became a hospital once more.

Army commanders rarely led attacks during the Civil War. At the battle of Wilson's Creek, *McCulloch* displayed the same recklessness that would cost him his life seven months later at Pea Ridge.

Although Sigel remained a hero to many German Americans despite his faults, Pvt. Otto C. Lademann was unforgiving. Years after the battle he recalled sarcastically how Sigel's placement of the bulk of the 3rd Missouri in column on the road behind the guns, limbers, and caissons of Backof's Battery spelled disaster when the Louisianans struck from the front and *Rosser's* force attacked from the flank: "The effects of [the *3rd Louisiana's*] volley were singular. . . . [T]he fright produced on the horses by the rattle of the musketry added to the discomfiture of the drivers; made them plunge, as with one accord, into the infantry columns of the 3rd Missouri volunteers. . . . While our battalion presented an indescribable mixture of men, horses, guns and caissons, the enemy, now only fifteen feet from our naked left flank, gave one tremendous cheer, and rushed in. Col. Sigel's tactical skill having deprived us of every opportunity of employing our arms, there was nothing left for us but to run, and run we did like good fellows." [6]

OPTIONAL EXCURSION: Sigel's Retreat, 9:00–9:45 A.M.

The roads Sigel followed during his retreat no longer exist. The route outlined below runs west of his actual route.

Directions

Returning to the Visitor Center, leave the battlefield, *turning left* from the entrance onto FARM ROAD 182. *Proceed* 0.1 mile to COUNTY ZZ. *Turn left. Drive south* 3.6 miles to HOLDEN ROAD. *Turn left. Proceed* along HOLDEN ROAD 1.2 miles to a low area of ground just before reaching the junction of KERR ROAD on your right. Sigel moved through this low area from right to left, heading for a ford of the James River. From its intersection with KERR ROAD, *continue* along HOLDEN ROAD 0.6 mile to MISSOURI 14. *Turn left*, heading east. *Proceed* 0.7 mile to DELAWARE TOWN ROAD; you will cross the James River en route. *Turn left* and *drive* 0.2 mile. *Turn left* into the Delaware Town Public Fishing Access Area. *Proceed* 0.2 mile to the boat-ramp parking lot on your right. You can view the James River from the ramp. Sigel crossed the James at a ford about 0.5 mile upstream. There is no public access by foot or automobile to the site.

What Happened

After reaching the Dixon farm, Sigel decided to move south circuitously rather than retrace the route he had used to reach the battlefield. The troopers of Carr's Company I, 1st U.S. Cavalry, soon joined him. Despite the colonel's instructions to stay with the column, Carr pushed ahead, leaving the infantry and the artillerymen hauling a lone gun to their fate. The Southerners dispatched by *McCulloch* caught up to them as they crossed the James River. Two companies from the *South Kansas– Texas Cavalry*, a cavalry company under Lt. Col. James *Majors* of *Clark's* division, Col. William *Brown's* cavalrymen from *Parsons's* division, and three other unidentified units from the Missouri State Guard made the attack. The odds were approximately even at about 400 men per side, but the Federals soon scattered in disarray, abandoning the gun. Although Sigel left the field only after further resistance was pointless, his swift horse got him back to Springfield ahead of Carr's cavalrymen or any other organized body of Federals.

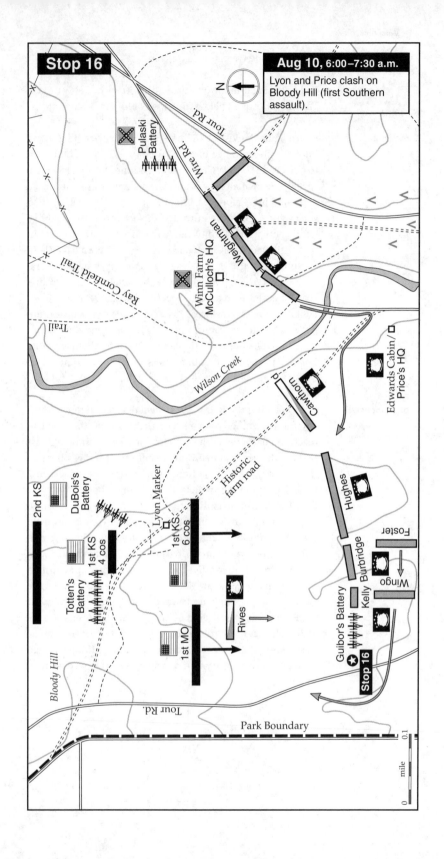

Stop 16

Aug 10, 6:00–7:30 a.m.

Lyon and Price clash on Bloody Hill (first Southern assault).

N

Pulaski Battery

Tour Rd.

Wire Rd.

Weightman

Ray Cornfield Trail

Trail

Winn Farm/ McCulloch's HQ

Wilson Creek

Cawthorn

Edwards Cabin/ Price's HQ

2nd KS

DuBois's Battery

Lyon Marker

1st KS 6 cos

Historic farm road

Hughes

1st KS 4 cos

Totten's Battery

1st MO

Rives

Guibor's Battery

Kelly

Burbridge

Foster

Wingo

Stop 16

Bloody Hill

Tour Rd.

Park Boundary

0.1

0

mile

Bloody Hill

STOP 16   Guibor's Battery, 5:15–8:00 A.M. (NB6)

Directions   *Proceed* 0.5 mile along the TOUR ROAD to the turnout on the right for *Guibor's Battery*. Upon leaving Stop 14, the road curves to the right and drops down to a modern bridge across Skegg's Branch, which runs west to east and joins Wilson Creek a short distance to your right. Probably dry on August 10, the streambed presented no obstacle for troops. The road continues north and west, briefly paralleling Skegg's Branch. At the time of the battle, a farm road ran parallel to the stream's north side, to the left of the TOUR ROAD (traces of it are visible in the winter). Southern troops used the farm road to march west, extending the left end of their battle line facing Bloody Hill. *En route* on your right you pass one of the two large ravines that scar the hill's south slope. The prairie grass, brush, and scattered trees here reflect the ground cover that characterized the whole of Bloody Hill in 1861. As the fighting developed, this narrow valley sheltered various Southern units as they either moved into position or fell back after a failed assault to regroup out of view of Union forces on Bloody Hill's crest.

After a short distance the TOUR ROAD climbs Bloody Hill. The small farm of T. B. Manley, the brother of Caleb B. Manley, was to the west (left side of the road). There is no access to the site. You are now near the left flank of the Southerners' battle line, from where they began the first assault against Lyon. *En route* toward the hillcrest, you will notice the second large ravine that cuts into the south slope. Also to your left is COUNTY ZZ, which marks the western boundary of the battlefield. After driving a short distance you will see a small parking area on your right and the guns marking the location of Capt. Henry *Guibor's* battery.

Orientation   Face in the direction of the guns marking *Guibor's Battery* (north-northeast), looking up the slope of Bloody Hill. Phase Six of the battle began as *Price* formed his infantry units on the south slope of Bloody Hill (to your right rear) to counter Lyon's battle line on the crest (to your front). This phase eventually encompassed the majority of the combat and the largest number of troops, approximately 10,000 men (4,000 Union and 6,000 Southern) and seventeen pieces of artillery (ten Union, seven Southern). Although you can see a large portion of the battlefield from this location, undulations of terrain and modern forestation prevent you from seeing the

Lyon Marker (Stop 19, to your right front) or the area where fighting occurred to your left outside the battlefield boundary (see "*Greer* Attacks Lyon's Right" below).

What Happened

(These events relate to Phase Six of the battle.) Around 5:15 A.M., to your right front and out of sight of the *Guibor's Battery* position, *Cawthorn* heard the exchange of fire between *Hunter* and Lyon on the northern spur of Bloody Hill. In response he led the remaining cavalry of *Rains's* division of the Missouri State Guard (the commands of Col. Robert *Peyton* and Col. James *McCowan*) to the main crest. Dismounting into line of battle along the northern face, they sheltered their horses on the hill's south side. *Hunter's* retreating men soon extended *Cawthorn's* right. From Bloody Hill's northern spur, Lyon assessed the situation, adjusted his line, and renewed his advance. After brief fighting, *Cawthorn's* men retreated over the crest of the hill, the Missourians racing to mount their horses. Lyon's lead units (the 1st Missouri, 1st Kansas, and Totten's Battery) reached the top of the hill about 6:00 A.M., while the remainder of his column followed more slowly, using farm roads skirting the ravine.

Only one small unit stood between Lyon and the main Southern camps along Wilson Creek. The 284 men of Col. Benjamin A. *Rives's* cavalry of *Slack's* division were camped below the hill's crest (to your right front about 450 yards away). The acoustic shadow prevented their hearing the opening phases of the battle, and the rolling terrain to the east and north blocked their view of *Cawthorn's* retreat. Earlier in the morning, one of the unit's officers had ridden north out of camp and stumbled onto the fighting. He raced back to camp and informed *Rives* of the attack. The colonel responded by sending a patrol to investigate, ordering his wagons to the rear, and beginning to form his regiment into a dismounted line. But before the line was formed and the wagons moved out of harm's way, the patrol raced back into camp confirming the Federal advance. Minutes later Lyon's forces appeared on the hilltop to the northeast. The 1st Missouri, on the Federal right, turned to face *Rives* and opened fire. While most of this fire was too high and *Rives's Cavalry* suffered only a few casualties, the Southerners fled in panic, breaking into two groups that did not reunite until the end of the battle. Even so, *Rives's* unexpected presence on Bloody Hill slowed Lyon, giving *Price* additional time to respond.

As *Cawthorn's* horsemen fled from the main crest, the Federals came under fire from the *Pulaski Light Battery*, across Wilson Creek near the Winn farm. While the 1st Missouri drove *Rives's* men down the hill, Totten's Battery deployed and returned fire against the Arkansas guns. The resistance Lyon encountered made him cautious. The area to his front seemed clear, but the broad undulations of Bloody Hill prevented him from seeing the Southern camps. Therefore, while waiting for the remainder of his force to arrive, he sent most of the infantry then present forward to probe for the enemy.

Phase Six of the battle, the struggle to control Bloody Hill, now began. From the crest (about 800 yards to your right front), Lyon ordered Lieutenant Colonel Andrews of the 1st Missouri and Colonel Deitzler with six companies of the 1st Kansas to advance down the hill's south slope; the remaining four companies of Kansans supported Totten. Since Lyon failed to place either Andrews or Deitzler in charge, their movement was uncoordinated. Some time after 6:00 A.M., the 1st Kansas advanced in column by company (to your right front), while the 1st Missouri on their right (to your front) marched in the standard line of battle. As the two commands advanced, they quickly lost contact with each other due to the tree-lined ravine (to your right) that scars that portion of the slope. When the two units blundered into the Missouri State Guard, a 60-yard gap separated them.

From his headquarters at Edwards Cabin (one-half mile to your right, out of view), *Price* had struggled since shortly after 5:00 A.M. to get his largely untrained and poorly disciplined men out of their camps, between Wire Road and Wilson Creek, and into position facing Bloody Hill. He formed his initial line of battle near the southeastern base of the hill and near the creek, using a portion of *Cawthorn's* horsemen and the 650 infantry of *Slack's* division, consolidated under the command of Col. John T. *Hughes*. By 6:00 A.M. he extended his line west (to your right) with Col. John Q. *Burbridge's* 270 infantrymen from *Clark's* division and the 142-man infantry battalion from *Parsons's* division under Col. Joseph M. *Kelly*. *Guibor's Battery* of four 6-pounders provided artillery support to their left. But the battery's precise location is uncertain. The position marked on the battlefield (your present location) may be fifty yards or more farther up the slope than the Southerners were when they initially encountered the Federals descending the hill about 6:30 A.M.

Due to the vegetation and the rolling nature of the ground, *Price's* Missourians could not initially see Lyon's men marching toward them, 1,200 strong. But soon the sound of so many soldiers moving through the prairie grass and brush, along with mounted officers and their shouted commands, announced their approach. Although *Price* had some 1,400 men ready for action, his battle line was still incomplete. Most of his soldiers were armed with short-range smoothbore muskets or shotguns brought from home, and they averaged only twenty-five rounds of ammunition apiece. Under these circumstances, *Price* decided to let the enemy approach closely before opening fire. When some guardsmen armed with military or civilian rifles violated orders by shooting at long range, Andrews and Deitzler apparently interpreted this as fire from skirmishers. The Federals were quite surprised when entire State Guard units rose up out of the tall prairie grass. They fought well, however. For some thirty minutes, at ranges varying from twenty to one hundred yards, both sides exchanged fire so intensely that the sounds of battle reached Springfield, nine miles away.

As the six companies of the 1st Kansas traded volleys with the commands of *Cawthorn*, *Hughes*, and *Burbridge*, Lyon ordered Maj. John Halderman to take the four companies that had supported Totten's Battery and join their regiment. Halderman's detachment formed on Deitzler's left, and the Southerners gave ground before them.

While this action was taking place on the ravine's east side (to your right), fire from *Guibor's Battery* (at or near your present position) halted the advance of the 1st Missouri. After a short time Andrews decided to charge the Southern guns. But before the attack could begin, he observed an enemy force moving around his right flank (to your left). This was the infantry from *McBride's* division, 600 men organized into two units led by Col. John A. *Foster* and Col. Edmond T. *Wingo*. *McBride* had moved to the left (west) of *Guibor's Battery*, extending *Price's* left flank and bringing the Southern strength up to 2,000 men. Andrews therefore sent a message to Totten asking for support and began a fighting withdrawal toward the hilltop. Totten detached one section (two guns) under Lt. George O. Sokalski, who took up a position on the far right of the Federal line. As the 1st Missouri neared the crest, Andrews halted and pulled his right companies back at an angle to face west and confront *McBride*, while the rest of the regiment continued to face south toward *Guibor's* guns.

McBride's advance marked a turning point in the fighting on Bloody Hill. For the first time, Southern forces were on the offensive on this portion of the battlefield. For the rest of the fight, Lyon stood on the defensive, responding to attacks from *Price*.

It is not clear whether *McBride* advanced on his own initiative, by a misunderstanding, or as part of a plan by *Price* for a general assault. In any case, shortly after *Foster* and *Wingo* moved up the hill, the entire Southern line began to move en echelon from left to right (west to east). A combination of terrain, ground cover, and uneven training caused units to advance at different rates, however, robbing the attackers of their numerical advantage even as additional forces arrived. While *Cawthorn* and *Hughes* advanced, the infantry from *Rains's* division, consolidated under Col. Richard H. *Weightman*, took up a position between them. The Southern advance forced the 1st Kansas to fall back as well, and Lyon brought up the 2nd Kansas, under Col. Robert B. Mitchell, for support. Arriving earlier, the regiment lay behind Bloody Hill's northern slope until Lyon called them out of reserve. While Mitchell's men moved into position, the general ordered the 1st Kansas to charge, hoping to halt the apparently relentless Southern advance. Only three companies of the regiment heard or understood the order, but their sudden counterattack scattered the Missourians in their immediate front. Once the Kansans returned to the crest, Lyon consolidated his entire force. Around 7:30 A.M. *Price* began pulling the State Guard back. Like the advance, this was a slow, complicated process. By 8:00 A.M. the forces on Bloody Hill were disengaged. Except for occasional artillery firing, a prolonged lull ensued.

Analysis

Although small in comparison to later battles, the forces that clashed on Bloody Hill exceeded the command-level experience of everyone on the field. Both Lyon and *Price* moved with caution and deliberation, while the common soldiers' minimal training and shortage of ammunition also slowed the pace of battle. Although intense, the small-arms firing during this initial engagement probably lasted no more than thirty minutes. Having more ammunition, artillery units on both sides were more active, firing almost continuously at various points on the field, even during lulls when the infantry rested.

Given the relatively open terrain, Lyon could have used his cavalry rather than his infantry to explore the area to his front. He might also have used his horsemen to locate and harass *Price's* left flank once the firing began. Instead, Lt. Charles W. Canfield's Company D, 1st U.S. Cavalry, and a mounted company of the 2nd Kansas under Capt. Samuel N. Wood (totaling 350 men) remained to the rear. The fight that occurred when Lyon sent the 1st Kansas and 1st Missouri forward unsupported did not slow *Price's* ongoing deployment appreciably, though it may have made him more cautious. While time was not on Lyon's side, a delay in order to concentrate all of his infantry for an attack en masse may have represented his best chance for victory. Once Lyon lost the initiative, his hope for success lay with Sigel, yet he sent no mounted forces to try to establish contact with the other portion of his army.

Price constructed his battle line slowly, leading many units into place himself. It is not clear whether he actually ordered the first advance up Bloody Hill. It may have occurred spontaneously, as *McBride's* infantry under *Foster* and *Wingo*, moving to *Guibor's* left, advanced farther than the rest of the State Guard. While the bold counterattack by the 1st Kansas helped stymie the Southern right flank, the overall advance stalled because units lost contact with each other on the uneven ground, and the fire from the Federal artillery unnerved many in the ranks. The remnants of *Rains's* cavalry fought dismounted, though *Price* might have used them mounted to threaten the Federals' left flank. Regardless, he apparently made no attempt to call upon the rest of his cavalry camped at the Sharp farm; it is not clear when he learned of the disaster there.

Vignette

While the terrain at Wilson's Creek was open compared to that on battlefields such as Shiloh or the Wilderness, two incidents testify to the confusion inherent in combat. During this early battle, the normal confusion was exacerbated by the fact that many combatants on both sides wore civilian clothes and that no standardization of color or style existed among those who did possess uniforms.

During the Southern advance, Captain *Guibor* rode ahead of his guns to examine some high ground to the northwest (your left front) as a possible location for his battery. He was soon cut off by the Federals but escaped by riding north into the enemy's rear. No one paid attention to a lone rider in civilian clothing. *Guibor* did not rejoin his unit until after the battle, and command of the battery fell to Lt. William P. *Barlow*.

During the charge of the 1st Kansas, the company under Capt. Powell Clayton became separated from the others and failed to hear the order for retreat. Clayton led his men farther down the slope but soon lost contact with the fleeing Missouri State Guard. When a unit of infantrymen appeared on his left and identified themselves as "friends," the two companies joined together and marched west, searching for "the enemy." Clayton's men wore blue and the newcomers wore gray, but the captain was not alarmed, for Lyon's Army of the West was a hodge-podge of colors. He became suspicious, however, when he noted that each of the gray-clad soldiers wore a distinctive red badge on his left shoulder, the likes of which he had not seen in the army. Coolly, he ordered his men to march obliquely, increasing the distance between the two companies. This drew the attention of the commander of the "friendly" company, who was Capt. James J. *Clarkson* of *Weightman's* brigade. The Kansans' actions, rather than their uniform color, caused him concern. *Clarkson* therefore sent his adjutant, Capt. Michael *Buster*, to confront the men in blue. *Buster* instructed the wayward company to halt and make identification. Drawing his revolver, Clayton pulled *Buster* from his horse and shouted, "Now, sir, God damn you, order your men not to fire on us, or you are a dead man."[7] At this point *Clarkson* instructed the Missourians to fire, disregarding the safety of his adjutant. Clayton promptly shot *Buster*, wounding him slightly, and ordered his own men to "run for their lives." For reasons that are not known, *Clarkson* failed to pursue the Kansans, who reached the crest of Bloody Hill without further incident.

A modern view of the site of Guibor's Battery, Missouri State Guard, looking north up the slopes of Bloody Hill. Courtesy National Park Service, Wilson's Creek National Battlefield.

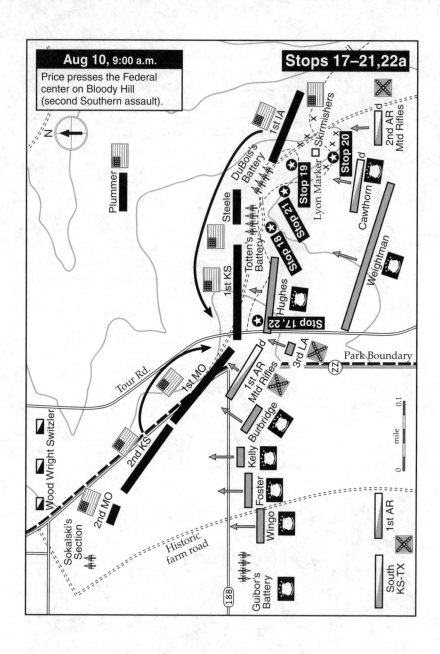

Aug 10, 9:00 a.m.

Price presses the Federal
center on Bloody Hill
(second Southern assault).

Stops 17–21, 22a

N

Plummer

1st IA

2nd AR
Mtd Rifles

DuBois's
Battery

Skirmishers

Stop 20

Steele

Lyon Marker

Stop 19

Cawthorn

Stop 21

Totten's
Battery

Stop 18

Weightman

1st KS

Hughes

Stop 17, 22

Tour Rd.

1st MO

1st AR
Mtd Rifles

3rd LA

Park Boundary

2nd KS

Kelly Burbridge

Wood Wright Switzler

2nd MO

Foster

Sokalski's
Section

Wingo

1st AR

Historic
farm road

188

Guibor's
Battery

South
KS-TX

0.1

mile

0

STOP 17   Bloody Hill, 5:15–8:00 A.M. (NB7)

Directions   *Proceed* 0.25 mile to the parking lot for Stop 17. *Follow* the
                           adjacent trail to the NB interpretative sign.

Orientation   As you stand viewing the interpretative sign, you are on the
                           crest of Bloody Hill, facing east. The Ray House is visible to
                           your front, more than 1 mile distant. Just in front of the
                           house, parallel split-rail fencing marks Wire Road. Closer to
                           you, about 0.75 mile away, on the plateau outlined with split-
                           rail fencing, is the Ray Cornfield. The unnamed northern
                           spur of Bloody Hill is to your far left, out of sight. Directly
                           to your rear the terrain of Bloody Hill encompasses a sub-
                           stantial amount of ground outside the battlefield boundary.
                           To your right front a walking trail begins that leads to the
                           Lyon Marker and other sites on Bloody Hill. To your right a
                           gun marks the position taken by Sokalski's section of Totten's
                           Battery to repulse the first Southern attack on Bloody Hill
                           (discussed at Stop 16). Do not confuse this with Sokalski's
                           position during the second attack, which is described below.

What Happened   (The events interpreted here relate to Phases Two, Three, and
                           Six of the battle. As the initial events relating to Bloody Hill
                           during Phases Two and Three have already been discussed in
                           relation to Stops 2, 3, 7, and 12, the focus here is primarily on
                           Phase Six.) During the night of August 9, most of *Cawthorn's
                           Cavalry* of *Rains's* division camped in the ravine between the
                           northern spur and this position. *Rives's Cavalry* of *Slack's* di-
                           vision camped approximately 250 yards to your right front.
                           About 5:00 A.M., after receiving word of Lyon's approach,
                           Cawthorn ordered his subordinate *Hunter* north to look for
                           the enemy. When *Hunter* moved his company up onto Bloody
                           Hill's northern spur, he observed the Federals at the Short
                           farm. After sending word back to *Cawthorn*, he placed his
                           men into line of battle. In response to *Hunter's* message, *Caw-
                           thorn* led the remainder of his horsemen up to the northern
                           face of Bloody Hill's main crest (about 250 yards to your left
                           front). Col. Robert L. Y. *Peyton's* regiment formed the left flank
                           of this line, Col. James *McCowan's* company the right. Both
                           units dismounted to fight.
                               When Lyon forced *Hunter's* men from the northern spur,
                           the retreating state guardsmen formed on the main ridge,
                           extending *Cawthorn's* right. Lyon continued his advance, driv-
                           ing *Cawthorn's* men down the southern slopes (to your right)
                           as well as *Rives's Cavalry* soon afterward.
                               Lyon reached the crest of Bloody Hill between 5:30 and
                           6:00 A.M. with only the 1st Kansas, 1st Missouri, and Totten's

Battery, having detached Plummer to seize Wire Road and instructed the remainder of his column to follow farm roads that would take them around the head of the ravine (to your left rear).

When Totten's Battery fired on *Rives's* horsemen, the noise and smoke attracted the attention of the *Pulaski Light Battery* near the Winn farm. Totten changed direction, and a duel ensued between the Federal and Arkansas gunners. As a result, Lyon made Totten's Battery the anchor of his line on the crest, sending the 1st Kansas and 1st Missouri forward to explore the ground to his front while waiting for the rest of his column to arrive. As this was going on, the four-gun battery commanded by Lt. John V. Du Bois arrived via a farm road. Du Bois placed his guns to Totten's left rear, taking up the duel with the *Pulaski Light Battery*. Totten shifted his battery to the right when the retreating 1st Missouri called for help. Later Lyon's adjutant, Capt. Gordon Granger, noted Plummer's men retreating through the Ray Cornfield toward Gibson Mill and directed Du Bois to cover their retreat. The Federal fire caused the *3rd Louisiana Infantry* and *2nd Arkansas Mounted Rifles* to withdraw in disorder.

By 9:00 A.M. Lyon had deployed the remainder of his troops. His line of battle faced roughly south (to your right), stretching about 0.6 mile. The 1st Iowa, with skirmishers to the front, anchored the left flank, near the steep eastern slope of Bloody Hill overlooking Wilson Creek. To their right, in order, were Du Bois's four-gun battery; a battalion of Regulars under Capt. Frederick Steele; two sections (four guns) of Totten's Battery, commanded by Totten; the 1st Kansas; the 1st Missouri; the 2nd Kansas; the 2nd Missouri; and one section (the remaining two guns) of Totten's Battery under Lieutenant Sokalski. Plummer's battalion, which had returned from the fight in Ray's Cornfield, formed the infantry reserve, while the mounted troops (Home Guard units, Kansans, and Regulars) remained to the rear. More than 3,000 men stood waiting to see what the Missouri State Guard would do next.

Vignette

Capt. James Totten was popular among both the Regulars and the volunteers in Lyon's Army of the West, in part because of the flair with which he directed his battery. He also habitually punctuated his orders with profanity. Eugene Ware, a soldier in the 1st Iowa, recalled that "Take that limber to the rear, G-d d—n you, sir" and "Wheel that caisson around, G-d d—n you, sir" as typical of the captain's style. Most of Totten's gunners were either Irish or German by birth. In the intense August heat, they shed their regulation blue blouses and fought in their shirtsleeves.

Analysis

When Lyon gave up the initiative, his chances for a decisive victory dropped sharply, but once he went on the defensive, he obtained a tactical advantage that the Federals maintained throughout the rest of the fighting on Bloody Hill. From his static position he was able shift his troops laterally in response to events while maintaining the overall cohesion of his lines. The Southerners, attacking uphill over broken terrain, faced much greater challenges in terms of command and control.

Vignette

A draconian disciplinarian, Lyon had little respect for volunteer soldiers and their easy ways, but the 1st Iowa, which anchored his left, won his respect in the days before the battle. They marched so quickly he nicknamed them "greyhounds." Each of the regiment's ten companies wore a different style and color of uniform, manufactured by loved ones in their home communities. Hard marching wore out much of this finery, and many now wore at least some civilian clothing obtained during the campaign. As many as 10 percent of the Iowans were barefoot, shoes being in critically short supply, but their spirits were high. Lt. Col. William Merritt led them during the battle, wearing a white coat and riding a white horse. The regiment's commander, Col. John F. Bates, remained in Springfield (his supporters insisted that he was ill, while his detractors claimed that he was drunk).

STOP 18   Totten's Battery, 9:00 A.M.

Directions   *Follow* the Bloody Hill Loop Trail, which begins to your right
front, for approximately 200 yards, *halting* at the four guns
marking the position of Totten's Battery. *Stand* behind the
guns, looking downhill (south).

Orientation   You are in the position held by Totten's guns as they supported
the retreating 1st Missouri (to your right front) as discussed
at Stop 16. From this position the battery also formed the
center of the left flank of the more extensive Federal battle
line when the second Southern attack up Bloody Hill began
(discussed below).

What Happened   (The stop relates to Phase Six of the battle.) After defeating
Sigel at the Sharp farm, *McCulloch* turned his attention to
Bloody Hill. As he led *Hyam's* battalion of the *3rd Louisiana*
toward the fight, he sent a messenger to *Pearce*, instructing him to direct all available units of the Arkansas State
Troops to join him. Before they could reach the scene, *Price*
sent the Southern battle line forward for a second attack. It
was shortly after 9:00 A.M. Elements from all three of the
brigades composing the Western Army were present in this
assault. They numbered about 3,500 men, but their intermin-
gled positions, which reflected the ad hoc Southern response
to Lyon's surprise attack, exacerbated command-and-control
problems. The *2nd Arkansas Mounted Rifles* of *McCulloch's* Confederate brigade, still fighting on foot, held the right flank
(to your left front), adjacent to Wilson Creek. They had joined
the fight on Bloody Hill after their retreat from the Ray Cornfield. *Cawthorn's* horsemen from *Rains's* division of the Missouri State Guard fought to their left, also on foot. Next in
line to the left were *Weightman's Infantry* from *Rains's* division
and *Hughes's Infantry* from *Slack's* division. About 100 men of
the *3rd Louisiana* supported their flank; *Hébert* had rallied
them after the fight at the Ray farm, bringing them across
the creek to join the struggle. Another Confederate unit,
Col. Thomas J. *Churchill's 1st Arkansas Mounted Rifles*, fought
dismounted to their left. Beside them, extending the line farther west, were additional infantry units of the Missouri State
Guard: *Burbridge's* men from *Clark's* division, *Kelly's* men from
Parsons's division, and the infantry under *Foster* and *Wingo*
from *McBride's* division. *Guibor's Battery* was to their left front,
having shifted from its earlier position (described at Stop 16).
On the far left flank (to your right front) and farther down
the slopes, awaiting orders, were two mounted units, *Greer's*
Confederate *South Kansas–Texas Cavalry* and Col. DeRosey

Carroll's 1st Arkansas Cavalry from *Pearce's* Arkansas State Troops. Another unit under *Pearce*, the *Pulaski Light Battery* (to your left front, across Wilson Creek), had shifted from its initial position near the Winn farm to higher ground across Wire Road, where it could lend supporting fire.

Cavalryman of the
U.S. Regulars, in 1861.
BLCW 1:289

STOP 19   The Lyon Marker, 9:00 A.M.

Directions   From Totten's Battery *follow* the Bloody Hill Loop Trail approximately 250 yards to the Lyon Marker.

Orientation   Viewing the marker, you are facing west. The Federal battle line stretched from near this location back toward the parking lot for Stop 17. In 1861 the ground cover was a mixture of scrub oaks, barren rocky patches, and prairie grass, but the contour of the hill prevented the Federals from seeing Wilson Creek (to your rear) or the Edwards Cabin (to your left).

What Happened   (These events relate to Phase Six of the battle.) Contrary to the claim on this monument, Lyon was not killed near this spot. When the second Southern assault on Bloody Hill began, skirmishers from the 1st Iowa occupied the ground where you are standing. They were not heavily engaged, but Lyon was wounded in his right calf as he inspected their position. A few moments later his distinctive gray horse was killed. (The horse's position was marked after the battle, creating a later misunderstanding about the site of Lyon's death.) Shortly thereafter Lyon was wounded a second time, a bullet grazing his head, as he moved back toward the center of his line. Although dazed for a few minutes, he received medical treatment, then obtained another mount and rode to the Federal center, which was sorely pressed and in danger of collapse. Lyon ordered Merritt to move his 1st Iowa from the left flank to a position between the 1st Kansas and 1st Missouri.

Vignette   Despite the heat of the morning sun, Lyon kept his uniform coat smartly buttoned up as he moved among his troops, waving his hat and sword while shouting encouragement. His leg and head wound, however, seemed to affect his spirit as well as his body. Maj. John Schofield, Lyon's chief of staff, joined the army commander just as a handkerchief was being wound around his head to stop the bleeding. "Major, I am afraid the day is lost," Lyon announced. There was no word from Sigel, and the pace of the battle was increasing rapidly. "No, General," Schofield replied, "let us try it again." With this firm support, Lyon returned to the fray.[8]

STOP 20   Loop Trail Overlook, 9:00 A.M.

Directions   *Continue* along the Loop Trail until you come to a junction.
                     Turn left and *follow* the trail to its end, where it overlooks the
                     valley of Wilson Creek.

Orientation   Look down into the valley of Wilson Creek, facing southwest
                     toward the Edwards Cabin in the distance. Wilson Creek
                     is to your left. The slopes of Bloody Hill stretch from your
                     present position back to Stop 17 and beyond the battlefield
                     boundary.

What Happened   (Events discussed here relate to Phase Six of the battle.) By the
                     time of the second Southern assault, the focus of the battle
                     had shifted farther west. Even so, the Edwards Cabin area re-
                     mained the scene of frantic activity. Soldiers carried wounded
                     comrades from the battle to one or more makeshift hospitals
                     along the creek (their exact location is unclear). Men who had
                     become separated from their units during the surprise attack
                     mingled with skulkers unwilling to face the danger and with
                     the members of the Missouri State Guard who had no weap-
                     ons. Abandoned horses and mules roamed freely. Some of the
                     women, children, and slaves who accompanied the Western
                     Army sought shelter in the shade of the tree-lined stream.

STOP 21   The Sinkhole, 6:30–11:00 A.M.

Directions   *Retrace* your steps along the trail. At the junction *continue*
                           straight until you come to the sinkhole, a distance of about
                           twenty-five yards.

Orientation   Face west, looking across the sinkhole. The trail leading back
                           to Stop 17 is visible in the distance. To your front the second
                           Southern attack up Bloody Hill moved from your left to your
                           right. The skirmish line of the 1st Iowa was to your rear.

What Happened   (The interpretation here relates to Phase Six of the battle.)
                           The first, second, and third Southern attacks crossed the
                           ground where you are standing as well as that to your front,
                           though the fighting was heaviest around the sinkhole during
                           the first assault.

                           When the battle ended near midday, 277 Southerners and
                           258 Federals lay dead on the field. Because of the heat, rapid
                           burial was necessary. The majority of the dead were interred
                           in two mass graves that have never been located. But a large
                           number were buried in this natural sinkhole. Their remains
                           were disinterred during the 1870s and moved to the National
                           Cemetery in Springfield and the adjacent Confederate cem-
                           etery, which was initially separate from it.

Maj. Samuel Sturgis,
who assumed com-
mand of Union forces
following Lyon's death.
Courtesy National Park
Service, Wilson's Creek
National Battlefield.

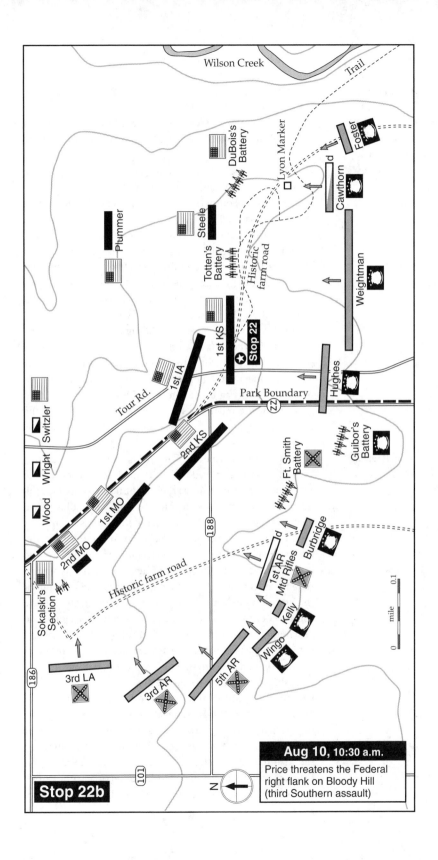

Wilson Creek

Trail

Foster

DuBois's Battery

Lyon Marker

Cawthorn

d

Plummer

Steele

Weightman

Totten's Battery

Historic farm road

Stop 22

1st KS

1st IA

Hughes

Tour Rd.

Park Boundary

ZZ

Switzler

2nd KS

Guibor's Battery

Wright

Ft. Smith Battery

Wood

1st MO

188

2nd MO

Burbridge

1st AR Mtd Rifles

d

Sokalski's Section

Historic farm road

Kelly

Wingo

186

3rd LA

3rd AR

5th AR

0   mile   0.1

101

N

Aug 10, 10:30 a.m.

Price threatens the Federal right flank on Bloody Hill (third Southern assault)

Stop 22b

STOP 22   Bloody Hill, 9:00–11:00 A.M.

Directions   *Follow* the trail back to Stop 17, about 500 yards. *Go* to the
                       artillery piece on your left as you return (to your right if you
                       are facing the NB display at Stop 17), marking the position of
                       Sokalski's section of Totten's Battery during the first attack.

Orientation   Face in the direction of the gun (south-southeast). You are
                       standing approximately in the center of the Federal line dur-
                       ing the second Southern attack (no guns stood here at that
                       time—Sokalski had shifted to the far right). Unfortunately,
                       the battlefield TOUR ROAD and COUNTY ZZ have destroyed the
                       key terrain to your right rear. The 1st Kansas was where you
                       stand, its right flank extending to the TOUR ROAD. To their
                       right (extending outside the battlefield boundary and just
                       across COUNTY ZZ) was the 1st Missouri, which faced south-
                       west to follow the contour of Bloody Hill. A small space ex-
                       isted between the two units. The Southerners used the ravine
                       to your right (the TOUR ROAD runs much of its length) and the
                       one just to the west of it (outside the battlefield) to press their
                       attack. Artillery could not cover this area, so Lyon responded
                       to the danger by calling upon the 1st Iowa. He ordered it to
                       move from the relatively secure left flank to reinforce the
                       Federal center.

What Happened   (Events interpreted here relate to Phase Six of the battle.)
                       When the Iowans arrived to fill the small space between the
                       1st Missouri and 1st Kansas, their right flank companies col-
                       lided with the left of the Missourians, who were falling back.
                       To disentangle them, Merritt ordered his Iowans to fall back
                       also, but two of his companies became separated from the
                       regiment and a significant gap developed in the Federal line
                       (to your right, about the center of the TOUR ROAD). As Merritt
                       rode to collect the detached companies, leaving the bulk of
                       the Iowans temporarily leaderless, Lyon arrived. The Federal
                       commander saw two mounted officers down the slope, one
                       of whom appeared to be Price. Lyon drew his revolver and
                       with his escort prepared to go after the State Guard com-
                       mander, but an aide advised him against it, and the general
                       turned his attention to fixing the break in the line. Maj. Sam-
                       uel Sturgis to this point had worked to rally the 1st Iowa in
                       Merritt's absence. When Lyon rode over to their position, the
                       men called for the general to lead them forward. But about
                       that time, Capt. Thomas Sweeny arrived, and Lyon directed
                       the Irishman to take charge of the unit. In all the confusion
                       the gap remained unfilled. While conferring with Sturgis
                       and Sweeny, Lyon sent orders for Colonel Mitchell to move

his 2nd Kansas from its position on the right of the 1st Missouri and fill the void.

Mitchell quickly formed his unit into column and passed behind the Missourians. As the Kansans came up, Lyon joined the colonel at the head of the column. A volley exploded to their front from the thick underbrush as the regiment moved into the gap. The fire caused some confusion as the men in the head of the column were cut down. Among those hit was General Lyon. He had the reins of his horse in his left hand and had turned back to his right and shouted to the Kansans, "Come on my brave boys, I will lead you forward!" At that moment a bullet from the volley plowed into the left side of his chest, cutting through both lungs and the aorta, and exited below his right shoulder blade. Lyon collapsed into the arms of his aide, Pvt. Albert Lehmann, and hoarsely whispered, "Lehmann, I am going." With these words the first Union general killed in combat during the Civil War lay dead on the field at Wilson's Creek.[9] (The spot where Lyon fell cannot be precisely determined, though it may well be within the path of either the TOUR ROAD or COUNTY ZZ.)

Lyon's body was taken a short distance to the rear, and his chief of staff, Major Schofield, went to inform Sturgis, the senior officer on the field, that he now commanded Union forces on Bloody Hill. The same volley that killed Lyon had wounded Mitchell. Unable to continue, he turned over command of his regiment to Lt. Col. Charles Blair. The 2nd Kansas recovered from the volley, finally closed the hole, and began exchanging fire with *Price's* Missourians.

Some twenty minutes or more passed before Schofield located Sturgis. During that time the leaderless Federals averted a second major threat. *Greer's South Kansas–Texas Cavalry* and *Carroll's 1st Arkansas Cavalry* struck the Union right flank but were driven off. (This action took place outside the NB boundary; see "*Greer* Attacks Lyon's Right" below). With this last effort, the second Southern assault came to an end. Around 10:00 A.M., another lull settled over Bloody Hill, though the artillery continued to fire at long range.

During the relative quiet, as both sides adjusted their lines and prepared to renew the fighting, *Price* received additional support from *McCulloch's* Confederate Brigade and *Pearce's* Arkansas State Troops. It is not clear whether *McCulloch* or *Price* primarily directed the subsequent action, but at around 10:30 A.M. the Western Army launched its greatest attack of the day. *Foster's Infantry* of *McBride's* division replaced the 2nd *Arkansas Mounted Rifles* as the anchor of the right flank; in response to a false report, the Arkansans were moved to guard Wire Road ford of Wilson Creek. To *Foster's* left were *Caw-*

thorn's dismounted horsemen and *Weightman's Infantry*, both of *Rains's* division, and *Hughes's Infantry* from *Slack's* division. To their left were *Guibor's Battery*, now under Lieutenant *Barlow*, and the *Fort Smith Light Battery*, shifted from its position across the creek. *Burbridge's Infantry* of *Clark's* division and the *1st Arkansas Mounted Rifles* guarded the Arkansas gunners' left. Beside them were *Kelly's Infantry* of *Parsons's* division and *Wingo's Infantry* from *McBride's* division. Two of *Pearce's* units came next: Col. Thomas P. *Dockery's 5th Arkansas Infantry* and Col. John T. *Gratiot's 3rd Arkansas Infantry*. The once separated battalions of the *3rd Louisiana Infantry* were reunited under *Hébert* on the far left flank. Well over 5,000 Southern soldiers participated in the third assault.

Sturgis stretched the Federal battle line perilously thin to meet this threat. If the Southerners had possessed enough ammunition for a sustained fight, they might have prevailed by weight of numbers. Shortly after 11:00 A.M., however, the fighting died down, and the Southerners retreated for a third time.

Analysis

While Lyon can be faulted for leading from the front, *McCulloch* and *Price* did so as well, as indeed did the most famous Civil War generals on occasion. Lyon monitored his situation accurately and was responding appropriately to a crisis at the time of his death. Although briefly discouraged earlier in the battle, he responded to the threat to his center with confidence and vigor.

McCulloch and *Price* directed their respective portions of the battle with skill, but many factors worked against them. Several of *Price's* units had been organized only a few weeks before the battle and had little practice in tactical maneuvers. Moreover, the Southerners attacked up a hill scarred with ravines, copses of trees, and undulating terrain features that blocked their view both to the left and right. Despite their best efforts, *McCulloch* and *Price* could not maintain a continuous line. The Southern assault broke up into a series of uncoordinated, piecemeal attacks. While all these factors played a role in frustrating the Western Army, its shortage of ammunition was even more crucial. Officers repeatedly cautioned their men to conserve ammunition. Finally, Federal artillery had a disproportionate effect. Although courageous, the Southern troops directly facing Du Bois, Totten, and Sokalski made little progress and suffered heavy casualties. It was no accident that the crisis in the Federal center that cost Lyon his life came at a part of the field that the Union batteries could not cover.

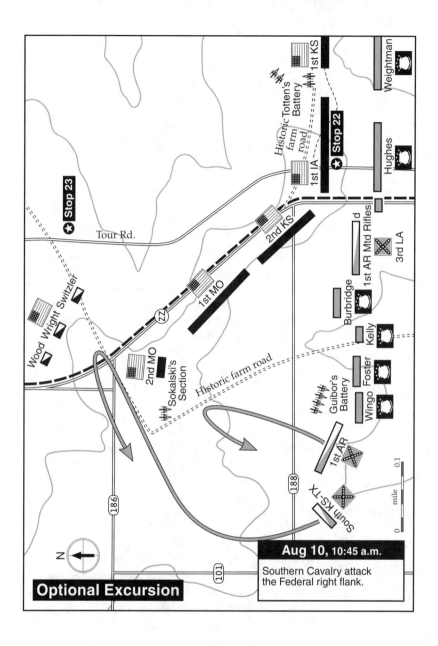

Optional Excursion

Aug 10, 10:45 a.m.

Southern Cavalry attack the Federal right flank.

Stop 23

Stop 22

Tour Rd.

Weightman

1st KS

Historic Totten's farm road

Hughes

1st IA

2nd KS

1st AR Mtd Rifles

3rd LA

Wood

Wright

Switzler

1st MO

Burbridge

Kelly

2nd MO

Sokalski's Section

Foster

Guibor's Battery

Wingo

Historic farm road

1st AR

South KS-TX

186

188

ZZ

101

N

0   mile   0.1

Vignette

Price fought the battle wearing a long white linen duster and a white hat. During the second Southern assault, he suffered a painful wound to his side but continued to direct the Missouri State Guard. According to one account, *Price* made light of his injury while also making fun of his own portly figure. After the bullet grazed him, he quipped, "That isn't fair; if I were as slim as Lyon that fellow would have missed me entirely."[10] About the same time, three bullets struck Colonel *Weightman*. Mortally wounded, he was taken to the Ray House, where he would learn of the Southern victory just before he died.

During the third assault, the Southern forces did not rush forward; they crept cautiously uphill, seeking to get within close range before expending any of their precious ammunition. Many received sharp surprises as Federal soldiers, who had been lying down for safety, rose suddenly from the waist-high prairie grass. Men on both sides frequently loaded their weapons while lying down, a clumsy, time-consuming process rarely followed during later, faster-paced battles. Pvt. Ras *Stirman* of the *3rd Arkansas* recalled: "They were lying down in the brush and grass until we were within one hundred yards of them, then they opened up on us bringing us down like Sheep but we never wavered. We did not wait for orders to fire but all of us cut loose at them like wild men, then we dropped to our knees and loaded and shot as fast as we could. We had to shoot by guess as they were upon the hill lying in the grass." More than 20 percent of *Stirman's* comrades fell during the battle.[11]

OPTIONAL EXCURSION: *Greer* Attacks Lyon's Right, 10:45 A.M.

Directions

This excursion does not offer an opportunity to leave your vehicle; sites must be viewed in passing. Returning to the Visitor Center, *leave* the battlefield, *turning left* from the entrance onto FARM ROAD 182. *Proceed* 0.1 mile to COUNTY ZZ. *Turn left. Proceed* 0.8 mile to FARM ROAD 188. *Turn right.* You are heading due west. The right flank of the Federal army faced southwest, occupying the ground to your immediate right. The right flank of the 1st Missouri ended just across COUNTY ZZ. To its right, in order, were the 2nd Kansas (before being pulled out of line by Lyon), the 2nd Missouri, and Sokalski's detached section (two guns) from Totten's Battery. *Proceed* 0.2 mile to the point where FARM ROAD 188 ends at FARM ROAD 101. Look to your left rear: *Greer* used the low ground there to cover his flanking movement. *Turn right* onto FARM ROAD 101. *Proceed* 0.2 mile to the point where it ends at FARM ROAD 186. *Turn right.* You are now heading due east. *Proceed* 0.2 mile to the point where FARM ROAD 186 ends at COUNTY ZZ. Sokalski's guns sat on the high ground to your right rear. *Greer* swept around them, moving east over the ground you just covered. The Southerners were repulsed, east of this intersection, and retired the same way they came. *Turn left* onto COUNTY ZZ to return to the battlefield entrance.

What Happened

(Events discussed here relate to Phase Six of the battle.) Upon receiving orders from *McCulloch* for a flank attack on the Federal right, *Greer* immediately drew his saber and ordered his *South Kansas–Texas Cavalry* to charge. He failed, however, to pass the order to either his own officers or to *Carroll's* adjacent *1st Arkansas Cavalry*. As a result only three companies spurred their horses forward with the colonel. If all 750 of his men and *Carroll's* 350 had moved en masse, they might have played a major role in the battle, but with only about 240 men following him, *Greer* was doomed from the start. Surprised, some of the Federals on the Union right panicked and ran in the face of the oncoming Texans, but most shifted their positions to meet the threat. From the Union rear, Wood's mounted company of the 2nd Kansas and the Home Guard units under Switzler and Wright fired into *Greer's* left flank. Company B, 2nd Kansas, pivoted from its new position at the Union center to fire into the face of the Confederate cavalrymen. Both Du Bois and Totten turned some of their guns on the Texans as well. They repulsed *Greer* quickly.

Although *Carroll* led his Arkansans forward to support *Greer*, the route he followed is unclear. He apparently opened fire on Sokalski, causing him to reposition his guns, but otherwise had no effect before retreating. With only eight rounds of ammunition per man, the *1st Arkansas Cavalry* could not accomplish much.

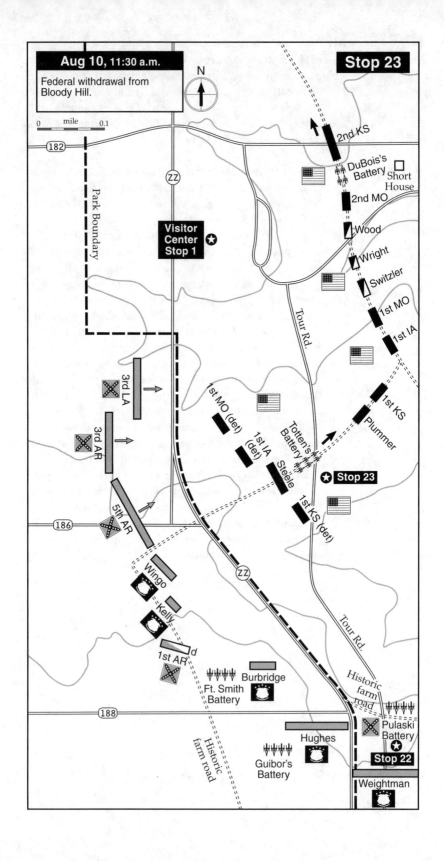

Aug 10, 11:30 a.m.

Federal withdrawal from Bloody Hill.

Stop 23

N

0 mile 0.1

182

ZZ

Visitor Center Stop 1

Park Boundary

Tour Rd.

2nd KS

DuBois's Battery

Short House

2nd MO

Wood

Wright

Switzler

1st MO

1st IA

1st KS

Plummer

3rd LA

3rd AR

1st MO (det)

1st IA (det)

Totten's Battery

Steele

Stop 23

5th AR

186

1st KS (det)

ZZ

Wingo

Kelly

1st AR

d

Ft. Smith Battery

Burbridge

Historic farm road

Pulaski Battery

188

Historic farm road

Hughes

Stop 22

Guibor's Battery

Weightman

STOP 23   Historic Overlook, 5:00–6:00 A.M.; 11:00 A.M.–12:30 P.M. (NB8)

Directions   *Proceed* 0.4 mile along the TOUR ROAD to the parking lot for
                            Stop 22 (NB8), on your right. A trail of 225 yards takes you to
                            the battlefield's interpretive site for the historic overlook.

Orientation   You are on the crest of the northern spur of Bloody Hill. As
                            you view the battlefield's interpretive sign, you are facing
                            east. The Ray House is to your right front, a distance of just
                            over 1 mile. The Short farm, where Lyon's column entered
                            the battlefield about 5:00 A.M., is to your far left on the rise
                            across the ravine and the TOUR ROAD, about 0.4 mile away.
                            The main body of Bloody Hill lies to your far right. *Cawthorn's
                            Cavalry* camped in the ravine to your right front, close to the
                            ford of Wilson Creek near the Gibson Mill.

What Happened   (The events discussed here relate to Phases One and Six, the
                            opening and closing scenes of the battle. Since Phase One ac-
                            tion has been discussed at previous stops, the emphasis here
                            is on Phase Six.) Sometime before 5:00 A.M., *Cawthorn* had
                            learned of Lyon's column and ordered *Hunter's* command to
                            find the enemy. He moved onto Bloody Hill's northern spur,
                            observed the Federals about 450 yards away to the north,
                            placed his 300 men in line of battle (to your front, facing to
                            your left), and sent word to *Cawthorn*. In response, the brigade
                            commander positioned *Peyton* and *McCowan* on the northern
                            crest of Bloody Hill.

                            Lyon attacked the northern spur with Plummer's battalion
                            of Regulars, Lt. Col. George L. Andrews's 1st Missouri, and
                            Maj. Peter J. Osterhaus's 2nd Missouri, supported by Totten's
                            Battery, driving the Southerners from their position. *Hunter*
                            retired across the ravine, joining *Cawthorn's* line atop the crest
                            of Bloody Hill (to your far right). From the northern spur,
                            Lyon assessed the situation and made the following disposi-
                            tions: He ordered Plummer's battalion to cross Wilson Creek
                            and advance in conjunction with the main column. Then he
                            aligned the 1st Missouri and 1st Kansas along the ridge (to
                            your front). With Totten's Battery firing in support from the
                            northern spur, the Federals moved down into the ravine and
                            up its far slopes to attack *Cawthorn*. The remainder of Lyon's
                            column followed a farm road leading west around the head
                            of the ravine.

                            (This ends the overview of the opening of the fight for
                            Bloody Hill. The following addresses the final phase of the
                            fight on Bloody Hill and the Union withdrawal.)

                            Around 11:30 A.M., during the lull after *Price's* third as-
                            sault had been turned back, Sturgis decided to abandon the

field. The Federals had been fighting for five hours and had eaten little if anything since leaving Springfield the night before. The 2nd Kansas was almost out of rounds, and there had been no word from Sigel. Sturgis ordered the 2nd Kansas back to the northern spur of Bloody Hill, where Du Bois's Battery and the 2nd Missouri soon joined them. Sokalski's section rejoined Totten, and the reunited battery moved next, with the Home Guard units, Canfield's cavalrymen, and Wood's mounted Kansans moving off about the same time. The 1st Kansas and 1st Iowa started back as well, with Steele's battalion of Regulars deployed to provide cover fire. Sturgis handled the retreat skillfully, but it was a close thing. Just as the Federals were leaving, Southern units came up the hill.

Sketchy reports make it difficult to determine the sequence of events for the Southerners' fourth assault, but the *3rd Louisiana* began the advance. *McCulloch* ordered *Hébert* to flank the Federals on their right, with the *3rd* and *5th Arkansas* in support. The remainder of the Southern forces crept cautiously up the slopes. They poured so much fire into the withdrawing Federals that Totten temporarily lost one of his caissons and Sturgis had to send detached companies from the 1st Iowa, 1st Kansas, and 1st Missouri back to support Steele. The fighting heated up briefly before the Federals safely completed their withdrawal. The *Pulaski Light Battery* arrived at the finish to fire a few long-range shots at the disappearing enemy. By 12:30 A.M. Bloody Hill was quiet except for the groans of the wounded. As the Western Army was exhausted and almost entirely out of ammunition, *McCulloch* and *Price* rejected pursuit.

Vignette

During the Federal retreat, the lead horses drawing one of Totten's caissons were killed, and the caisson became entangled in a sapling. Although the crew fled, Cpl. Lorenzo Immell raced back from his gun to rescue the vehicle. Pvt. Nicholas Bouquet of the 1st Iowa joined him. Working together, they got the caisson clear and brought it to safety, a feat that earned them the Medal of Honor.

Pea Ridge

The Union right wing under
General Carr at Pratt's Store,
second day of battle.
BLCW 1:300

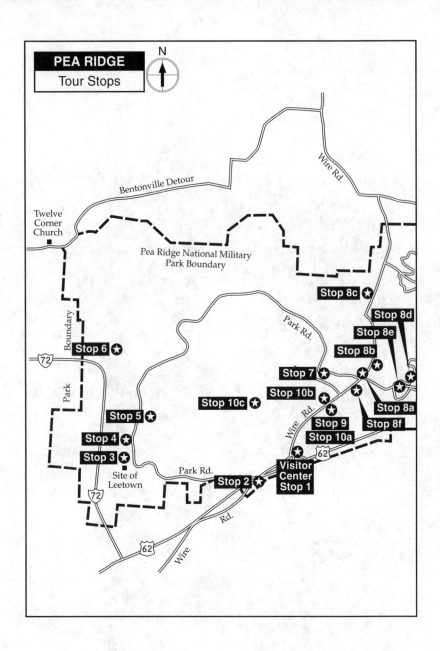

Overview

The battle of Pea Ridge on March 7–8, 1862, was perhaps the best-known engagement in the Trans-Mississippi and represented the turning point in Federal efforts to dominate the upper part of that vast frontier region. It involved the use of Native American troops on the Confederate side, numerous German American troops on the Federal side, and a bold gamble by the Rebel commander to capture or destroy a Union field army. His crushing defeat effectually ended Confederate hopes of seizing control of Missouri.

Military moves that took place after the battle of Wilson's Creek (August 10, 1861) served as a prelude to the campaign that resulted in the engagement at Pea Ridge. Maj. Gen. John C. Frémont launched his ponderous campaign to reclaim southwestern Missouri following Maj. Gen. Sterling *Price's* capture of Lexington on September 20, 1861. Taking an army of nearly 30,000 troops, the largest field force ever raised in the Trans-Mississippi, he slowly advanced toward Springfield in October only to have *Price* easily slip away from his grasp. Brig. Gen. Benjamin *McCulloch* once again massed his forces near the Missouri border to defend Arkansas if Frémont decided to continue southward, giving aid to *Price's* Missouri State Guard. But the expected major clash never took place. Lincoln had grown tired of Frémont's ineptness and was appalled at the rampant corruption that existed among his administrative officers. The president also was convinced that such a large force was not needed to deal with *Price* and *McCulloch*. He therefore replaced Frémont with Maj. Gen. David Hunter and instructed the new commander to evacuate Springfield. For the second time in the war, the Federals gave up their prize and retreated to Rolla. Frémont's large army was dispersed, and many of his regiments were sent to support the projected invasion down the Mississippi Valley. Those units remaining took post at Rolla and farther west to watch *Price.*

Hunter also was soon replaced. Maj. Gen. Henry W. Halleck arrived in St. Louis on November 19 to become commander of the Department of the Missouri. This was a major turning point in Union efforts to control the Trans-Mississippi. Halleck brought a strong sense of professionalism and competence to the administration of the department, and he energetically organized efforts to secure southwestern Missouri and thereby launch a major drive down the Mississippi. He put Brig. Gen. Samuel R. Curtis in charge of a new field army, called the Army of the Southwest and consisting of the troops at and near Rolla, on December 25. Curtis, a

West Point engineer who had not yet commanded troops in combat, was given the task of clearing the state of *Price's* force so St. Louis and the Missouri River line would never again be threatened. He concentrated his units at Lebanon, about sixty miles from Springfield, and prepared for a winter campaign over the Ozark Plateau.

On February 10, 1862, after Brig. Gen. Ulysses S. Grant had launched the Union strike down the Mississippi Valley by capturing Fort Henry, Tennessee, Curtis moved out from Lebanon with more than 10,000 men. *Price* was outnumbered and decided to give up Springfield without a battle. The Federals entered the town on February 13 and rested only a short while before setting out on a heated pursuit of the Missouri army. *Price* conducted a rapid retreat along Wire Road, the van of Curtis's army snapping at his heels, until he crossed the state line into Arkansas. There he was joined by *McCulloch's* troops and fought two small skirmishes with the Federals at Pott's Hill, just below the state line, and at Little Sugar Creek, just south of Elkhorn Tavern. The combined Rebel force continued to retreat southward in an effort to draw Curtis ever deeper into Confederate territory and stretch his supply line to the breaking point. *Price* and *McCulloch* evacuated Fayetteville and finally stopped in the Boston Mountains, where they established camps so their tired men could recuperate from the exhausting campaign.

Curtis refused to overextend himself but faced a perplexing problem. He had accomplished his mission with speed and precision: southern Missouri was cleared of all organized Rebel troops, and the Mississippi Valley campaign was proceeding with spectacular results. In Tennessee, Grant's capture of Fort Donelson on February 16, the day that *Price* entered Arkansas and fought the skirmish at Pott's Hill, was the first major Union victory of the war. It resulted in the Confederate abandonment of southern Kentucky and western and central Tennessee. Nashville became the first Confederate state capital to fall into Union hands. Curtis had contributed to this great triumph, but his little army could not continue to move south along Wire Road indefinitely. His logistical support already was stretched as far as it could go. He received supplies by rail from St. Louis to Rolla but had to rely on wagon trains to make the 250-mile trip from there to Little Sugar Creek, where Curtis decided to position his army. Even vigorous foraging through the countryside, which was only marginally productive, could not ensure that the Federals would have enough to eat let alone provide them with the necessary ammunition and equipment. With Halleck's approval, Curtis decided to stop and await developments. He blocked Wire Road and guarded Missouri against a possible invasion.

Curtis did not have to wait long, for the Confederate forces on the frontier received a new commander. Maj. Gen. Earl *Van Dorn* was put in charge of the Trans-Mississippi armies and reached *Price's* and *McCulloch's* encampments in the Boston Mountains on March 2. He immediately combined the two forces, calling them the Army of the West, and planned a strike against Curtis. *Van Dorn* was an aggressively ambitious general who burned to make his mark in the world. With very little planning or preparation, and with only three days' worth of food issued to the soldiers, he pushed his new army of about 16,000 men forward on March 4. *Van Dorn* optimistically expected to crush the Army of the Southwest and then invade Missouri, capture St. Louis, and perhaps even cross the Mississippi River to invade Illinois. No previous leader on either side in the Trans-Mississippi took the field with such ambitious plans. His men were enthusiastic, but they had to contend with a fierce winter storm that blew in from the west on March 5, causing a great deal of suffering.

The Federals learned of *Van Dorn's* advance that day as the snow and cold wind descended over the area. Curtis immediately ordered all of his outlying units to concentrate at the point where Wire Road crosses Little Sugar Creek, two miles south of Elkhorn Tavern, where he hastily dug fortifications to make a stand. *Van Dorn* hoped to pull off a smashing victory by cutting off half of Curtis's army, encamped several miles west of this position, before it could march to the entrenchments. But the Federals managed to reach Curtis in time, though a small rear guard under Brig. Gen. Franz Sigel was intercepted and had to fight its way out of encircling Rebel cavalry to rejoin the rest of the column on March 6.

That night *Van Dorn* decided against attacking the strong fortifications and opted instead for a grand flanking movement. By marching along a road known as the Bentonville Detour, he hoped to bypass Curtis's position and place his army on Wire Road north of Elkhorn Tavern, thereby trapping and capturing the Federals. It was a typically ambitious move by a general who preferred to play an all-or-nothing game. But the troops were not up to the daunting task. They were tired after several days of very hard marching in difficult weather, and their food was already gone. Moreover, the Federals cut timber across the detour, further delaying *Van Dorn's* march. Trudging throughout the night of March 6–7, the Confederates simply could not reach Wire Road until well past dawn. *Van Dorn* was forced to divide his army into two wings, ordering *McCulloch's* command to retrace its steps and advance toward the Federal position from the west around a commanding eminence called Big Mountain (sometimes erroneously called Pea Ridge), while Price continued to march south down Wire Road past Elkhorn Tavern.

Thus the battle of Pea Ridge was a divided affair, with two separate engagements fought within two miles of each other on March 7. Curtis was alerted to the Rebel flanking maneuver in time to reposition his forces and fight both wings of *Van Dorn's* army separately. While his men soundly defeated *McCulloch* and killed the Rebel general north of a small village called Leetown, they had a much more difficult time holding *Price* at bay in the hollows just north and east of Elkhorn Tavern. Here occurred the heaviest fighting of the battle, which resulted in the Confederates gaining ground at tremendous cost. Yet the Missourians failed to achieve a decisive breakthrough.

The next day, March 8, Curtis reconcentrated his army to launch an attack, preceded by a major artillery bombardment, against the remnants of *Price's* command and the few units that had joined it from *McCulloch's* shattered column. This last assault of the battle cleared the field of Confederate troops, and *Van Dorn* was forced to retreat to Van Buren by swinging widely to the east and south, making a complete circuit around Curtis's embattled army.

Pea Ridge was a smashing Union victory that garnered a lot of public attention. Coming as it did after the Union triumph at Fort Donelson and during the process of occupying huge stretches of abandoned territory in Kentucky and Tennessee, it was yet another sign of accelerating Union success that might bring the war to a close before the end of 1862. Although the battle of Shiloh in early April overshadowed it and brought an air of gloom to the North, Pea Ridge still remained the turning point of Union efforts to dominate the Trans-Mississippi. It was the culmination of Federal efforts to secure Missouri that had started with Nathaniel Lyon's capture of the Missouri militia at Camp Jackson. And it turned back the largest, most aggressive Confederate offensive yet launched in the Trans-Mississippi.

Van Dorn, his ardor undiminished, quickly accepted a suggestion to transfer his Army of the West east of the Mississippi to join the large Confederate army gathering at Corinth, Mississippi. This force, later to be named the Army of Tennessee, would attack Grant's invading army at Pittsburg Landing. In so cavalierly giving up his own theater of operations, *Van Dorn* essentially abandoned the Trans-Mississippi to the Federals. Ironically, he did not make it to Corinth in time to

take part in the battle of Shiloh, and his actions left pro-Con-
federate elements in Arkansas in the lurch.

Curtis also moved his army away from Pea Ridge, slowly
marching eastward across northern Arkansas to shadow *Van
Dorn's* move across the river in case he decided to turn north
and try to invade Missouri again. But when it became apparent that would not happen, Curtis turned his attention to
Little Rock. His attempt to march to the city, which would
have become the second Confederate state capital to fall into
Union hands, was stymied in the summer of 1862 by a combination of growing Rebel resistance and his own logistical
difficulties. Rebel units were rapidly moved in from Texas to
defend the city, and Curtis found that his long, vulnerable
supply line from Rolla was insufficient to support his army
all the way to Little Rock. Finally, in July he cut his supply
lines and marched across the delta land of eastern Arkansas
toward Helena on the Mississippi River, where his tired men
regained contact with the North through river transport.

Although Curtis failed to take Little Rock, his Pea Ridge
campaign was one of the most successful Union efforts of
the early part of the war. With a minimal force, the doughty
engineer had secured Missouri, cleared northern Arkansas
of enemy troops, and threatened the central part of the state
along with its capital. *Van Dorn's* impetuous decision to take
his army eastward relieved Curtis of a difficult strategic problem, whether to retain his army along the Arkansas-Missouri
border or to drive deeper into Confederate territory. The
course of the war in the Trans-Mississippi seemed almost at
an end that summer of 1862.

Major-General
Samuel R. Curtis.
From a photograph.
BLCW 1:315

Leetown, March 7, 1862

STOP 1   Visitor Center

Directions   *Approach* Pea Ridge National Military Park on U.S. HWY 62. *Turn off* the highway; the Visitor Center is the first building you will encounter.

Orientation   As you park and walk across the lot toward the building, keep in mind your location on the battlefield. It will be helpful to read the description of the Pea Ridge campaign in the introduction to this section before you begin your exploration of the park. A quick walk to the rear of the Visitor Center will give you a good view of the field. The building is located adjacent to the historic Wire Road, which served as the avenue of invasion for Samuel Curtis's Army of the Southwest into northwestern Arkansas. By early March 1862 the Federals had established a fortified defensive position on the northern bluff of Little Sugar Creek, straddling the road, about 2.5 miles to the south. About 1 mile to the north is Elkhorn Tavern, the most famous landmark at Pea Ridge. The Leetown battlefield is 1.5 miles to the west. Thus the Visitor Center is located to the rear of all Union positions on both days of the battle. Pea Ridge National Military Park is one of only two parks that contain original stretches of Wire Road, though much of it is paved in asphalt. Wilson's Creek National Battlefield has an original stretch of the road that is unpaved, except with a gravel underbase.

Look northward to the great open expanse of the March 8 battlefield. You cannot see all the way to Elkhorn Tavern from here because of the lay of the land, but Welfley's Knoll, where Curtis's artillery had an excellent vantage point from which to bombard the Confederates, is visible to the left. The most prominent geographic feature on the battlefield, Big Mountain (also known as Elkhorn Mountain or Pea Ridge), is also plainly visible. Keep the location of Big Mountain in mind as you make a long loop around the battlefield. The tour will take you to the top of it and a panoramic vista of the field.

The Visitor Center is an essential place to begin your tour of Pea Ridge. Not only does it have numerous brochures and publications available, but there are also exhibits of maps, explanatory films, and a number of artifacts. A recent painting by Andy Thomas entitled *On the Battery*, depicting the Confederate attack on the Union position at Elkhorn Tavern on the evening of March 7, hangs in the center. A mountain howitzer like the kind used by Maj. William D. Bowen's Missouri Cavalry Battalion is on display. Recruited largely from among Unionist refugees from southwestern Missouri, the battalion had four 12-pounder mountain howitzers in its arsenal. These are smaller versions of the 12-pounder howitzer widely used to support infantry regiments. They could be easily disassembled and the component parts packed on mules for easier travel through mountainous terrain. There are very few examples of this ordnance surviving and on display.

Another significant exhibit is the uniform coat and forage cap belonging to Capt. Henry Curtis Jr. of the 37th Illinois Infantry. He was shot in the right shoulder and abdomen during the fighting at Leetown but survived his wounds. Not so lucky was Alva Bevins of the 9th Iowa Infantry, who died of wounds received on March 7 at Elkhorn Tavern. His waist belt, cap pouch, canteen, diary, and photographs are on display as well.

Major-General
Earl Van Dorn, c.s.a.
From a photograph.
BLCW 1:318

STOP 2   Pratt's Store, March 7–8

Directions   *Drive* from the Visitor Center parking lot into the park, *turn-ing left* onto the paved stretch of the original WIRE ROAD. *Drive* about 0.5 mile and *stop* at Pratt's Store, Curtis's headquarters site (NB1).

Orientation   The precise spot where the store stood is somewhat unclear. Various maps and a painting by Hunt *Wilson*, who served in Capt. Henry *Guibor's* Missouri battery, clearly indicate the store was located immediately on the east side of WIRE ROAD, yet until recently there was a stone foundation on the *west* side of the road. *Wilson's* painting has a log cabin located on the west side of the road where the stone foundation stood. It is not known when Pratt's Store was demolished, though Franz Sigel, Curtis's second in command, noted that it was still standing when he visited the battlefield on July 6, 1887. It is possible that the store site is farther from the park's ser-vice road, perhaps now covered by U.S. 62.

If you wish, you may later visit the site of a marker erected by a family that lived at Winton Springs (immediately west of Pratt's Store) in 1935. It is a stone monument with a plaque commemorating the site of Curtis's headquarters. The family located it a short distance south of here. When leaving the park entrance, *turn right* on U.S. 62 and *drive* for 0.5 mile to the monument, which will be on your left. The gravel road that you see a bit farther down the highway to the left is an original stretch of WIRE ROAD. It rejoins U.S. 62 about 0.5 mile farther south.

What Happened   Curtis's headquarters was the nerve center of the Union army at Pea Ridge. It was here, at his tent, that the general re-ceived the first word of *Van Dorn's* turning movement, which threatened to cut the Federal line of communications to the north and trap the Army of the Southwest between Little Sugar Creek and Elkhorn Tavern. Here also Curtis called a council of war at 9:00 A.M. on March 7. After some discussion he decided to send a mobile force to the northwest to locate the enemy and force him to deploy and develop his strength. Curtis quickly dispatched a force of cavalry and three light guns under Col. Cyrus Bussey toward Leetown. Three infan-try regiments and two batteries were ordered to follow. Col. Peter J. Osterhaus was given overall command of this strike force. The council of war continued until word arrived from the Federal pickets near Elkhorn Tavern that the Rebels were already on WIRE ROAD. The situation was now becoming des-perate, and Curtis dismissed his subordinates at 11:00 A.M.

with the admonition to prepare for a general battle. He sent a force under Col. Eugene A. Carr to the tavern to stop whatever enemy force was approaching from the north.

Thus the battle of Pea Ridge had assumed its basic character as an oddly fragmented engagement. Two battles, barely related to each other, were to take place at Leetown and at Elkhorn Tavern, more than two miles apart. The results of both engagements would determine the victor and the vanquished in this exciting battle.

When evening descended over the field on March 7, the Federals were victorious at Leetown and had stopped the Rebels at Elkhorn Tavern after much bloody fighting. The area around Pratt's Store was crowded with a mass of supply wagons, draft animals, wounded soldiers, and stragglers. Newspaper correspondent Thomas W. Knox remembered that the sound of braying mules disturbed his sleep as he tried to rest that night. "Their usually hoarse tones gradually softened to a low, plaintive moan that was painful to hear," he wrote.[1]

On the morning of March 8, anyone standing near Pratt's Store would have seen one of the more impressive martial displays of the war. Across the open fields to the north, Curtis arrayed his entire army of nearly 10,000 men to drive the remnants of *Van Dorn's* army from the field. A noisy artillery barrage preceded the general advance of the infantry, dealing destruction to the Confederate position atop and to the east of Big Mountain. When the infantry closed in, *Van Dorn* ordered a retreat, and the battle of Pea Ridge came to a close by midday on March 8 with much rejoicing by Curtis and his men.

Analysis

Pratt's Store was the most strategic spot on the battlefield. The road junction here connected the Leetown battlefield with WIRE ROAD and, by extension, the Little Sugar Creek position and Elkhorn Tavern as well. As long as the Federals held this spot, they could use the advantage of interior lines of march to send troops to any place on the battlefield more quickly than *Van Dorn*, who had to march many more miles along exterior lines to reach the same spot. Curtis could rapidly receive dispatches from all the scattered wings of his army, and he could easily ride to any of them personally to see what was happening. In contrast, *Van Dorn's* army was split into two wings, separated by the towering, bulky rise of Big Mountain. *Van Dorn* chose to accompany the wing that attacked Elkhorn Tavern, and he waited in vain most of March 7 for timely dispatches from the Leetown area. As a result, there was literally no coordination of the two Confederate wings that day. This was a key factor in the Union victory.

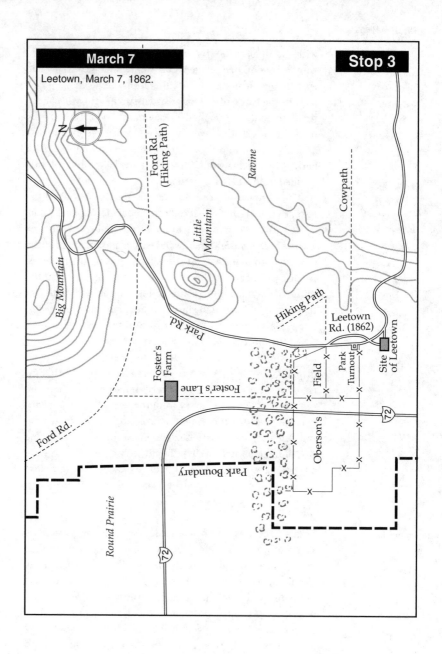

N

Big Mountain

Little Mountain

Ravine

Ford Rd. (Hiking Path)

Cowpath

Hiking Path

Park Rd.

Leetown Rd. (1862)

Site of Leetown

Foster's Farm

Foster's Lane

Field

Park Turnout

Oberson's

Ford Rd.

72

Park Boundary

Round Prairie

72

STOP 3   Site of Leetown, March 7

Directions   *Drive* from Pratt's Store along the TOUR ROAD as its leaves the historical WIRE ROAD and heads west. It now approximates the wartime road connecting Pratt's Store with Leetown. The actual road ran along the northern bluff of the hollow, where a hiking path now exists, but the TOUR ROAD remains mostly on the hollow's floor.

Continue driving west and *stop* at the Leetown site parking lot (NB2). *Walk along* the path southward a short distance and *turn right* onto the hiking path that runs along the wartime road as it enters the town site from the east.

Orientation   This rectangular cleared area was the location of Leetown, founded in the 1830s by John W. Lee. While many of the inhabitants fled at the approach of the armies, Lee and his wife, Martha, remained behind. Leetown had a school, a church, a blacksmith shop, a tannery, two stores, and a Masonic lodge.

Bussey's cavalrymen and Osterhaus's infantry and artillery approached Leetown from Pratt's Store and then headed northward along Leetown Road to meet the Confederates. Although this road is now covered by vegetation, you can find the traces of it by walking along the northern side of the cleared area and looking into the brush that borders the site. Leetown Road headed northward through the thicket to Oberson's Field, about 0.25 mile away, where much of the fighting at Leetown took place. The Federal troops sped along this road at midday of March 7, not knowing what dangers lay ahead.

What Happened   Federal surgeons commandeered a number of buildings for use as hospitals, and the damage from this use and from wanton destruction was extensive. Many residents decided not to return to their ruined homes, and the village quietly disappeared in the years following the war. The only physical remnant is a grave marker for a two-year-old child named Robert Braden just outside the southwest corner of the cleared area.

STOP 4   Oberson's Field, March 7, afternoon

Directions   *Drive* north from the Leetown site parking lot about 0.25 mile
                             to the Leetown battlefield parking area (NB3).

Orientation   You are in the southeastern corner of an expansive cornfield
                             owned by several residents of Leetown, including Samuel
                             Oberson, Wix Mayfield, and George Lee, but best known
                             simply as Oberson's Field. To the north and east lay Little
                             Mountain, also known as Round Mountain (visible above
                             the treeline). The western end of Big Mountain is a bit far-
                             ther north. Leetown Road went northward toward both emi-
                             nences and connected with a west–east route named Ford
                             Road, which crossed the saddle of high ground between Little
                             Mountain and Big Mountain. *McCulloch's* Division was march-
                             ing along Ford Road as it tried to make its way eastward from
                             the Bentonville Detour. *McCulloch's* aim was to rejoin *Price's*
                             Division somewhere near Elkhorn Tavern, just north of Ford
                             Road's intersection with WIRE ROAD. Looking north and a bit
                             to the west, you will see a belt of timber on the north side
                             of Oberson's Field that is about 500 yards thick and extends
                             west to east, forming a natural barrier between Oberson's
                             Field and the Round Prairie and a farm owned by Wiley Fos-
                             ter just north of the trees. The only break in this belt was
                             Foster's Lane, which ran west from Leetown Road along the
                             north edge of Oberson's Field and then north through the
                             middle of the trees to give access to Foster's farm. Ford Road
                             runs along the northern edge of both the Round Prairie and
                             Foster's farm. Off to the right, or east, of Leetown Road is
                             a heavily wooded thicket owned by Elizabeth Morgan and
                             known as Morgan's Woods. All of the wooded areas were
                             filled with post oak, blackjack oak, white oak, hickory, pop-
                             lar, elm, and a variety of briers and vines.

                             Now that you know the landscape of the Leetown battle-
                             field, walk west along the southern edge of Oberson's Field to-
                             ward ARKANSAS 72, a modern highway that bisects the battle-
                             field. The trace of the original fencerow, with a reconstructed
                             fence, is clearly visible, its southern end marked by a small
                             tree, about ninety paces east of the highway. This was the
                             fence that divided Oberson's Field into two nearly equal sec-
                             tions west and east. As you look northward the fence crosses
                             the 400-yard expanse of Oberson's Field. The fencerow con-
                             tinues into the belt of trees but lessens progressively until it
                             is faintly visible on the northern edge of the timber. Foster's
                             Lane ran on the right side of this fencerow.

Stop 4

N

March 7, afternoon

McCulloch and McIntosh attack.

Pike on Foster's Farm

Park Boundary

Hébert in Morgan's Woods

Foster's Lane

72

Park Rd.

16th AR McIntosh
McCulloch falls **x** falls **x**

2nd AR Mtd Rifles

Skirmishers
∧ ∧ ∧ ∧ ∧

36th IL

Fence

Park Rd.

Oberson's

Field

Park Turnout

Leetown Rd. (1862)

4th OH Battery

12th MO

Ind MO Battery

22nd IN

Park Boundary

Osterhaus

Site of Leetown

72

What Happened   Oberson's Field is the heart of the Leetown battlefield—it was as far as the Confederates got in their attempt to join with the other wing of the Rebel army and attack the Federal rear. Curtis's quick dispatch of Bussey's cavalry and Osterhaus's infantry and artillery brought the fighting to this cornfield and to Foster's farm a bit farther north. The Union presence here forced *McCulloch* to stop his eastward march, deploy his entire division facing south, and engage the enemy. Thus

Curtis was able to keep the two halves of *Van Dorn's* army separated and defeat them in detail.

Bussey's small command passed along Foster's Lane to the farmstead north of the belt of timber and took position. It opened the battle against *McCulloch* and was attacked by the cavalry brigade, led by Brig. Gen. James *McIntosh*, of *McCulloch's* Division. Bussey was quickly defeated and forced to retreat (this action is detailed under Stop 6 below). As Bussey's men fell back to Oberson's Field, they found Osterhaus's infantry and artillery, which had followed them, already forming a solid battle line along the southern edge of the cornfield. Capt. Peter Davidson's Battery A, 2nd Illinois Artillery, took position in the southeastern corner of the field later in the engagement. (The placement of the artillery piece is a bit misleading, for the paved TOUR ROAD is several yards farther east than the original roadbed of Leetown Road. The wartime road angled off toward Round Mountain, and the TOUR ROAD joins it only at the northern side of Oberson's Field.)

Under Osterhaus's direction, Col. Nicholas Greusel positioned the 22nd Indiana Infantry in the southeastern corner of Oberson's Field, then Capt. Martin Welfley's Independent Battery of Missouri Artillery deployed to the left, the 12th Missouri Infantry was next (where you are now standing at the midfield fencerow), Capt. Louis Hoffmann's 4th Independent Battery of Ohio Light Artillery, and finally the 36th Illinois Infantry, whose position extended well past ARKANSAS 72. This line would hold for the remainder of the day.

After chasing Bussey away from Foster's farm, most Confederate units regrouped and waited for orders north of the belt of timber. *McCulloch* ordered the *16th Arkansas Infantry* forward to reconnoiter the belt and personally rode behind its skirmish line. Because there is a crown of land in the middle of the belt, he was perfectly silhouetted against the sky as he rode through the short timber. On the Union side, Companies B and G of the 36th Illinois had been sent across to the northern edge of Oberson's Field as skirmishers. The Federals opened fire as soon as the Arkansans neared the field, and *McCulloch* was instantly killed, shot through the heart at about 1:30 P.M. The battle line of the *16th Arkansas* moved forward and recovered the body but stopped inside the edge of the timber to exchange shots with the Union skirmishers.

Command of the division thus fell on the shoulders of *McIntosh*, who impulsively led his old regiment, the *2nd Arkansas Mounted Rifles*, in a dismounted advance through the belt of timber. He foolishly neglected to give instructions to any of the other units deployed, and they remained idle at Foster's farm. Greusel had ordered the 36th Illinois to move forward into the middle of Oberson's Field and cover the retreat of Companies B and G. Thus it was close enough to fire a heavy volley at the *2nd Arkansas Mounted Rifles*. Just as *McCulloch* before him, *McIntosh* was killed as he approached the northern edge of the cornfield, dying instantly from a shot through the heart at about 2:30 P.M. The commander of the *2nd Arkansas Mounted Rifles* quickly decided to retreat, forcing the *16th Arkansas* to withdraw as well. This was the only serious effort by any Confederate units to penetrate the belt of timber and test the strength of Osterhaus's line.

The sites of *McCulloch's* and *McIntosh's* deaths were marked by two cairns of stone after the war, but those markers have since disappeared. *McCulloch* probably fell about 100 yards west of ARKANSAS 72, and *McIntosh* probably fell about 200 yards east of the highway, just a few yards west of Foster's Lane.

Before leaving Oberson's Field, walk across it to get a better idea of its expanse and what it might have felt like for the men of Companies B and G to advance across the cornrows toward an unseen enemy in the woods beyond. The 36th Illinois played a key role in the Union victory. By quickly shooting down the first and second in command of *McCulloch's* Division, it broke the Confederate chain of command and immobilized most of the regiments in this large, powerful force of nearly 8,000 men. The division never had a chance to recover from the confusion and lack of direction for the remainder of the day, and Osterhaus's outnumbered troops were able to hold firm.

Vignette

Ben *McCulloch* was a Tennesseean by birth and a Texan by adoption. He narrowly missed dying at the Alamo with his friend Davy Crockett when illness delayed his journey to Texas. *McCulloch* served the Republic of Texas well as an Indian fighter and congressman, fought in the Mexican War, and hunted for gold in California. He was a capable general despite his lack of military training, having served well at Wilson's Creek. But his performance at Leetown was dismal. *McCulloch* did not want his staff members to expose themselves to danger in the belt of timber and told them, "I will ride forward a little and reconnoiter the enemy's position. You boys remain here; your gray horses will attract the fire of the sharpshooters."[2] He rode his red sorrel and was clothed not in Confederate gray but in a black velvet suit, a brown hat, and high boots, with a Maynard rifle slung over his shoulder. Gallant it was of him to do the scouting himself, but it also was very foolish. The commander of half of *Van Dorn's* army rode into the teeth of danger, while his staff members idled their time at Foster's farm, and no one was given instructions about what to do next.

The man often credited with killing *McCulloch* was Pvt. Peter Pelican of Company B, 36th Illinois. Actually, it is impossible to credit an individual for that deed since the Rebel general fell before a volley of fire. But Pelican was the first of several Yankees who managed to enter the woods and scavenge what they could from the fallen officer after the Rebel skirmishers withdrew and before the battle line of the *16th Arkansas* arrived. He grabbed the general's gold watch, which he later gave or sold to Greusel, his brigade commander. Other soldiers grabbed the Texan's rifle and field glasses.

When the Arkansans found *McCulloch*, he was "lying full length on his back. The calm, placid expression of his face indicated that death was instantaneous and that he died without a struggle."[3] Someone covered his face with his coat, and officers decided not to spread word of the general's death for fear of demoralizing the men. Yet that only worsened the crisis of command that ensued. *McIntosh* was quickly informed of his new responsibilities by staff officers, but he was killed before taking full charge of the division and directing its movements. The next in command, Col. Louis *Hébert*, never knew of his increased responsibilities, for he had already taken his infantry brigade on a charge east of Leetown road (an action that is the subject of the next tour stop).

There are few other cases in the Civil War where the chain of command was so quickly and effectively cut as at Leetown. If the full weight of *McCulloch's* large division could have been directed in a coordinated fashion, it is quite possible that the Confederates would have smashed Osterhaus and the other Union brigades that later showed up on the battlefield, resulting in a massive Union disaster. "If Gens. *McCulloch* and *McIntosh* had not been killed," a Confederate officer later mused, "we would have gained a complete victory."[4]

Oberson's Field, ca. 1939, looking northeast from a point on the left of the Union Line. Little Mountain is the lone eminence in the middle distance. Big Mountain can be glimpsed on the far left as it begins to ascend from the saddle of land between it and Little Mountain. Morgan's Woods are on the far right, and the belt of timber stretches across the picture in the distance. Courtesy Clyde T. Ellis Papers, Special Collections, University of Arkansas Libraries, Fayetteville.

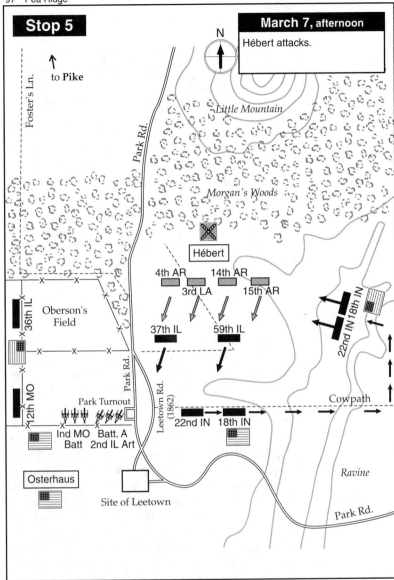

Stop 5

↑
to **Pike**

Foster's Ln.

March 7, afternoon

Hébert attacks.

N
↑

Little Mountain

Park Rd.

Morgan's Woods

Hébert

4th AR   14th AR
3rd LA   15th AR

37th IL   59th IL

22nd IN 18th IN

36th IL

Oberson's
Field

12th MO

Park Rd.

Park Turnout

Leetown Rd. (1862)

22nd IN   18th IN

Cowpath

Ind MO   Batt. A
Batt   2nd IL Art

Osterhaus

Site of Leetown

Ravine

Park Rd.

STOP 5

Morgan's Woods, March 7, afternoon

Directions

Walk back to the parking lot at the southeastern corner of the field, *cross* the TOUR ROAD, and *enter* Morgan's Woods along a hiking path easily visible in the edge of the thicket. This trail takes you some distance into the woods. *Stop* where it makes a sharp return to the left, which leads back toward the TOUR ROAD and the eastern edge of Oberson's Field.

Orientation

You are standing on ground where the 37th Illinois Infantry and the 59th Illinois Infantry deployed and began to advance forward to meet the most serious Confederate assault at Leetown, conducted by four of *Hébert's* infantry regiments. To the east is a ravine, about ten feet deep, running northwest to southeast, which was as far as the two Illinois regiments went. The remnants of a wartime road running northeast toward Ford Road by skirting the east side of Little Mountain can be found just on the other side of the ravine. A few yards to the south is another ravine, deep and well timbered, that runs east to west. A cowpath ran along the southern edge of this depression, connecting Leetown Road with the road running toward Ford Road; its slight remnants can also be found after some searching. While still standing at the sharp turn in the hiking path, near the ravine, look northward into Morgan's Woods. Soldiers deployed here could not see more than seventy-five yards into this thicket, which is preserved today exactly as it appeared in 1862.

What Happened

When *McIntosh's* cavalry deployed to attack Bussey at Foster's farm, *Hébert's* Infantry Brigade continued marching along Ford Road toward Elkhorn Tavern. When it reached the saddle between Little Mountain and Big Mountain, a shell fired by one of Osterhaus's guns in Oberson's Field came screeching overhead, alerting *Hébert* to the presence of sizeable forces somewhere to the south. He felt it his duty to stop, face his men in that direction, and meet this unknown danger. Thus all of *McCulloch's* Division played directly into the Federal plan to keep the two Confederate wings separated.

Hébert deployed part of his command west of Leetown Road on Foster's farm, where they waited in vain for instructions from *McCulloch* and *McIntosh*. The rest formed line of battle east of the road under *Hébert's* personal direction. Hearing the sound of fighting between the *16th Arkansas* and the Illinois skirmishers following *McCulloch's* death, *Hébert* decided to take it upon himself to lead an attack east of Leetown Road. Thus he was well into Morgan's Woods when *McIntosh* was killed, and no one could get word to him that he now commanded the division. *Hébert* led the *4th Arkansas*, *3rd Louisiana*, *14th Arkansas*, and *15th Arkansas* through the tangled vegetation, a passage made worse by a recent tornado that had knocked down many of the larger trees.

The Confederates encountered two regiments of Col. Julius White's brigade, the 37th Illinois and the 59th Illinois. They had just arrived on the battlefield to reinforce Osterhaus as part of Col. Jefferson C. Davis's 3rd Division of the Army of the Southwest. Davis placed Davidson's Battery A, 2nd Illinois

Light Artillery, in the southeastern corner of Oberson's Field, then deployed White's two regiments where you are standing. They advanced a few yards north and ran into the Rebels. A fierce battle ensued for the next forty-five minutes, with each side pouring in a heavy volume of fire. The Federals often lay prone for better protection, but the superior weight of numbers enabled the Confederates to wear them down, and slowly the Illinoisans fell back fighting. Many of them crowded near Davidson's battery, which placed White's command in danger of collapsing altogether.

Just then help arrived. Col. Thomas Pattison brought up the 18th Indiana Infantry, and this regiment, joined by the 22nd Indiana Infantry, already on the field, moved along the cowpath just south of the east-west ravine several yards behind White's slowly retreating men. The Hoosiers crossed the northwest-southeast ravine and the road that ran toward Ford Road and entered the tangled vegetation just to the east. Then Pattison halted his men and ordered them to conduct a left wheel so they could take *Hébert* on his left flank. It was a difficult maneuver to make, but these green troops did it magnificently. They opened a raging fire into the Rebels, who recovered from their initial surprise to return fire. A static fight developed, with Pattison unable to push farther forward, as much because of the terrain as because of enemy resistance, but he had the upper hand.

Hébert also was threatened from the west. Many of his men had managed to emerge from Morgan's Woods and race across the open space to capture most of Davidson's guns, pushing White's infantry even farther south. This alerted Osterhaus to the danger. He ordered the 36th Illinois, which had since returned to the southern edge of Oberson's Field after putting the *16th Arkansas* and the *2nd Arkansas Mounted Rifles* to flight, back into the open expanse of the cornfield. Then the regiment faced east and began to fire into the woods. The 12th Missouri did the same. This was too much. *Hébert's* command broke into pieces and tried to retreat anyway it could. Many of the men were captured; *Hébert* himself became separated from the retreating mass and fell into Federal hands. The fighting at Leetown sputtered to an end as the refugees streamed back toward Little Mountain. It was a smashing Union victory against great odds.

Analysis

The fighting in Morgan's Woods vividly illustrates a particular difficulty of Civil War combat. A portion, large or small, of nearly every battle took place in tangled woods, thickets, or open forests. A rough estimate is that about half of all combat in the war occurred on terrain similar to that of Morgan's

Woods. Soldiers North and South had to learn how to operate in it if they hoped to win the war. Fighting in the woods greatly reduced their visibility and made maneuvering in linear tactical formations extremely difficult. The men had to rely more fundamentally on themselves as individuals rather than feel the union with their fellow soldiers that tight formations in an open field provided. The woods could also become more dangerous in another way. Twigs, branches, and leaves were clipped as if by a machine and flung into their faces. Artillery projectiles screeching through the trees lopped off limbs, which fell on soldiers and injured them. The physical environment of combat became more noisy, confusing, and disorienting in the woods, thus increasing the psychological pressure of battle.

The effect of massed musketry and rapid artillery firing on the forest was immense. A surgeon treating the wounded in the Leetown hospitals after the battle noted that for 200 yards in front of White's position in Morgan's Woods, there was not a tree, bush, or sapling that was unmarked by the firing: "you see the sturdy Oaks pierced by cannon, canister, or death dealing shell," he wrote home. "Here you meet with a tree through which a twelve pound cannon ball has gone crashing through, fraught with death to man and horse farther on."[5]

The same was true on other parts of the battlefield as well. When Federal troops occupied this area again in October 1862, they were amazed at the appearance of the vegetation. An Iowa soldier named Benjamin McIntyre wrote: "The woods present a scene as if a tornado had passed through it and spent its vengeance in snapping limbs and twisting huge trees from the main trunk. I noticed many cannon balls still remaining in the trees." It literally took many decades for the woods to heal properly. A Kansan named Noble Prentis visited the battlefield in 1888 and wrote of "the broken tops of the old oaks, wounded so that a quarter-century has not healed them. It is doubtful if a human being ever entirely recovered from a square blow from an ounce or half-ounce ball, and trees do not seem to outgrow their battle scars. Saying nothing of the effects of artillery fire, the mark of a musketball is permanent."[6]

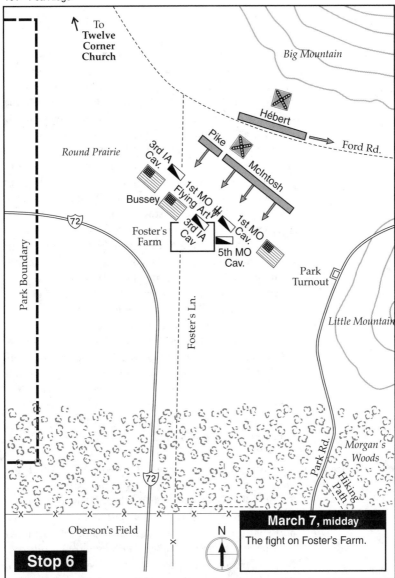

March 7, midday
The fight on Foster's Farm.

Stop 6

STOP 6   Foster's Farm, March 7, midday

Directions   *Walk* back to the parking lot in the corner of Oberson's Field and *drive* north to a small turnout with a marker referring to the fighting at Foster's farm (NB4). The cannons here point toward the Federal side of the battlefield because this spot is near the deployment site of Capt. John J. *Good's Texas Battery*, one of the few Confederate artillery units to go into action at Leetown.

Orientation

You are standing just to the west of Little Mountain, roughly on the ground where *Hébert* deployed his regiments before starting his bloody advance into Morgan's Woods. To the north is the western end of Big Mountain, to the west is an open field extending beyond the boundaries of the park. This was the location of Foster's farm, though in 1862 the cleared area was less expansive. There are no cannon, markers, or even a footpath here, but it is worth your while to walk across the field due west to locate the spot where the fighting took place. Go to the northern edge of the belt of trees. Foster's Lane emerged from the thicket about 50 paces east of ARKANSAS 72; you can still detect slight remains of the fencerow as it continues northward into the open area. Walk 313 paces along the row and see the remains of another fence row that runs west to east—this apparently was the southern edge of the Foster homestead. Continue walking due northward, continuing to count your steps. At 512 paces north of the belt of trees is the lowest spot of the landscape; it drained westward toward the Round Prairie adjacent to Foster's farm. Here you are about halfway between the belt of timber and the western end of Big Mountain. Bussey's position was probably about here or just a few paces farther north. If you continue walking northward and counting your steps, you will encounter another west to east ditch at 745 paces north of the belt of trees. This probably marked the northern edge of Foster's homestead. Ford Road lay many paces farther north, but there are no remaining traces of it.

What Happened

McCulloch's Division advanced along Ford Road late in the morning when the opening shots of the battle were fired by Capt. Gustavus M. Elbert's 1st Missouri Flying Battery on Foster's farm, partly shielded by a skirt of timber just to the north of the homestead. *McIntosh's* Cavalry Brigade deployed to deal with this threat while *Hébert's* Infantry Brigade continued marching east. Bussey had only 600 cavalrymen and three light guns to oppose *McIntosh's* roughly 3,000 horsemen, so the outcome was never in doubt. The Rebel troopers launched a spirited charge through a large break in the trees, attacking toward the southwest across open farmland. They easily and quickly overwhelmed the Federals, sent the Union cavalry fleeing from the farm, and captured the three guns. Two regiments of Cherokee troops, one of them dismounted, under Brig. Gen. Albert *Pike*, attacked to the right of *McIntosh* through the trees. They hit a small contingent of the 3rd Iowa Cavalry and sent it flying as well. The Confederate victory was complete.

Bussey's fleeing troopers streamed south along Foster's Lane and through the belt of timber as best they could, finding Osterhaus forming his infantry and artillery in a solid line at the southern edge of Oberson's Field. They later regrouped to Osterhaus's rear and guarded his left flank. During the next two hours, both *McCulloch* and *McIntosh* rode forward into the belt to meet their deaths, and *Hébert* started his attack through Morgan's Woods. Most of the division, cavalry and infantry, remained inert on and near Foster's farm, vainly awaiting orders and wasting their strength.

But an unusual incident occurred during this time. The two Cherokee regiments became unmanageable, and the men began to wander about the farm, refusing to obey orders from anyone. It was during this time that some Cherokees scalped and mutilated about a dozen dead and wounded Federals at Foster's farm, some of them belonging to Elbert's battery and others belonging to the 3rd Iowa Cavalry. *Pike*, an inept political general with no combat experience, could not prevent the Cherokees from taking random shots "at every one having on a blue coat, whether friend or foe," according to an observer.[7] The general even had to argue with them for nearly an hour before he could convince enough of them to drag the three captured cannon into the woods, where they were recovered by the Federals at the end of the day.

Thus, after a colorful and brilliant cavalry charge, the scene on Foster's farm was marked by confusion and wasted opportunity for the rest of the day. The men could easily hear the sound of battle on Oberson's Field and in Morgan's Woods and see the powder smoke ascend into the sky, but they had no orders to advance. *Pike* was the ranking officer left, but he was too incompetent to seize the opportunity to go in and win the day. This ranks as one of the most frustrating moments in Civil War history for Southern partisans. When *Hébert's* command was finally defeated and retreated to Foster's, there was no hope of continuing the struggle. *Pike* managed to evacuate the remnants of *McCulloch's* Division from the field, taking most of them around Big Mountain that evening to join the other half of *Van Dorn's* army to the east. But this took place not along Ford Road, south of Elkhorn Tavern, but along the Bentonville Detour, north of that spot. The Confederate army was partially reunited, but it had failed to achieve a decisive victory on March 7.

Vignette

Why were there Cherokee regiments in the Confederate army at Pea Ridge? It came about because the Five Civilized Tribes, including the Cherokee, had been forced from their ancestral homes in southern Appalachia during the 1820s and 1830s by the U.S. government and given land in the Indian Territory, now the state of Oklahoma. This was done both to clear them from areas wanted by white Americans in Georgia and elsewhere and to place them beyond the reach of white greed. The Civil War disturbed this naive arrangement. The Cherokees were the largest and most sophisticated of the Five Tribes, having gone furthest in their assimilation of white culture. Many Cherokees dressed as did the Americans, had developed a written language, published newspapers, and argued cases before the U.S. Supreme Court. Some even owned large plantations in the Indian Territory worked by African American slaves.

The Cherokee Nation was deeply divided by the war. A minority remained loyal to the Union, while the rest more or less sided with the South. The Confederacy signed treaties of alliance with each of the Five Tribes and raised troops from them that were supposed to operate only for home defense. But *Van Dorn* wanted to have all the guns he could get when he attacked Curtis's army and prevailed on *Pike*, Confederate commander in the Indian Territory, to bring help. *Pike* managed to reach *Van Dorn* with only two Cherokee regiments in time to take part in the first day of fighting, with little glory added to Indian arms.

In fact, the scalping incident greatly embarrassed *Pike* and many Cherokee leaders. It was the first of at least four confirmed incidents of scalping by Confederate Indian troops during the war, and it became a major weapon in the hands of Northern propagandists. The incident also inspired a sharply worded exchange of letters between Curtis and *Van Dorn* and forever marred *Pike's* reputation, but the perpetrators were never identified or punished.

Analysis

The small engagement at Foster's farm was a turning point in the battle. If Curtis had not dispatched Bussey and Osterhaus as soon as he did on the morning of March 7, *McCulloch's* division could have moved far enough east on Ford Road to attack the Federals at Elkhorn Tavern from the rear or to seize Pratt's Store and attack the Little Sugar Creek fortifications from the rear. The battle would have been fought in a vastly different way, and it likely would have resulted in a Confederate victory. As it was, Elbert's opening shots diverted *McIntosh's* Cavalry Brigade from its mission. The other incidents that followed took the stream of events to their conclusion, which was a Confederate disaster. By winning the engagement at Leetown, the Federals brought the first half of the battle of Pea Ridge to a successful close.

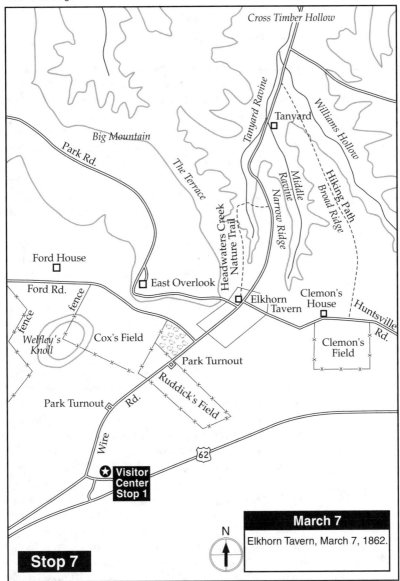

Elkhorn Tavern, March 7, 1862.

March 7

Stop 7

Elkhorn Tavern, March 7, 1862

STOP 7 East Overlook, March 7–8

Directions Return to your car and *drive* north on the TOUR ROAD up the
side of Big Mountain. A turnout is provided at the West Overlook (NB5) that offers a view of the saddle connecting Little
Mountain to Big Mountain, and parts of Ford Road are visible. You will also have a superb view of Little Mountain itself
and can even glimpse Oberson's Field. *Continue* to the East

Overlook (NB6), which offers a more spectacular view of the countryside south of Big Mountain.

Park your car and walk the short distance to the pavilion situated on an exposed point of rocks, a natural balcony from which to view the battlefield below. You are about 170 feet above the surrounding landscape and about 1,610 feet above sea level. The vegetation on Big Mountain is probably about as thick as it was in 1862. Franz Sigel found that during his visit here in 1887, the woods had grown much more dense since the battle took place—they even covered the rocky promontory so that he could not see it from below—but the fields were even more cleared. He also noted that the Ford House and barn were still standing.

As you face southward look off to the right, or west, where you can see a narrow mowed strip that approximates the course of Ford Road. Parts of the road, such as the stretch that connects with WIRE ROAD, are preserved. Note how the mowed strip crosses the saddle between Little Mountain and Big Mountain. Notice too that the Leetown battlefield is mostly hidden from view by Little Mountain and by the thick woods that cover part of it.

Now scan to the left and you will see most of the battleground of March 8 (discussed at Stop 10). Since the TOUR ROAD allows only for one-way travel, you will not have an opportunity to return to this spot after concluding this tour (unless you wish to drive around the circuit once more). Take the time to understand the terrain now. Curtis's army arrayed itself in one continuous line on the morning of March 8, crossing WIRE ROAD about where it sharply angles just north of the Visitor Center. The battle line extended west from there to the small knoll, named Welfley's Knoll after the Federal artillery officer who occupied it with his guns that morning. This was a key feature of the fighting, for it gave the Union gunners a marvelous, elevated platform from which they could bombard the Confederates at relatively short range. They directed their fire at Rebel guns and infantry in the skirt of timber, adjacent to WIRE ROAD and extending south from Ford Road. The Federal fire also was directed against the small number of Confederate troops stationed atop Big Mountain, about where you are standing.

Finally, look off to the left, or east, where you can see part of Ruddick's Field. It is the open space east of WIRE ROAD and north of the sharp angle in the road. Ruddick's Field is bounded on the north and south by strips of woods. Curtis's right wing was positioned in the woods on the south side of

the field and played only a minor role in the spectacular attack that followed up the artillery bombardment and drove
Van Dorn's army from the field by midday of March 8. For your
reference, Elkhorn Tavern is at the eastern end of Big Mountain, off to your left, hidden from your view by the bulk of
the eminence.

What Happened

While most of the fighting on March 7 took place off to the
north and east of the East Overlook, the land below was
a broad arena for the fighting on March 8, and this rocky
promontory naturally received a great deal of attention from
Union gunners positioned in the open ground. For two hours
on the morning of March 8, Curtis's artillery pounded the top
of Big Mountain and the skirt of timber just below, twenty-
one guns belonging to six batteries made the biggest noise
ever heard in this pastoral region. *Van Dorn* could answer only
with twelve guns because of the constricted area in which he
deployed his army. Only three of the fifteen batteries available to him had room to set up, and they were badly overwhelmed by the hail of Federal fire. While the Confederates
suffered numerous casualties, there were only four known
fatalities in the Union army resulting from enemy artillery
fire that morning.

Van Dorn had dispatched a small force to hold the top of
Big Mountain, Col. Stand *Watie's 2nd Cherokee Mounted Rifles.*
Later in the war *Watie* would become the only Native Ameri-
can to be commissioned a general in the Confederate army.
But on this day, he had only enough men to form a picket
line, and they were badly harassed by the Union artillery.

When the barrage lifted in late morning and Curtis ordered
his infantry forward in a general advance, the extreme left
wing crossed the open space and began to ascend the slope
of Big Mountain at an angle, approaching the rocky promontory from the southwest. The 2nd Missouri, 3rd Missouri,
15th Missouri, 17th Missouri, and 36th Illinois climbed up
the steep side and easily chased the Cherokees away, securing
the top of the mountain. The soldiers were appalled at the
destruction wrought by their colleagues serving the cannon.
They found mangled corpses and realized that shells striking
the exposed sandstone had fractured it and sent chips flying
as projectiles. The trees were shattered and stripped as well,
and everywhere lay the scattered debris from soldiers who
discarded their equipment and fled in haste.

The well-served Union artillery had done an excellent job
of softening up *Van Dorn's* position and played a key role in
the final Union triumph at Pea Ridge.

STOP 8a   Elkhorn Tavern, March 7, late morning

Directions   Return to your car and *carefully drive* down the mountainside
                           until you reach Elkhorn Tavern (NB7) at the base of the slope.
                           Park and prepare for a long walk. You are only on the edge
                           of the March 7 battleground—there are no park TOUR ROADS
                           into the interior part of this site. The only way to truly under-
                           stand the landscape and the action that took place there is to
                           walk on graveled or dirt hiking paths. The full walk around
                           this portion of the battlefield is about 3 miles, and part of it
                           demands a modest climb.

Orientation   This is the most famous building associated with the battle;
                           in fact the Confederates preferred to call the engagement
                           the battle of Elkhorn Tavern. The original structure was built
                           sometime between 1842 and 1858 to take advantage of traf-
                           fic on WIRE ROAD and was purchased from William Ruddick
                           in the latter year by its wartime owner, Jesse Cox. The tavern
                           was never an official stop on the Butterfield Overland Stage
                           route, but it often was used by travelers of all kinds. Cox
                           placed elk antlers on its roof to give it the distinctive name.
                               The hostelry did not survive the war. Bushwhackers burned
                           the building sometime in 1863, and it was not rebuilt until
                           after the war, when Joseph Cox became the new owner. When
                           Noble Prentis visited the battlefield in 1887, he found that
                           Cox had turned a ground-floor room into a primitive visitor
                           center, with a map of the battlefield that marked troop posi-
                           tions hanging on the wall. Cox told Prentis that five tons of
                           expended ordnance had already been picked up in the area
                           by relic hunters.
                               The U.S. government reconstructed the tavern according
                           to its 1885 appearance when Pea Ridge National Military Park
                           was created. This structure is almost identical to the wartime
                           tavern. Only the fireplace and chimney on the southern side
                           exists from the antebellum building. The original elk antlers
                           were taken off the roof by Eugene Carr as a memento of the
                           battle that made him famous. He returned them in 1885, and
                           when last heard of they were in a private museum in the
                           area. The tavern is the only wartime building on the battle-
                           field that has been reconstructed.
                               Cox's hostelry was located at a strategic spot. The Hunts-
                           ville Road joins WIRE ROAD here, connecting the area with
                           the seat of Madison County to the southeast. The Ford Road
                           joins WIRE ROAD 0.25 mile south of the tavern. Also to the
                           south is an expansive collection of fields owned by several
                           area residents, including Benjamin Ruddick, Jesse Cox, and
                           George Ford.

To the north of the tavern, the land is very rugged. Cox's building was located at the northern edge of the Pea Ridge Plateau. The ground descends northward nearly 300 feet in about 0.5 mile until reaching the bottom of Cross Timber Hollow, which is formed by a fanlike series of smaller ravines draining the slope north of the tavern. The WIRE ROAD entered Tanyard Ravine, located immediately north of the tavern. Two hundred yards to the east is the parallel Middle Ravine. About 400 yards farther to the east is Williams Hollow, a much larger feature that curves and drains from the south and east to connect with the others. Together all three ravines form the head of Cross Timber Hollow, through which WIRE ROAD ran its course. The ravines and the ridges that lay between them—Narrow Ridge is between Tanyard Ravine and Middle Ravine; Broad Ridge is between Middle Ravine and Williams Hollow—were covered with a growth of large trees. But there was relatively little undergrowth, making for a much more open battleground than existed in the belt of timber and Morgan's Woods at Leetown.

What Happened   By late morning of March 7, *Price's* Division of Missouri troops, accompanied by *Van Dorn*, had reached WIRE ROAD after its long flanking march along the Bentonville Detour. The Rebels intended to hit the rear of Curtis's position at Little Sugar Creek, but instead they met resistance before they could ascend the slope leading out of Cross Timber Hollow. Curtis had earlier been alerted to the danger by Maj. Eli W. Weston, commander of the 24th Missouri Infantry and in charge of a number of supply wagons parked around the tavern. A portion of Weston's command had already fought a long skirmish with the cavalry that preceded *Price's* infantry to Cross Timber Hollow, and the major informed Curtis that a large enemy force was on its way from the north.

Curtis then dispatched Col. Grenville M. Dodge's brigade to the tavern, placing 4th Division commander Carr in charge of the action there. Dodge deployed his units along Huntsville Road at 11:30 A.M., stretching the 35th Illinois Infantry and the 4th Iowa Infantry eastward from the tavern in a line positioned along the top of the slope. The 24th Missouri stood just to the west of the tavern, but Carr realized that this force was far too small. He sent a plea for help to Curtis, who dispatched Col. William Vandever's brigade. Carr believed the heavy force of Rebel infantry already forming in the hollow a half mile away would strike before Vandever reached him, so he decided to advance his artillery and open the battle himself, hoping to catch the Rebels off guard and delay their deployment.

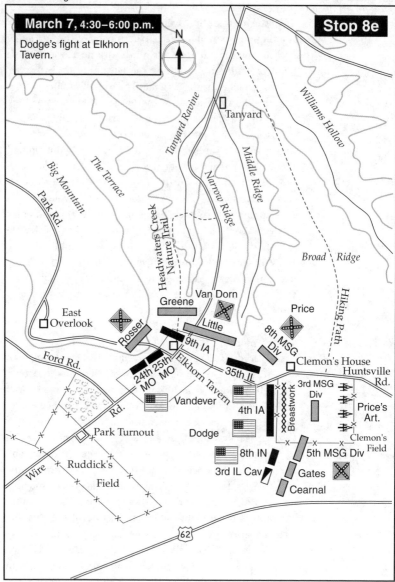

March 7, 4:30–6:00 p.m.

Dodge's fight at Elkhorn Tavern.

N

Stop 8e

STOP 8b　　Jones's Battery, March 7, early afternoon

Directions　　*Walk* along the hiking path to the north, which follows the original roadbed of WIRE ROAD, and *stop* about 300 yards from the tavern. The original roadbed ran atop Narrow Ridge as long as possible until it sharply curved to the left to enter Tanyard Ravine near the tanyard, about 0.33 mile ahead of you.

Orientation

Here is where Carr decided to place his artillery. He advanced two 6-pounders, later joined by two 12-pounder howitzers, of Jones's 1st Independent Battery, Iowa Light Artillery. They deployed about 300 yards forward of the infantry and just east of WIRE ROAD. Their opening salvo was the beginning of a costly and hard-fought engagement that would last until sunset.

What Happened

Jones's salvo reached *Price* just as he was completing his deployment. He put his best unit, Col. Henry *Little's* 1st Missouri Brigade, in Tanyard Ravine and onto Narrow Ridge and placed Col. William Y. *Slack's* 2nd Missouri Brigade to *Little's* right on the west side of the ravine. A long line of guns was laboriously hauled partway up the slope of Broad Ridge to answer Jones's fire. They found an excellent position from which to fire through the open woods.

As the Rebel guns opened, Vandever's brigade arrived on the scene. Carr placed it on his far left, squeezing the men between the tavern and Big Mountain so they could oppose *Slack's* Missourians. Vandever took advantage of a sizeable bench of land extending from the base of the mountain toward the western edge of Tanyard Ravine. He advanced the 9th Iowa Infantry and 25th Missouri Infantry to meet *Slack's* command in a vicious firefight that began a little after 1:00 P.M. *Slack* was mortally wounded, but his Missourians traded rounds with the Federals until Vandever decided to retire. After regrouping, the Yankees advanced again, and a second firefight ensued. *Price* moved reinforcements to the west side of Tanyard Ravine, assembling a total of some 3,000 men there. Vandever was forced to retire a second time to a point between the tavern and Big Mountain.

While Vandever fought the Rebels on the left, Jones's battery engaged in the fight of its career, suffering heavy casualties, and was eventually forced to rejoin the rest of Carr's command. The Federals at this point, about midafternoon, had established a firm battle line, but they were badly outnumbered, about two to one in troops and four to one in artillery. Their only advantage was their excellent position and the rough terrain *Price* had to deal with in order to come to grips with his foe.

Vignette

Jones's Iowa battery was in an exposed position, unsupported to right or left by infantry, and it paid the price for such boldness. A concentration of twenty-one Confederate guns was only a quarter mile away on the lower slope of Broad Ridge, sending a hail of projectiles at the harried gunners. Carr boldly rode up to the battery to encourage the men. "Give them hell, boys," he shouted. "Don't let them have it their own way, give them hell."[8] For acts of bravado like this, Carr would later be awarded the Medal of Honor.

The Rebel artillery was particularly well served that day, and soon a shell scored a direct hit on a caisson. The ammunition chest went up in a spectacular explosion that rained debris on Jones's gunners. Then a second ammunition chest blew up only a few minutes later, so terrifying the draft horses that they dragged another caisson into Tanyard Ravine, where it tumbled out of control. The gunners too were hit, one by one, and Jones was seriously injured when a round glanced against his leg. Even Carr was slightly wounded as he sat his horse amid the noise and flying metal; shell fragments bruised and scratched his neck and ankle. The losses were becoming so heavy that the guns were progressively falling silent, but everyone who could still work them stayed at their posts. "I believe every man at the guns had made up his mind to die there," remarked Sam Black, "for it did not seem possible any of us could get out alive."[9]

Finally, the injured Jones ordered his remaining men to pull their guns back up the slope before he transferred command to his ranking lieutenant and sought medical aid to the rear. The Confederates had won their first small victory in this fight.

Morgan's Woods. This painting depicts the 37th Illinois as it fought against Hébert's Brigade on March 7, 1862. George W. Herr, *Episodes of the Civil War: Nine Campaigns in Nine States* (San Francisco: Bancroft, 1890), frontispiece.

STOP 8c   Tanyard, March 7, morning and early afternoon

Directions   *Walk* roughly 0.33 mile along the hiking path, *taking* the left
                               fork, as it descends Tanyard Ravine. A short distance north
                               of the fork is the junction of Headwaters Creek Trail on your
                               left. This walkway was cut by the park service to serve pri-
                               marily as a nature trail, but it leads across to the west side
                               of Tanyard Ravine and thus gives some access to Vandever's
                               battleground. You may elect to walk a short distance along
                               this trail, which loops to the west and then the south and
                               ends at Elkhorn Tavern, and then return to this spot.

                               If you decide to walk along Headwaters Creek Trail, keep
                               in mind that, in the latter stages of the fighting, a portion of
                               Little's 1st Missouri Brigade and part of Col. Colton *Greene's* 3rd
                               Missouri Brigade advanced up the ravine toward the tavern.
                               Note how wide and deep the ravine is and imagine the dif-
                               ficulty encountered by the Rebels as they tried to climb it.
                               When you reach the west side, take note of the lay of the land
                               that Vandever and the 2nd Missouri Brigade, now led by Col.
                               Thomas *Rosser*, fought on.

                               Retrace your steps across the ravine and return to the hiking
                               path. *Continue* walking northward. Just before you reach the
                               bottom of the ravine, look to the right and see where the
                               original WIRE ROAD rejoins the hiking path. Farther on, in the
                               level bottom, is the location of the Civil War–era tanyard.
                               Stop here.

Orientation   All that remains of the tanyard are the vats used to soak the
                               raw hides in lime water until the hair could be scraped off.
                               Then the hides were soaked again in tannic acid, obtained
                               from the bark of oak trees, to soften the leather. All in all it
                               was a process lasting from eight to ten months. A small build-
                               ing likely was erected here as well, but it was gone and the
                               tanyard was out of operation by 1888.

What Happened   This area was the scene of the first clash of the battle at Elk-
                               horn Tavern early on the morning of March 7. Weston had
                               gotten word at his command post at the tavern that Confed-
                               erate cavalry was approaching from the north along WIRE
                               ROAD. He sent a company of the 24th Missouri under Capt.
                               Robert Fyan to investigate. Fyan advanced to the tanyard,
                               where he encountered the horsemen and opened fire. Pvt.
                               John Franklin was the first Union soldier to fall in the battle.
                               Later Fyan received help in the form of four more compa-
                               nies sent by Weston, and the skirmish escalated into a fire-
                               fight. Fyan sent a courier to the major at about 10:00 A.M.
                               with word that Rebel infantry was approaching the tanyard.

When Weston relayed this news to Curtis, the army leader realized that *Van Dorn* had gotten completely around his right flank and had cut him off from his base of supplies at Rolla, Missouri. This was the reason he called off the council of war at his headquarters tent and ordered Dodge and Carr to Elkhorn. Weston hurriedly moved the supply wagons from the tavern to Pratt's Store, clearing the area for the battle that was to come.

The bottomland here, where the three ravines connect to Cross Timber Hollow, was the best place for *Price* to deploy his division from a marching column into battle formations. This was done almost entirely by the Missourian, who was mostly given a free hand by *Van Dorn* because the army leader was ill. He had caught a very bad cold and fever while traveling across Arkansas to take command of the Army of the West and impulsively started the campaign against Curtis before recovering. *Van Dorn* was forced to ride in an ambulance.

He retained command of the army throughout the battle but at this point had received little word from his other division. A dispatch arrived from *McCulloch* a little after noon informing *Van Dorn* that he was marching along Ford Road and expected to join *Price* presently. The army commander was therefore sure the victory would be his. Then at 2:00 P.M. *Price's* quartermaster, who had ridden around Big Mountain, told *Van Dorn* that *McCulloch* was fighting at Leetown, not racing toward Elkhorn Tavern. Soon after that *Price* was hit by a stray bullet that ripped through his right arm and went on to severely bruise his side. He refused to give up command of his division and remained on his horse "as though nothing was the matter."[10] Yet *Price's* mobility and energy was curtailed, and *Van Dorn* tried to exert more influence on the course of events, becoming in essence a co-commander of one division of his little army. The two managed to patch together a tactical plan to deal with the rough terrain and Carr's embattled command.

STOP 8d   Huntsville Road, March 7, late afternoon

Directions   Prepare for an extended *walk* of about 1 mile that will take
                           you over the ground of *Price's* advance out of Williams Hol-
                           low. *Continue* northward along the hiking path that follows
                           WIRE ROAD, *past* the tanyard and *across* a footbridge that spans
                           a creek. A bit farther beyond is another creek, but the bridge
                           over it, used by local traffic before the creation of the park,
                           has been disassembled to prevent access to the battlefield
                           from the north. Beyond that point and outside the park, WIRE
                           ROAD is still used by local residents as a public thoroughfare.
                           You are now standing only about 2 miles south of the Ar-
                           kansas-Missouri state line. Near the footbridge over the first
                           creek, you will see a trail junction leading off to the right.
                           Take it and *walk* along the bottom of Williams Hollow for a
                           while. Then the trail will begin to ascend the slope, heading
                           generally south. As you *walk up* the grade, keep in mind that
                           you are passing over the general area where *Price* positioned
                           his battery of twenty-one guns. Look toward the right and
                           front and imagine the approximate location of Jones's battery.
                           Also keep in mind that the Missouri State Guard advanced up
                           this ground in the late afternoon during *Price's* major push
                           to seize control of the high ground where Dodge's men were
                           positioned. The trail soon reaches the edge of the Pea Ridge
                           Plateau and intersects with Huntsville Road. *Stop* there.

Orientation   Catch your breath and look down the road to the west. You
                           are about a third of a mile east of Elkhorn Tavern and about
                           forty miles northwest of Huntsville. The farm owned by
                           Rufus Clemon is about a quarter mile to the west; it is the
                           cleared field bordering the south side of Huntsville Road. The
                           foundation of Clemon's house is on the north side of the road
                           opposite the western edge of the field. The house was gone by
                           1888. The cleared fields of Clemon's farm were more exten-
                           sive in 1862 than they are today. The current clearing is about
                           two-thirds the size of the farm in 1862, with woods covering
                           what was the southeast corner of the field.

What Happened   The battle began to turn against the Federals when *Price's*
                           men made it to this spot. The Confederates had earlier tried
                           to move forward against Carr's advantageous position at
                           midafternoon, when *Little* ordered Col. Elijah *Gates's 1st Mis-
                           souri Cavalry* to advance up the Middle Ravine and try to take
                           Jones's battery. *Gates's* dismounted horsemen were confronted
                           by Dodge's two infantry regiments, which the colonel had
                           ordered forward about a third of the way down the slope
                           to spoil any such Rebel advance. The Union soldiers poured

several volleys down the ravine and easily forced the cavalry-men to flee. Dodge later pulled his men back to the top of the slope. This action took place more than halfway between the spot where you are standing and Elkhorn Tavern.

Then *Price* received word from his cavalry that the Union right flank along Huntsville Road was short and could be out-flanked. He and *Van Dorn* began to laboriously shift his nu-merous State Guard units, headed by Col. James T. *Cearnal's Missouri Cavalry Battalion* and *Gates's* reassembled regiment, along the bottom of Williams Hollow toward the southeast. Roughly 2,000 infantrymen and eleven guns carefully picked their way along the hollow and aligned so as to climb the slope when given the command and close with the Federals. At the same time, *Price* and *Van Dorn* repositioned units in the center and on the right. *Little* took a leading role in this movement. He inched his 1st Missouri Brigade about halfway up the slope of Narrow Ridge until his men were able to lie prone on the ground to avoid the rain of shell and musketry that began to pour down. He was ready to storm the position at Elkhorn Tavern when called on. *Guibor's Missouri Battery* also advanced along Narrow Ridge to bombard the Federal line, and *Rosser* and *Greene* realigned their brigades west of Tanyard Ravine to outflank Vandever.

By 4:30 P.M. the Confederates were ready for their first all-out push to get out of Cross Timber Hollow. The far left had no initial difficulty. As soon as Dodge realized such an over-whelming force was rising up from the depths of Williams Hollow, he quickly re-fused his thin line, bending it back along the western edge of Clemon's Field. The Missouri State Guard easily gained the top of the slope and advanced to the eastern edge of the field. The stage was set for one of the most vicious engagements within the battle of Pea Ridge.

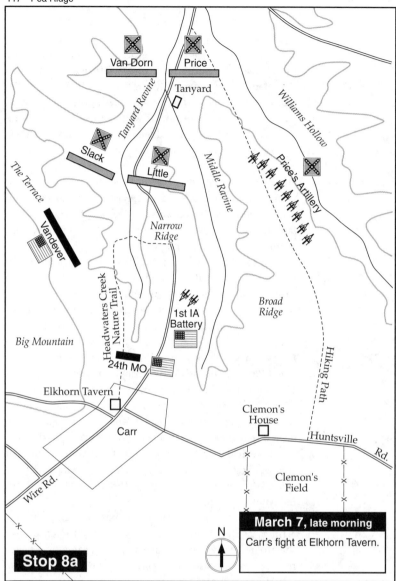

Stop 8a

N

March 7, late morning
Carr's fight at Elkhorn Tavern.

STOP 8e   Clemon's Field, March 7, 4:30–6:00 P.M.

Directions   *Walk* westward along Huntsville Road to Clemon's Field and
                     position yourself either at the eastern or western edge of it,
                     depending on whether you want to view the field from the
                     Confederate or Union position.

Orientation   Whichever side of this cornfield you choose to occupy, which
                     is about 200 yards wide, note that the ground rises slightly

in the middle to form a crown running north to south. It is six to eight feet high and offered the attacking Confederates some shelter when lying prone behind it. Also note that Dodge's men built a crude breastwork of logs and brush, uprooted the previous winter by farmer Clemon when he cleared some land, on the western edge of the field. This offered them some protection as well. Both sides took advantage of the lay of the land and the vegetation to improve their chances of survival and success.

What Happened   *Price*, who personally accompanied his left wing, took charge of operations. He ordered an artillery barrage to soften up Dodge's position. The outburst of fire was the signal to *Van Dorn* to start the right wing in motion for its final assault against the Federals at Elkhorn Tavern.

Dodge had two guns of Jones's battery, the 4th Iowa, and the 3rd Illinois Cavalry arrayed in an attenuated line on the west side of the field. The 35th Illinois was forced to stretch its thin line even farther to cover the space between the tavern and Clemon's farm, a distance of about a quarter mile.

After twenty minutes of artillery fire, *Price* ordered an infantry attack. He foolishly sent in Col. John B. *Clark's 3rd State Guard Division*, only 500 men, unsupported on either flank. They started on the double quick but were immediately met with a hailstorm of artillery and musket fire. *Clark's* horse was killed, toppling the colonel, and his men fell by the dozen. They managed to make it past the crown in the middle of the field to within a few yards of the Federals, but then stopped, hesitated, and retreated. Some of the men dropped behind the crown for shelter while the rest fled to their starting point.

Price tried to soften up the Union position again with his artillery as Dodge recklessly exposed himself to encourage the troops. A shell fragment ripped his pants, a canister round grazed his hand, and a branch cut off by another projectile knocked him from his horse, cracking two ribs. All told, Dodge lost three horses that day and later found six bullet holes in his coat.

The Missouri general sent in his infantry a second time but once again committed the same grave error. He inexplicably ordered the *3rd Division* to attack alone. This time they went across the field with less enthusiasm but bravely made it as far as the line of dead and wounded men they had left behind, then once again retreated. *Price* was so moved by the slaughter that he rode partway into the field, his arm still dangling in a sling, to rally his men. "I mowed them down in mounds," Dodge later bragged. "They charged us time and time again but they could not move us." [11]

Now *Price* was forced to do the proper thing. He sent the *8th State Guard Division* to swing north of Huntsville Road and through the woods to attack the northwest corner of the field, where the 4th Iowa joined the 35th Illinois at a ninety-degree angle. The *5th State Guard Division* would hit Dodge's right, the 3rd Illinois Cavalry, by moving through the woods south of the field. Price had the manpower to overwhelm both of Dodge's flanks while he kept up a raging artillery fire on his center.

The Federals received a small reinforcement. A battalion of the 8th Indiana, sent by Curtis, took post to the right of the 4th Iowa to help the Illinois cavalrymen.

As the Confederates pressed forward, Dodge's line came under tremendous stress and weakened. The men of the 4th Iowa manfully stood to their posts. Dodge later wrote, "Many who were too badly wounded to leave the field stuck to their places, sitting on the ground loading and firing." The regimental flag bearer was hit and the staff was splintered; the fabric, Dodge mentioned, was "riddled—nothing left of it." [12]

By 6:00 P.M., after a half hour of relentless pressure, the Federal position began to crumble. The 35th Illinois was attacked not only by the *8th Division* on its right but also by *Little's* brigade advancing against its left. That regiment was forced to retreat from Huntsville Road to the south. The 3rd Illinois Cavalry and the 8th Indiana also gave way before the advance of the *5th Division*, and both of Dodge's flanks were driven away. His old regiment, the 4th Iowa, now had to flee or be captured. The men stopped firing, about faced, and headed due west into the woods with as many wounded comrades as they could carry. Carr's right wing was gone.

Analysis   The vicious little fight at Clemon's Field demonstrates a typical element of Civil War tactics. Throughout the first two years of the conflict, many commanders sent out small units to either attack an enemy position or to defend against an assault without placing supporting units to either flanks. *Price* was guilty of a particularly blatant example of that when he foolishly sent *Clark's* division into the open. Even worse was his insistence on trying it again, with predictable results. This was a difficult lesson for poorly trained commanders to learn. But to *Price's* credit he learned that lesson quickly. His coordination of available manpower to reduce Dodge's position by moving through the protective woods and hitting vulnerable flanks was a textbook example of how to conduct a battle, achieving the tactical goal with minimal casualties. But the brave men of *Clark's* division had to pay a heavy price in blood for their commander's lesson.

Major-General Sterling Price, C.S.A. From a photograph. BLCW 1:272

STOP 8f   Elkhorn Tavern, March 7, evening

Directions   Walk westward along Huntsville Road to Elkhorn Tavern.
                              Along the way think about the harried 35th Illinois, which
                              tried desperately to hold this road against great odds in the
                              waning hours of March 7, and how it was forced to give way
                              and retreat into the woods to the south.

Orientation   Place yourself in front of the tavern, east of WIRE ROAD and
                              south of Huntsville Road, near the cannon that mark the ap-
                              proximate location of *Guibor's Battery* on the evening of March
                              7. Face north toward the tavern and up WIRE ROAD.

What Happened   Imagine the scene around the tavern in the last hour or two
                              of daylight. This is the moment depicted in the Andy Thomas
                              painting you saw in the Visitor Center as the Missouri Reb-
                              els finally drove away the Federals from the tavern. As first
                              the 35th Illinois and then Vandever's command withdrew,
                              the Confederates moved up onto the plateau to occupy the
                              area where you are standing. There was great confusion as
                              Little's brigade and *Rosser's* brigade came together around the
                              building, even some friendly fire was exchanged between
                              the two before the men realized their mistake. Many Rebels
                              were amazed to find stockpiles of commissary stores Weston
                              had not been able to move south, and they rooted around
                              for something to fill their empty stomachs; most of *Price's*
                              soldiers had not eaten since breakfast the day before. *Guibor's
                              Battery* advanced to the open area in front of the tavern and
                              set up four guns, becoming the first Confederate artillery to
                              open fire along the ground that sloped down toward Pratt's
                              Store. The nearby cannon accurately mark the spot.

                              It was about this time, when *Price's* Division finally achieved
                              its objective, that *Van Dorn* received the chilling news that
                              both *McCulloch* and *McIntosh* had been killed at Leetown and
                              that the army's other wing had been defeated. There was
                              nothing to do but grimly push on.

                              The battle was not yet over; the final scenes were played
                              out in the thickets and fields just south of here (see Stop 9).
                              But before you leave the tavern, keep in mind that it was not
                              just a hostelry but a home as well. Jesse Cox happened to
                              be away on business when the battle occurred, but his wife,
                              Polly; son Joseph; daughter-in-law Lucinda; and two young
                              sons had taken shelter in the cellar. All of them survived the
                              battle without injury. Most of the wounded Federals who
                              were sheltered in the tavern also had been moved before
                              Price's men came crashing by. The only known damage to the
                              building, despite the hail of artillery fire, was a solid shot

that smashed into a bedroom on the second floor and landed in the hearth on the southern end of the first floor. Several outbuildings near the tavern were riddled. Corpses, dead artillery horses, and a profusion of equipment and supplies lay scattered about the grounds that evening. Thousands of milling, hungry, and exhausted men added to the scene of confusion.

That night, after the fighting died down, the Confederates crowded sixty wounded soldiers into the tavern. Its complex of buildings along with Clemon's house were the only structures on this part of the battlefield, and they were filled with the injured. A man who passed by Clemon's saw a pile of amputated limbs outside the door, with the "arms in sleeves and legs with boots still on the feet." [13]

Before leaving the area walk over to the two small, unpretentious monuments near the tavern across the parking lot. These are the only markers erected by veterans on the battlefield. Ex-Confederates raised one of them, about 100 yards south of the tavern, on September 1, 1887, as a memorial to their dead. It bears the names of *McCulloch*, *McIntosh*, and *Slack*. The other was raised two years later (and only a few yards away from the first) by both Union and Confederate veterans as a symbol of sectional reconciliation. The text avoids any controversial statements. The only other battle-related monument is one erected by the state of Texas to memorialize its troops engaged in the fighting. It was placed in the postwar town named Pea Ridge several miles west of the battlefield.

Major-General
Eugene A. Carr.
From a photograph.
BLCW 1:325

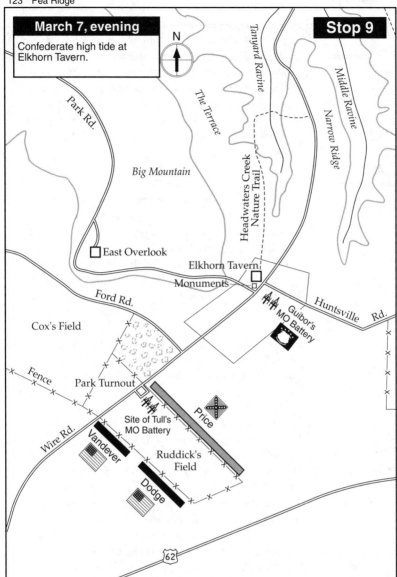

March 7, evening

Confederate high tide at Elkhorn Tavern.

N

Stop 9

Tanyard Ravine

Middle Ravine

The Terrace

Narrow Ridge

Park Rd.

Big Mountain

Headwaters Creek Nature Trail

East Overlook

Elkhorn Tavern

Monuments

Ford Rd.

Huntsville Rd.

Guibor's MO Battery

Cox's Field

Fence

Park Turnout

Price

Wire Rd.

Site of Tull's MO Battery

Vandever

Ruddick's Field

Dodge

62

STOP 9   Ruddick's Field, March 7, evening

Directions   Return to your car and *drive south* on WIRE ROAD. *En route* note
                   on your right the junction of Ford Road and the skirt of tim-
                   ber, which played a key role in the fighting of March 8. Then
                   stop at Ruddick's Field (NB8), where a small turnout is avail-
                   able on the left.

Orientation

This was the high-water mark of *Price's* advance out of Cross Timber Hollow. A spacious cornfield at the time, it was owned by Benjamin Ruddick and extended to the east of WIRE ROAD. It is bounded north and south by thick woods. You are about a half mile north of the Visitor Center, less than a half mile from Elkhorn Tavern, and more than one mile from *Price's* starting point in Cross Timber Hollow. The cannon here mark the location of Capt. Francis M. *Tull's Missouri Battery* on the morning of March 8.

What Happened

As Dodge's command retreated from Clemon's Field into the woods that bordered the north side of Ruddick's Field, Vandever fought his way from his position west of the tavern and down WIRE ROAD. It was a dogged retreat, the units harassed by *Rosser's 2nd Missouri Brigade* and *Greene's 3rd Missouri Brigade*. Vandever held for some time in the woods between Big Mountain and the tavern but eventually was forced to withdraw. Col. Francis J. Herron of the 9th Iowa Infantry boldly exposed himself in the fighting retreat, "too brave for his own good," thought an admiring officer.[14] A canister ball broke Herron's ankle and toppled his horse. The colonel was pinned to the ground by the animal and taken prisoner by the advancing Confederates. He was later awarded a Medal of Honor, one of four to be given for service at Pea Ridge.

Vandever's Iowa and Missouri troops fought their way southward through the thickets bordering both sides of WIRE ROAD until they established a new line of battle in the edge of the woods on the south side of Ruddick's Field. Dodge's retreating command took position to their right. The Federals had a total of thirteen guns on this line. Soon the first Confederates appeared from the treeline on the north side. The Rebels were disorganized but buoyed by their success. They assembled in a mass of hundreds, barely controlled by their officers, and impulsively charged across the open space. The Unionists opened a heavy fire but the Rebel yell could distinctly be heard above the roar. Many of *Price's* men had been issued white uniforms made of undyed wool just before the battle, and now they shone dimly in the gathering dusk, making easy targets. Asa *Payne*, a Confederate infantryman, heard a bullet strike his lieutenant. "He was so near me that he almost brushed me as he fell. He threw up his hands and said 'O Lord,' and fell upon his back and was dead." Another Rebel recalled that, as dusk descended, his comrades were so close to the raging Federal cannon that "the fire from the guns would pass in jetting streams through our lines."[15] Although outnumbering the Yankees, *Price's* men could not break this last position. They left their dead and wounded behind and retreated into the protective cover of the trees, ending the last Confederate attack of the day.

The only remaining action was a counterattack by the Federals. Now that the fighting at Leetown was over and the battle at Elkhorn Tavern was coming to a close, Curtis decided to personally lead a small reinforcement to the scene. He and Brig. Gen. Alexander S. Asboth, commander of the 2nd Division, rode at the head of an assortment of 500 men, parts of two infantry regiments and two batteries, northward along WIRE ROAD. They shored up Vandever's hard-pressed line.

For the first time in his life, Curtis took personal control of troops under fire. He optimistically believed a counterstrike could drive the Rebels back into Cross Timber Hollow and ordered an artillery barrage to precede it. The Confederates were forced to withdraw deeper into the woods to avoid this fire. Then Curtis instructed Dodge to lead the advance with his 4th Iowa. The colonel was willing but pointed out that his regiment had no cartridges left. Curtis told him to attack with the bayonet. The Iowans were game for it; they tossed their hats into the air and started across Ruddick's Field with a shout as the sun began to slip behind the horizon. "Such a yell as they crossed that field with, you never heard," exulted Dodge. "It was unearthly and scared the rebels so bad they never stopped to fire at us or to let us reach them." [16]

The Yankees penetrated far into the woods, though only because *Price's* Division was badly disorganized by its success. Most of the Rebel artillery was still in Cross Timber Hollow, and the infantry was scattered by heavy losses, exhaustion, and the confusion resulting from maneuvering over darkened, unfamiliar ground. But they retained enough power in sheer numbers so that the Missourians ground Dodge's advance to a halt well short of the tavern. Even Curtis came under fire as Rebel resistance stiffened. He and Asboth rode up WIRE ROAD just behind the advancing troops. An aide to the army commander was hit and a member of his headquarters guard was decapitated by an artillery projectile. Asboth was painfully wounded in the arm but refused to leave the field. When the attack came to a halt, Curtis was forced to withdraw to the southern edge of Ruddick's Field and rest his exhausted men.

Save for a few more defiant rounds of noisy artillery fire on both sides, the first day of the battle of Pea Ridge was over.

Analysis

The fighting at Elkhorn was the heaviest of the entire battle, and it was the nearest the Confederates came to achieving a decisive breakthrough. Curtis committed fewer troops there than to the Leetown sector for good reason. The terrain gave Carr the opportunity to offset his disparity of numbers, while the landscape at Leetown was very favorable to a Rebel success. Several strokes of good fortune aided the Federals at Leetown, but gutsy decisions by Carr and Dodge and stiff fighting by the rank and file saved the day at Elkhorn. Carr's 4th Division suffered twice as many casualties as any other Union division at Pea Ridge; indeed, it sustained half the army's entire losses. By holding the Missouri Rebels as far northward as possible, Carr played a key role in the Union victory. Curtis had a complete success at Leetown and a successful but costly holding action at Elkhorn Tavern. Now he had to prepare for the final action on March 8.

Elkhorn Tavern. This is the current structure, restored to its 1885 appearance. The Civil War building was burned by guerrillas after the battle but rebuilt after the war. The original was very similar but not identical to the current structure. Courtesy William L. Shea.

Elkhorn Tavern, after 1885. This was the model for the current restoration of the tavern. Courtesy Western History Collections, University of Oklahoma, Norman.

Elkhorn Tavern, early twentieth century. The elaborate portico was later demolished by the National Park Service to bring the building back to something like its original style. Courtesy Western History Collections, University of Oklahoma, Norman.

Victory and Defeat, March 8, 1862

STOP 10a   Ruddick's Field, March 8, morning

Directions   Remain at the turnout for *Tull's Missouri Battery* in the northwest corner of Ruddick's Field.

Orientation   Look southwest across the road to the vast open field west of
WIRE ROAD, called Cox's Field.

What Happened   During the night of March 7–8, Davis marched his 3rd Division from the Leetown area and deployed it astride WIRE ROAD
to support Carr's battered 4th Division. He placed White's brigade on the left of the roadway and Pattison's brigade on the
right while Carr shifted his tired troops into the woods eastward. Sigel's 1st and 2nd Divisions bivouacked near Pratt's
Store that night. Many of his men had fought and won the
Leetown battle, while the rest had been held in reserve all
day at the Little Sugar Creek fortifications waiting for a possible Rebel attack.

The rising of the sun on March 8 led Davis to test the enemy. He ordered the remaining three guns of Davidson's Illinois battery, positioned just to the west of WIRE ROAD, to
fire into the forest on the north side of Ruddick's Field. These
twenty rounds were the opening shots of that day's action.
The Rebels quickly opened a heavy counterbattery fire, and
Davidson was forced to pull back. When the Federal infantry
also came under this bombardment, Davis bent back his left
wing to get it out of the open field. Having felt the strength of
the enemy, Davis remained quiet and waited for instructions
from the army commander.

Curtis was determined not to let this momentary waver-
ing get out of hand. He ordered Davis to move White's brigade into the treeline south of Ruddick's Field and reform
his position. Then he urged Sigel to make haste in deploying
his half of the army to Davis's left. Osterhaus was sent ahead
to scout out the rolling and open landscape. He quickly saw
that a prominent rise of ground several hundred yards to
the northwest of Davis's left flank, now known as Welfley's
Knoll, was the key to this part of the battlefield. Osterhaus
suggested that Sigel simply extend the Union line westward
from Davis's left and then move the men forward some 300
yards to cover the knoll. This was begun. By 8:00 A.M. Curtis's
army was concentrated for the first time since the morning
of March 7. It stretched in a continuous line of battle for
three quarters of a mile through wooded and open country.

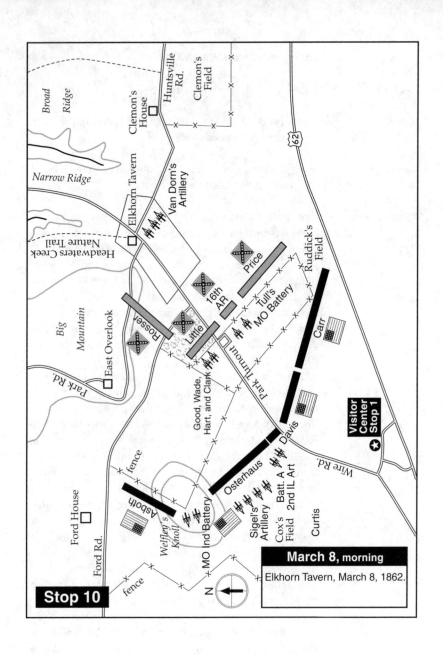

Broad Ridge

Clemon's House

Huntsville Rd.

Clemon's Field

62

Narrow Ridge

Elkhorn Tavern

Van Dorn's Artillery

Headwaters Creek Nature Trail

Ruddick's Field

Price

16th AR

Tull's MO Battery

Rosser

Big Mountain

Little

Carr

East Overlook

Park Rd.

Good, Wade, Hart, and Clark

Park Turnoff

Visitor Center Stop 1

Davis

fence

Osterhaus

Wire Rd.

Ford House

Asboth

Sigel's Artillery

Cox's Field

Batt. A 2nd IL Art

Curtis

Ford Rd.

Welfley's Knoll

MO Ind Battery

N

March 8, morning

Elkhorn Tavern, March 8, 1862.

fence

Stop 10

Most importantly, the men were ready to attack and drive the Rebels from astride their line of communication with the North.

Soon an artillery duel ensued as the Union guns opened fire to cover Sigel's advance. Rebel cannon instantly replied, but it was not a fair fight. *Van Dorn* failed to bring more than twelve guns of his available fifteen batteries into play at any one time, while the Federals used twenty-one guns. The Yankee artillery gained an even greater advantage when Sigel's line occupied Welfley's Knoll. This high ground was a superb gunnery platform, located only 400 yards from the Confederate position and about fifty feet higher than the Rebel guns. Welfley's Independent Missouri Battery occupied the top and began pouring rounds into the enemy.

Vignette

Franz Sigel was a very controversial figure in the Civil War. Born in Baden, a German dukedom, he had a professional military education and served in high places in the failed revolutionary movement that swept the German states in 1848–49. Sigel was among the flood of German refugees who fled to America following that bloody affair. His years in the United States were spent in relative obscurity until the Civil War catapulted him into the public eye. Sigel's handling of a small flanking column at Wilson's Creek was disastrous; in fact his unstable conduct that day greatly contributed to the Union defeat. He later lobbied for command of the Army of the Southwest and was deeply offended when Curtis was named instead. Sigel threatened to resign and enlisted the aid of the public and a number of influential politicians. The large German American population of the Northern states rallied to his cause, and Curtis felt compelled to name him his second in command, placing the German in charge of two of his four divisions. Both of those units consisted largely of regiments filled with European immigrants.

It was too bad that Sigel's political savvy was not matched by his military ability. He played no significant role in the fighting of March 7, mainly because Curtis carefully avoided giving him any important tasks. Now the situation demanded more of the German. He had to decisively handle half of Curtis's army and deliver the final blow in this long battle.

Fortunately for the Union cause, Sigel was up to the task. He quickly deployed his two divisions and began a slow but steady advance across the rolling landscape toward Welfley's Knoll. When his artillery opened up, Sigel, who had been trained as a gunner in Germany, personally supervised the firing. The effectiveness of his barrage was one of the best examples in the Civil War of how field artillery could pave the way for a successful infantry assault.

But this burst of efficiency was not unblemished. Unlike the other field commanders, who either shared Curtis's view that the advantage was on the Federal side in this day's fight or who simply obeyed their orders without comment, Sigel was convinced that the Union army was trapped by *Van Dorn*. His energy was inspired by a sincere belief that only prompt and desperate action could clear WIRE ROAD and save the Army of the Southwest from capture. When the final push came and the Rebels fled the battlefield, Sigel violated Curtis's wishes and raced northward along WIRE ROAD with a large portion of his command, not in pursuit of the enemy, but in a desperate effort to escape while there was a hole in the Rebel trap. He even sent a message urging Curtis to bring the rest of the army on a retreat into Missouri. The irritated Union commander had to send a strong message of his own before he convinced Sigel of his error, compelling the flighty German to rejoin the army on the battlefield. Only then did the surprised Sigel realize that a great victory had been won.

Original chimney of Elkhorn Tavern. Located on the south side of the building, the chimney and the foundation are all that remain of the Civil War-era tavern. It is difficult to verify the construction date of 1833, which is depicted on the homemade sign on the photograph. Courtesy Western History Collections, University of Oklahoma, Norman.

STOP 10b   Skirt of Timber, March 8, morning

Directions   *Walk across* WIRE ROAD *and enter* the field, *following* the tree-
                      line, which is the southern border of the skirt of timber. *Fol-
                      low* it to the corner of the wooded area. *Stop* here and look
                      into the thin tree cover.

Orientation   This skirt of woods, projecting southward, was the most for-
                      ward Confederate position on the morning of March 8. Rebel
                      guns and infantry here were exposed to the concentrated fire
                      of the Federal artillery on Welfley's Knoll. The skirt had been
                      used as a woodlot before the battle, and thus the tree cover
                      was thin and scattered. The artillery was positioned just
                      south of the treeline, but the infantry deployed in the skirt.

What Happened   *Van Dorn's* position on the morning of March 8 was less than
                      desirable. His army was still disorganized. A portion of *Mc-
                      Culloch's* Division had joined *Price* the night before, led by the
                      incompetent *Pike*, but the rest was far to the southwest near
                      Camp Stephens. Worse than that was the incredible fact that
                      the ammunition train of the Army of the West was nowhere
                      to be found. Poor staff work and *Van Dorn's* own negligence
                      had allowed the wagons to stray to Camp Stephens the day
                      before. The Rebel artillery had only a few rounds left for the
                      coming fight.

                      Worse still, the terrain was not suited to *Van Dorn's* tacti-
                      cal needs. Big Mountain blocked the full deployment of his
                      available strength to the west, where Sigel was assembling
                      his host for a decisive strike. The Confederate commander
                      placed the Missouri State Guard on his left, opposite Carr,
                      and put a portion of *McCulloch's* Division astride WIRE ROAD.
                      Little's 1st Missouri Brigade held the skirt of timber, and
                      Rosser's 2nd Missouri Brigade and some of *McCulloch's* units
                      stretched from *Little's* right flank back to Big Mountain. Most
                      of *Van Dorn's* artillery was parked in the open fields around
                      Elkhorn Tavern because only a few batteries could go forward
                      into the skirt to fire at the Federals massing in Cox's Field.
                      Any artillery fire delivered from the tavern area toward Si-
                      gel's troops would be ill-directed, for the gunners could not
                      see their targets.

                      When the massive barrage began, there were only two Con-
                      federate batteries here, *Good's Texas Battery* and Capt. William
                      Wade's Missouri Battery. Both units were quickly overwhelmed
                      and withdrew. *Van Dorn* was forced to send in replacements,
                      which also retreated after a few minutes of exposure to the
                      Federals' thunderous hail. The Rebel infantry also suffered;
                      Little's Missouri soldiers were pelted with limbs and splinters

from the shattered trunks of trees as they crouched behind stumps and clung desperately to the ground.

Sigel also directed his sweaty gunners to fire up the slopes of Big Mountain, causing *Van Dorn* to order *Rosser's* command to retire. Under cover of this sheet of flame, Sigel instructed his infantry line to continue its slow advance. The troops passed around Welfley's Knoll and its belching cannon to eventually extend the Union left to the foot of Big Mountain. The units on the extreme left paused only briefly before beginning the ascent. Each successive regiment in the line began the climb until five regiments were advancing up the smokey slope.

By now it was a bit later than 10:00 A.M. After two hours of maneuvering and softening up, Curtis rode to the left and met Sigel at Ford's farm. The two generals were talking when a stray Confederate shell arched across the open field and buried itself in the ground directly under the feet of Curtis's horse. Neither man moved a muscle while a thin column of smoke rose from the hole, but the fuse burned itself out before it exploded the charge. Curtis calmly looked at Sigel and said, as if it were a casual thought, "General, I think the infantry might advance now." As he rode away Curtis was convinced that, as he later put it, "victory was inevitable." [17]

Vignette

It was a particularly frustrating and deadly day for the Confederate gunners. *Price's* artillery had played a key role in the fighting at Elkhorn Tavern the day before, but they were not given an opportunity to repeat that performance on March 8. *McCulloch's* artillerymen had been mostly idle at Leetown and also found themselves in a similar situation this day. Those units sent into the skirt of timber later wished they had not been ordered to do the impossible.

At first *Good's* Texas and *Wade's* Missouri gunners tried their best to counter the overpowering weight of the twenty-one Union guns. Half of *Good's* men fell in the first thirty minutes. A lieutenant in the battery counted as 100 rounds fell within twenty feet of his position. The battery limbered up and retired, but someone left the unit's silk flag behind on the ground. *Good* later wrote, "it is a perfect myracle [sic] that any of us ever came out." *Wade's* Missourians were subject to "a cyclone of falling timber and bursting shells," according to one gunner. They fired until they ran out of ammunition and then retired in great disorder. [18]

Van Dorn next relied on Capt. William *Hart's* Arkansas Battery and Capt. S. Churchill *Clark's* Missouri Battery. The Arkansas unit moved into the skirt and retreated even before *Clark* had time to deploy. No one recorded whether *Hart's* men actually remained long enough to fire a round. The captain later explained that "he found the fire so severe he could not stay in it any longer."[19] *Van Dorn* ordered him placed under arrest and told *Clark* to use the Arkansas ammunition, which had been left behind in the skirt, for his own guns. He also instructed the young officer to deploy at the junction of Ford Road and WIRE ROAD so he would be slightly less exposed. There would be no more artillery batteries sacrificed in the skirt of timber, and *Clark* had little chance to counter the Union firepower.

His battery remained in place and bravely fired its cannon when the Confederates began to evacuate the field. A hail of artillery projectiles descended on the unit. *Clark* was about to order a withdrawal when a solid shot literally tore off the top of his head. He was only nineteen years old and was widely known and admired among *Price's* troops, but his gunners had to leave his mangled body on the ground where he fought his last, hopeless battle. The Missourians pulled their cannon away, but an observer who later came across the spot was appalled at the destruction left behind. *Clark's* artillerymen were "lying across each other and mingled with dead horses, all scorched and burned blak from the explosion of [an] ammunition wagon."[20]

Brigadier-General
William Y. Slack, C.S.A.,
mortally wounded
at Pea Ridge. From
a photograph. BLCW
1:302

STOP 10c Welfley's Knoll, March 8, morning

Directions *Walk* from the southwest corner of the skirt of timber over Cox's Field to the top of Welfley's Knoll. There is no trail or path, but the ground is completely open.

Orientation Look northward to the skirt of timber and observe the commanding position this ground offered the Federal gunners.

What Happened While the Federal artillery continued to bark, the infantry readied for its last charge of the battle. *Van Dorn* consulted with *Price* at about this time, and the two decided it was time to give up the fight. Ammunition for the Rebel guns was nearly gone, and the staff mix up that separated the ordnance wagons from the army meant there was no chance to resupply them. *Van Dorn* would pull his army out to the east along Huntsville Road and circle south to reach Van Buren, some 100 miles away on the north side of the Arkansas River. Disengaging and escaping Curtis's well-managed army, only a few hundred yards away, would be a challenge. All the wounded who could be moved were collected in ambulances and wagons, and the idle units of *McCulloch's* Division were to follow them eastward. The other troops, already in line, would have to cover the retreat as best they could. *Rosser's* withdrawal from *Little's* right flank not only left Big Mountain undefended but also opened up *Van Dorn's* right flank to an enveloping movement. The Rebels would have to act fast if they wanted to escape intact.

The Yankees started their final attack at 10:30 A.M. On the extreme left the 17th Missouri, 2nd Missouri, 3rd Missouri, 15th Missouri, and 36th Illinois pushed up the imposing slope of Big Mountain but met little resistance. But the troops assigned the task of attacking the skirt of timber had tougher going. The 25th Illinois and 44th Illinois advanced from Sigel's right, just west of WIRE ROAD, to hit *Little's* brigade in the southern portion of the trees. The two regiments entered the edge of the woods and found the enemy positioned only seventy-five yards away. A static firefight erupted as the Illinoisans' progress ground to a halt.

The momentary stalemate was broken when Osterhaus ordered one of his units, the 12th Missouri, into the fray. Osterhaus had formerly commanded this regiment and yelled to the men, "Boys, now strike [so] that the chips fly!"[21] They cheered lustily and started from a point in Sigel's line just to the east of Welfley's Knoll. This brought them to the southwest corner of the skirt of timber, where the regiment was able to hit *Little's* command on its right flank. The Rebels withdrew to WIRE ROAD and held briefly, delivering fire to the west against the advancing 12th Missouri. But the whole Rebel line began to collapse when Davis's 3rd Division attacked across Ruddick's Field to the east of WIRE ROAD on Curtis's orders. There clearly was no hope for a prolonged defensive stand. *Van Dorn's* attempt to conduct an orderly retreat fell apart as *Little* instructed his men to pull out and march along Huntsville Road. Each State Guard unit in the line from west to east did the same, and the Rebel position disappeared from Sigel's and Davis's front, passing behind the cover of the thick woods that fronted Carr's division.

Not all of *Van Dorn's* army retreated along Huntsville Road. Many units of *McCulloch's* Division that had remained idle all morning around Elkhorn Tavern and were still waiting their turn to file eastward were caught up by the sudden collapse of Confederate resistance. Faced with a surging Federal army to the south and a crowded escape route to the east, they chose to retire northward along WIRE ROAD. Some then took the Bentonville Detour west and south around Big Mountain. Others missed the junction and marched nearly twenty miles to Keetsville, Missouri, before they detoured eastward to make their laborious way back to the army. It was a confusing retreat that baffled the Federals as much as the Rebels.

The triumphant Yankees converged around Elkhorn Tavern just before noon, restoring their line of communication with the North and bringing the battle of Pea Ridge to a spectacular close. The grounds were littered with Rebel casualties, dead horses, and the discarded possessions of hastily fleeing soldiers. The Federals rejoiced without restraint. Curtis rode up WIRE ROAD cheering and waving his hat in the air, shouting "Victory! Victory!" He and Sigel shook hands in the road in front of Elkhorn Tavern. Other officers gave impromptu speeches to their commands, briefly interrupting the need to find out in what direction the enemy had retreated. Everyone shouted themselves hoarse. "May be you know what joy is," wrote Capt. Silas Miller of the 36th Illinois, "but you do not and never can know the wild delerious extacy which crazes the soldier . . . when they know they have met and put to route an enemy twice or three times their number." A man in the 59th Illinois admitted that it "was sometime before I could convince myself we had indeed won, so hard had been the fighting, so hopeless the issue for two days." There was no wonder that celebration took precedence over pursuit and that these were the most memorable moments of the war for many of Curtis's troops.[22]

After a day and a half of fighting, *Van Dorn's* attempt to bag the Army of the Southwest had ended in dismal failure.

A number of mistakes are apparent in *Van Dorn's* handling of the fight on March 8, and he could not shift the blame to anyone else. *Price* played no significant role in directing the day's events, for *Van Dorn* awoke to find his fever gone and his ability to take full control of the army restored. One of the biggest mistakes he made was to allow the imposing eminence of Big Mountain to constrict his deployment. If several of the idle infantry units and artillery batteries had been placed on top of the mountain by dawn, *Van Dorn* would have had a superb artillery platform that could have challenged Sigel's guns for dominance that morning. Well-placed infantry could also have prevented Sigel from advancing his line up the imposing slopes of the mountain. Curtis would have been forced to attack across Ruddick's Field or with Carr's depleted division on the far right, where thick woods and *Price's* tough Missourians could easily have halted such assaults. The failure to keep the ordnance wagons up with the army was just one of the more blatant examples of *Van Dorn's* failure as an army administrator. Even worse was his inability to see the big picture. He had spent the early part of his military career commanding cavalry companies on the Texas frontier and still had not adjusted to the much more complex task of managing a sizeable field army of mixed arms. What was, in hindsight, a disarmingly simple Federal victory on March 8 could have been the toughest day of fighting during the whole campaign. It might have somehow resulted in a Confederate victory after all, if *Van Dorn* had been more thorough and thoughtful in disposing of his available manpower.

For their part the Federals hardly made a mistake on March 8. They failed to damage the Rebel army in the latter stages of the battle and could not find or pursue it after the fighting ended. But Curtis can not be blamed too much for these lapses. The lay of the land and the thick woods hid his view of Huntsville Road, and thus no one knew which way the Rebels had fled for some hours after the battle. It was almost as if *Van Dorn* had disappeared into the hollows and woods. If Curtis had known of his enemy's escape route in time, and if Carr's division had been stronger and more aggressively led, the 4th Division might have advanced and cut off Huntsville Road. This would have forced *Van Dorn* to retreat northward over the same route he had taken to come to Curtis's rear. Yet the small number of Union cavalry on the battlefield would have made any hot pursuit very difficult, and Curtis could not afford to send his tired infantrymen off into the countryside on a march of uncertain length and duration on the hope that he might catch up with the fleeing Confederates. Curtis was content to hold the field and restore his communications, and *Van Dorn* was happy to move unmolested toward his base of operations on the other side of the Boston Mountains, bringing the Pea Ridge campaign to a close.

Leaving the Battlefield

Retrace your steps from Welfley's Knoll along the southern edge of the skirt of timber, *cross* WIRE ROAD, and *go back* to your car at the turnout for *Tull's Missouri Battery*. *Drive* south down the road from Ruddick's Field, but *stop briefly* at the last turnout (NB9), located at the bend of WIRE ROAD. Cannon placed here mark the position of Davidson's Illinois Battery early on the morning of March 8. Look around to obtain a slightly different perspective on the battlefield. Remember that the 25th Illinois and the 44th Illinois began their attack on *Little's* brigade in the skirt from this location, just to the west of WIRE ROAD. The 12th Missouri began its attack a bit farther west of those units. Note how the land rises as you look northward up WIRE ROAD. This crown not only hides most of Elkhorn Tavern but also during the battle it helped shield *Van Dorn's* army as it retreated eastward along Huntsville Road. Note also the view toward the skirt of timber and toward Big Mountain from this spot.

You have now finished your tour of the Pea Ridge battlefield. *Exit* the park by driving south down WIRE ROAD and *leaving* by way of the Visitor Center's parking lot.

OPTIONAL EXCURSION: Driving Tour of Pea Ridge Campaign

This portion of the tour will guide you to seven sites associated with the Pea Ridge campaign that are only a few miles outside the boundaries of Pea Ridge National Military Park. All of them can be visited in half a day of leisurely driving and are a good way to end your visit to the battlefield. The driving tour offers a good view of the countryside of northwestern Arkansas and allows for a better understanding of the strategic problems both commanders faced. Refer to the introduction for a brief narrative of the campaign and keep in mind that the sites included here span its pivotal phase. The tour covers the last portion of Curtis's pursuit of *Price* from Springfield, Missouri, when the two armies crossed the state line into Arkansas. The skirmish at Pott's Hill on February 16 and the larger fight at Little Sugar Creek the next day are detailed. The last Confederate stronghold, Cross Hollow, is also included. When *Van Dorn* started north with *McCulloch's* and *Price's* commands to attack Curtis, the scene of events shifted to McKissick's Creek, with Sigel's retreat from

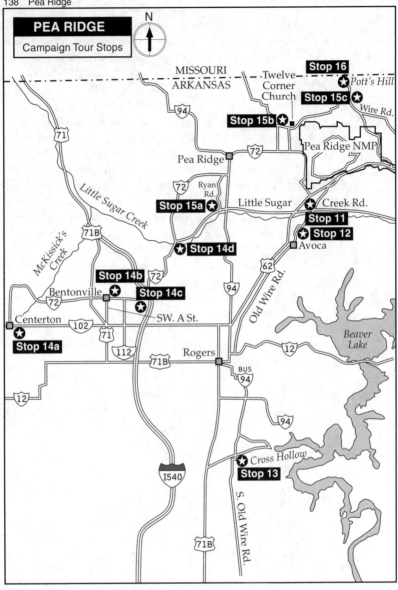

Bentonville meriting extended discussion. A stop at Curtis's fortified position at Little Sugar Creek is also included as is a retracing of *Van Dorn's* flanking movement along the Bentonville Detour to WIRE ROAD. This excursion will take you on a wide circuit around the battlefield park so you can understand how the armies came to fight at Pea Ridge. Keep in mind that part of the tour will take you on gravel roads, so caution is strongly advised while driving.

STOP 11   Curtis's Fortifications at Little Sugar Creek, March 6–8

Directions   Leave the park and *drive south* on u.s. 62 for 0.5 mile. *Turn left*
                           onto an UNMARKED GRAVEL ROAD (described in Stop 2). This
                           road, which curves for 0.5 mile before rejoining the highway,
                           is a short stretch of the original WIRE ROAD. *Drive* a very short
                           distance (about 0.12 mile) south on u.s. 62 after rejoining the
                           highway and *turn left* onto NORTH OLD WIRE ROAD, which also
                           is gravel and is the continuation of WIRE ROAD. After about 1
                           mile you will descend steeply into the valley of Little Sugar
                           Creek. *Turn right* at the bottom of the bluff onto LITTLE SUGAR
                           CREEK ROAD (COUNTY 44). *Proceed* nearly 0.25 mile until you
                           come to a fork in the road. The left fork, which crosses the
                           valley, is the original WIRE ROAD. *Stop* at the park turnout just
                           ahead on the right fork.

Orientation   Pea Ridge National Military Park owns a section of the creek
                           bluff here, but the footpath up the slope to the earthwork is
                           closed and in very poor condition. If it were open, you could
                           walk up the sixty-foot-high bluff and position yourself next
                           to the Union fortifications. Face south, in any case, so you can
                           see the wide creek valley.

What Happened   Curtis had selected this site as the place to make a stand in
                           late February, after deciding not to pursue the Rebels any
                           farther into Arkansas. He knew it offered a commanding de-
                           fensive position, guarding WIRE ROAD as it crossed the valley
                           of Little Sugar Creek. Curtis was careful to position most of
                           his available manpower within a one- or two-day march from
                           here so as to quickly concentrate his army if *McCulloch* and
                           Price showed any sign of moving northward.
                               On March 3 Curtis decided to bring his divisions together
                           and prepare fortifications, but there was no immediate hurry
                           as there were yet no indications of a Rebel advance. Two days
                           later he received word from a loyal citizen and a Federal
                           scout that *Van Dorn* was on his way. The need for urgency was
                           paramount. Most of his outlying units rushed to the bluffs;
                           Curtis moved his headquarters from Cross Hollow early on
                           the morning of March 6 only to learn that nothing had been
                           done to strengthen the Little Sugar Creek position. Davis's
                           3rd Division had been there for several days but had not yet
                           turned a shovelful of earth. A West Point engineer, Curtis
                           took charge of the operation. He personally laid out a line of
                           works along the bluff straddling WIRE ROAD. He ordered two
                           redoubts for artillery dug on either side of the road and a line
                           of infantry trenches constructed to connect them. A lighter
                           line of works was made partway down the slope. The men cut

down trees in all directions to afford a clear field of fire. The work was essentially done by the afternoon of March 6.

Davis placed Pattison's brigade just to the west of WIRE ROAD and positioned White's brigade to the east. Carr's 4th Division went into line to White's left. Sigel was to post the remaining two divisions to Pattison's right when he and his men arrived from Bentonville. Meanwhile, Curtis established his headquarters at Pratt's Store two miles to the rear.

The earthworks that remain on the bluff above the turnout lie west of WIRE ROAD and are the extreme Union right, prepared for elements of Sigel's command. They are simple fortifications by the standards of later Civil War campaigns, but they made for an incredibly strong defensive position. Unfortunately for Curtis, this was exactly why *Van Dorn* refused to attack it. The works so hastily planned and prepared were never tested in battle.

Analysis

This was one of the earliest uses of field fortifications in the Civil War. The simplicity of the earthworks is the result of the haste with which the Federals constructed them. Northern and Southern soldiers had little experience at this stage of the war with digging works and utilizing them in battle. If *Van Dorn* had elected to attack the position frontally, however, he certainly would have been bloodily repulsed.

The Rebel commander wisely chose to outflank the position, but he was mistaken to attempt a complete envelopment. It was very difficult to move all the way around Big Mountain to the north of Elkhorn Tavern, requiring many hours of tedious marching by his tired troops. The longer it took them to do this, the greater opportunity Curtis had to discover the maneuver and reposition his forces to foil it, which is exactly what happened. *Van Dorn* sacrificed surprise for a marginal chance to pull off something unique in military history, trapping an enemy army in the open field. The gamble failed.

Far better it would have been to conduct a shorter, less risky turning movement around Curtis's right flank. The Federal position was open and vulnerable to the rear. *Van Dorn* could have marched a short distance up the Bentonville Detour and headed east toward Leetown with his army intact, emerging at dawn of March 7 and catching Curtis by surprise. It could have been a Federal disaster, with the Yankees rapidly retreating up WIRE ROAD hounded by *Van Dorn's* much larger cavalry force. But the decision to risk all was typical of *Van Dorn's* breakneck career as an army officer. He pined for glory more than most commanders and rushed to take whatever shortcuts he could to achieve it.

STOP 12   Skirmish at Little Sugar Creek, February 17

Directions   *Return* to the fork in the road and *turn right* onto NORTH OLD
WIRE ROAD. *Drive south* across the valley of Little Sugar Creek.
En route notice that to your right, about a quarter of the
way across the valley, is the approximate location of Enoch
Trott's store. The Federals burned it on March 6 while preparing their defensive position on the bluff so that Rebel sharpshooters could not use the building for shelter.

You will encounter another fork in the road near the south
side of the valley just past a Masonic Hall. The right fork,
which is now blocked and inaccessible, is the original WIRE
ROAD. It climbs the bluff rather abruptly to reach the level
top as quickly as possible. *Continue driving* along the left fork,
which ascends the bluff through a long, deep hollow; curves
right; and rejoins the original WIRE ROAD on top. *Stop* at this
junction, where the road makes a ninety-degree turn to the
left. A historical marker for Dunagin's Farm is on the right.

Orientation   You are on the battlefield of Little Sugar Creek, also called the
battle of Dunagin's Farm, fought on February 17 near the end
of Curtis's pursuit of *Price* out of Missouri. It was the biggest
clash between the opposing armies before the battle of Pea
Ridge. Tree cover prevents you from viewing the valley to the
north, but the landscape to the south is roughly similar to
its appearance in 1862, except that the treelines and the outlines of the fields are different. The engagement started approximately where you are standing and extended perhaps
as much as a quarter mile south.

What Happened   *Price* had been sending shrill messages to his Confederate
counterparts in Arkansas for some time, asking for their help
in holding southwestern Missouri. No troops arrived because
McCulloch was determined not to be drawn into an uncertain
adventure in that state, especially if it meant cooperating
with the contentious *Price*. But on February 14 word reached
Louis *Hébert*, commander of *McCulloch's* infantry brigade at
Fayetteville, that *Price* had evacuated Springfield three days
before and was rapidly retreating toward Arkansas. *Mc-
Culloch*, who was at Fort Smith, ordered *Hébert* to advance and
join *Price* in defending the border. Some of *Hébert's* regiments
marched to Cross Hollow, twelve miles south of Little Sugar
Creek. Other units, already there, received orders to advance
up WIRE ROAD and meet *Price* as soon as possible. The latter
units joined the Missouri army on the afternoon of February
16 at Elkhorn Tavern, following the little skirmish at Pott's
Hill on the state line, and took position as *Price's* rear guard.

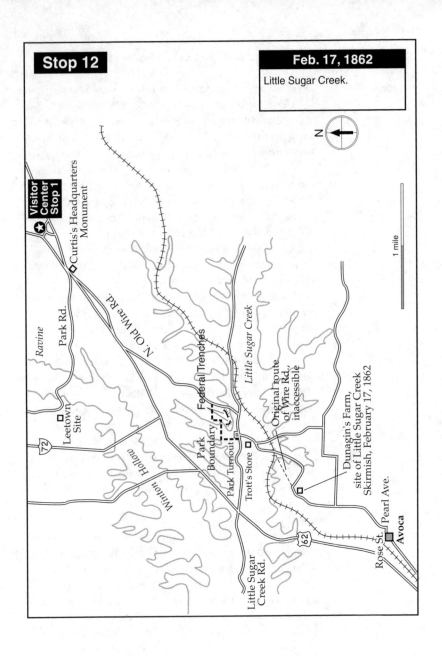

Stop 12

Feb. 17, 1862

Little Sugar Creek.

N

1 mile

Visitor Center Stop 1

Curtis's Headquarters Monument

Ravine

Park Rd.

N. Old Wire Rd.

Little Sugar Creek

Federal Trenches

Original route of Wire Rd., inaccessible

Leetown Site

72

Winton Hollow

Park Boundary

Park Turnout

Trott's Store

Dunagin's Farm, site of Little Sugar Creek Skirmish, February 17, 1862

Little Sugar Creek Rd.

62

Rose St.

Pearl Ave.

Avoca

The combined Rebel force was not bothered for the rest of the day.

Curtis's men crossed the state line early on the morning of February 17, cheering and playing patriotic tunes to celebrate their success. The vanguard, consisting of Col. Calvin A. Ellis's 1st Missouri Cavalry and Maj. William D. Bowen's Missouri Cavalry Battalion, reached the northern side of Little Sugar Creek at about 1:00 P.M. Ellis reported to the army leader that the enemy was making a stand, and Curtis hurried forward with reinforcements in the form of a battalion of the 6th Missouri Cavalry, a battalion of the 3rd Illinois Cavalry, and Capt. Mortimer M. Hayden's 3rd Iowa Battery. While the artillery set up on the northern bluff and fired indiscriminately into the trees across the valley, Curtis left Bowen's battalion behind as their support and ordered the rest of the cavalry to advance and feel out the Rebel position.

The horsemen were to find more than they could handle. *Hébert* had joined *Price* earlier that morning and agreed to remain on the south side of Little Sugar Creek while the Missouri army continued its retreat to Cross Hollow. He positioned the *3rd Louisiana*, *4th Arkansas*, and *15th Arkansas* at the bluff's edge so the pursuing horsemen could see them. Then *Hébert* pulled away, assuming the Yankees had halted for good. Hayden's guns opened up after the Rebel infantry pulled out, but the fire forced *Hébert* to halt and establish a line about a half mile south of the bluff's edge. He positioned his three regiments to the east of WIRE ROAD on the southern edge of a large field owned by farmer James Dunagin and sent for help. When *Little's* 1st Missouri Brigade came racing forward, *Hébert* placed it to the west of the road. The two commands made a formidable front, especially when reinforced by *Clark's Missouri Battery*.

Ellis, commander of the cavalry column, rode hard up the bluff and raced along the road onto Dunagin's farm. The opening salvo from *Clark's* guns convinced him to scatter his men. The 1st Missouri Cavalry swung left and was followed by the 3rd Illinois Cavalry, while the 6th Missouri Cavalry deployed to the right. Only a small group of the 1st Missouri Cavalry remained on the road and continued to ride toward the Rebels. The regiment's lead battalion, under Maj. James M. Hubbard, failed to understand the order to deploy and came under a hail of small-arms fire and artillery rounds before reaching the Confederate line. The battalion came to an abrupt halt, and many horses and horsemen littered the roadway before Hubbard ordered the survivors to retreat.

Meanwhile, the rest of Ellis's command had advanced on

both sides of the road, pressing back the *1st Missouri Cavalry* of *Price's* army, which was acting as skirmishers. When the Federals got far enough to accurately gauge the strength of *Hébert's* line, they withdrew to a safer distance.

Curtis did not know that this small fight had essentially ended. He remained on the northern bluff of the valley in order to hurry forward reinforcements. Vandever's brigade of Carr's division was the first infantry force in column; his Iowa and Missouri soldiers raced at the double quick across the valley and reached Ellis's men at 3:00 P.M., after the firing had stopped. Hayden's Iowa Battery came up with Vandever and briefly reopened the engagement by shelling *Hébert's* position, prompting *Clark's Missouri Battery* to reply. A few Confederate infantrymen were hit in this exchange. Dodge's brigade also raced across the valley, but it was not needed. *Hébert* pulled out at 4:00 P.M., and Curtis decided not to pursue. Casualties in this little engagement amounted to thirteen men killed and twenty wounded on the Union side. *Hébert* never reported his losses, but the Federals claimed to have found twenty-six Rebel dead on the field.

Vignette

The skirmish at Little Sugar Creek was the first exposure to combat for most of the Federals, but the Confederates had already seen a much bigger and bloodier battle at Wilson's Creek the previous August. As the wounded were carried to Trott's Store and the dead were buried, many Union soldiers saw the effects of battle for the first time. Lt. George E. Currie of the 59th Illinois watched with awe as details hauled corpses to their burial ground. "The heads covered with blood were hanging out at the back end of the ambulance, the tail gate not being closed, jarring and knocking with every jerk of the wagon. A ghastly sight. I followed it and when it stopped went up and saw a soldier's burial on the battlefield. Two men were digging a trench about three by seven feet, and into this side by side with an army blanket under and one over them, the soldiers were placed and the dirt, which was being removed for graves for the next dead comrades, covered them from sight forever." [23]

While the Federals generally viewed the skirmish as a big and exciting affair, the Rebels took the fight in stride. "I never thought it was much of a battle," a member of *Little's* brigade later confided, "but I have talked with some Federal soldiers, since, who claimed it was a stunner." [24]

STOP 13   Cross Hollow, February 17–19

Directions   *Continue south* along OLD WIRE ROAD to Avoca, a postwar
                                town. OLD WIRE ROAD becomes PEARL AVENUE at the town lim-
                                its; *bear right* where it becomes ROSE STREET. Then *turn left*
                                to continue on OLD WIRE ROAD. As it leaves Avoca, the road
                                shadows a railroad, which was built through northwestern
                                Arkansas in the 1880s. Immediately on the other (west) side
                                of the track is U.S. 62. If you prefer to drive quickly south,
                                cross over the tracks and *take* the highway to Rogers, another
                                postwar town. But if you want to more closely approximate
                                the original route of WIRE ROAD, *stay east* of the railroad all
                                the way to Rogers. As you enter the city, OLD WIRE ROAD be-
                                comes ARKANSAS STREET. *Continue driving south*, keeping east of
                                the railroad, *past* LOCUST AVENUE and *doglegging* to the right
                                across ARKANSAS 12. Set your odometer as you pass this junc-
                                tion and *continue driving south*. At 0.8 mile south of LOCUST
                                AVENUE, the road *curves left* onto OAK STREET at Maple Grove
                                Park, then *right* onto C STREET, and *left again* onto MULBERRY
                                STREET. *Take* another curve *to the right* out of town and *head
                                south* again. This is MONTE NE ROAD. At 2.2 miles south of LO-
                                CUST AVENUE, MONTE NE ROAD intersects NEW HOPE ROAD (AR-
                                KANSAS 94) and becomes SOUTH OLD WIRE ROAD (COUNTY 83).
                                   Cross Hollow is 4.6 miles south of LOCUST AVENUE. SOUTH
                                OLD WIRE ROAD descends into its deep valley to meet CROSS
                                HOLLOW ROAD, which runs nearly the length of the hollow
                                west to east. *Stop* at this junction.

Orientation   You have been skirting a series of ravines that drain west to
                                east and empty into White River, the main watercourse of
                                northwestern Arkansas, as you have continued tracing the
                                route of the Confederate retreat from the battlefield at Little
                                Sugar Creek. Cross Hollow extends farther west than most of
                                these ravines, thus it is the only one that WIRE ROAD crosses.
                                You are in the upper reaches of the hollow, which begins
                                about one and a half miles west of the junction. The valley
                                is narrow at this point but widens only a half mile to the
                                east. There the Confederates had built an extensive winter
                                encampment in November 1861. Two-room huts were con-
                                structed in two rows, extending more than a mile through
                                the hollow. Many of the men of *Hébert's* infantry units were
                                snugly resting in their wooden huts when they were ordered
                                to move out and support *Price*. Of course nothing is left of the
                                encampment, but you may drive east for a half mile or more
                                to see its location. The hollow is, as yet, largely unspoiled by
                                development. The stream that flows eastward along its floor
                                is called Monte Ne Branch.

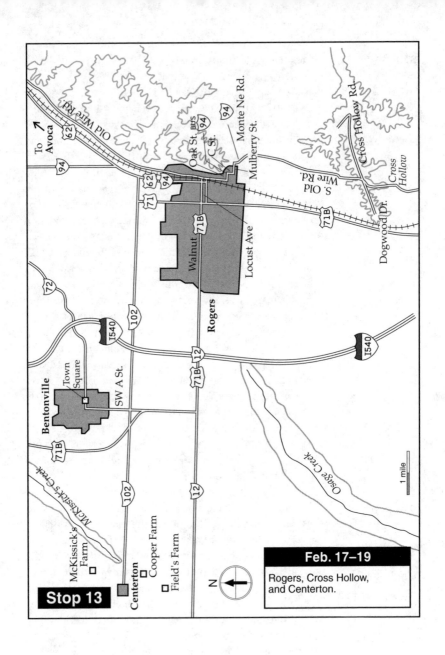

Feb. 17–19

Rogers, Cross Hollow, and Centerton.

Stop 13

Centerton
Cooper Farm
Field's Farm
McKissick's Farm

Bentonville
Town Square
SW A St.

Rogers
Walnut
Locust Ave
Oak St.
C St.
Monte Ne Rd.
Mulberry St.

Cross Hollow

N

1 mile

Osage Creek

McKissick's Creek

To Avoca

Old Wire Rd.
S. Old Wire Rd.
Cross Hollow Rd.
Dogwood Dr.

72
102
1540
71B
12
71B
12
94
62
71
94
62
94
Bus 94
71B
71B
1540

What Happened

Curtis stopped and pondered his next move after the skirmish at Little Sugar Creek. He had accomplished his primary task of clearing southwestern Missouri of Rebel forces but found himself at the end of an ever-lengthening supply line. He was dependent on wagon trains rumbling some 250 miles from his supply depot at Rolla, Missouri, and there apparently was no end to this pursuit. The Rebels could easily continue withdrawing all the way to Fort Smith and the Arkansas River. Curtis had to decide that enough was enough. He could afford to drive the Rebels out of Cross Hollow but to go any farther south would be too risky.

The Confederate position appeared to be very strong. Curtis had received several reports that Cross Hollow was fortified (which were untrue), and he now knew that *McCulloch's* men had reinforced *Price*. He had to move much more cautiously than before. Consequently the Federal general planned a turning movement to pry the Confederates out of their stronghold.

Before he sent his infantry west over the level landscape to outflank Cross Hollow, Curtis wanted to make sure there were no Confederates lurking in the area. He sent Asboth with a cavalry force to reconnoiter toward Bentonville, nine miles west of his position at Little Sugar Creek. This raid netted a few Rebel stragglers but demonstrated that there were no sizeable numbers of troops in the vicinity. Curtis planned his turning movement to begin on February 19.

But the Confederates preempted him by evacuating the hollow. *McCulloch* joined *Price* and *Hébert* there on the evening of February 18 and engaged in a heated debate about strategy. *Price* wanted to make a stand, but *McCulloch* correctly pointed out that the topography was not suitable. The position could easily be turned from the west, and there was no terrain advantage for a force defending against an attack from the north. The Texan wanted to continue the retreat all the way to the Boston Mountains to draw Curtis farther from his base of supplies. Although two-thirds of the subordinate officers agreed with *McCulloch*, *Price* stubbornly refused to concur, and the conference ended late that night with no decision having been made.

Then in the early morning hours, a civilian brought word of Asboth's raid on Bentonville. He also incorrectly informed *McCulloch* that the Federals were on their way to Elm Springs, twelve miles south of Bentonville and ten miles southwest of Cross Hollow. This alarmed *McCulloch* and *Price* alike, for it meant that any stand at Cross Hollow would place the combined armies in a trap. *Price* reluctantly agreed to a hasty pull out.

The Confederates burned all they could and marched away early on the morning of February 19 under freezing rain. They reached Fayetteville the next day and ransacked the large supply of army stores there. The doors of the warehouses were flung open, and each soldier was allowed to carry all the food and clothing he could handle. Whatever remained had to be burned due to the fact that the army's draft animals were wintering farther south. Things got out of hand as some soldiers began to loot private houses as well. Fires set at the government warehouses inevitably spread to civilian property, and several blocks in the center of town were leveled in the inferno. War had come, done its worst to the principal town of northwestern Arkansas, and gone on its way.

McCulloch and *Price* moved on to Strickler's Station and Cove Creek, some seventeen miles south of Fayetteville, where they encamped and rested their men. Curtis was ecstatic with his easy capture of Cross Hollow and established his army in encampments to cover WIRE ROAD crossing of Little Sugar Creek. His only attempt to move troops farther south was another cavalry raid by Asboth. The Hungarian took 1,200 troopers down WIRE ROAD to reconnoiter. He captured about thirty Confederate stragglers and surveyed the charred remains of downtown Fayetteville. For three days the Unionists who lived in the area were delighted with their blue-coated visitors, but Curtis saw no need to keep Asboth there indefinitely. The column mounted and rode north on February 26, leaving Fayetteville in the middle of a no-man's land that was uncontrolled by either army.

Remnants of Union field fortifications, Little Sugar Creek, ca. 1939. These fieldworks were built on the creek bluff and supported a Union defensive position so strong that the Confederates decided to outflank rather than attack them. Clyde T. Ellis Papers, Special Collections, University of Arkansas Libraries, Fayetteville.

Sigel's Retreat from Bentonville, March 6

STOP 14a   McKissick's Creek

Directions   *Retrace* your route from Cross Hollow by *driving north* on
SOUTH OLD WIRE ROAD (COUNTY 83/MONTE NE ROAD) to the
eastern section of Rogers. *Turn left* onto WALNUT STREET rather
than continuing north on ARKANSAS STREET (WIRE ROAD). *Follow* WALNUT, which becomes U.S. 71B, west and north 6 miles
into Bentonville to the intersection with ARKANSAS 102. *Turn
left* (west) onto ARKANSAS 102. *Drive through* southern Bentonville and *continue* to Centerton, 5 miles farther west. *Stop* at
a convenient place in the eastern part of Centerton, a small
postwar town.

Orientation   Get out of your car and survey the landscape to the northeast
and the south.

What Happened   Sigel encamped his 1st and 2nd Divisions in this area following the capture of Cross Hollow, making up Curtis's right
flank. The land was owned by a farmer named McKissick, and
Asboth placed his 2nd Division near a spring on the farm that
provided a reliable source of fresh water. Sigel's headquarters were located a bit to the southeast on the Cooper farm,
and Osterhaus's 1st Division encamped one mile south on a
farm owned by John A. Field. McKissick's Creek begins just
east of Centerton and flows northeast into Little Sugar Creek.

The Federals had only a few days to rest in these camps.
Van Dorn took charge of *McCulloch's* and *Price's* commands and
advanced northward, compelling Curtis to order the two divisions from McKissick's on March 5. But Sigel took his time.
It was nearly dawn of the next morning before his men finally marched out of their camps and stumbled toward Bentonville, passing through that town by midmorning on their
way to the position overlooking Little Sugar Creek.

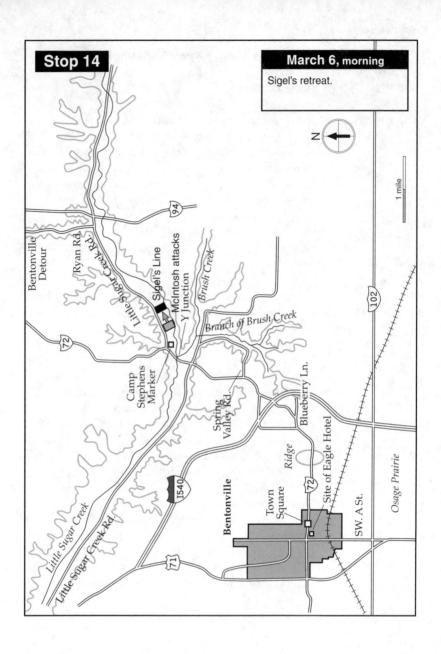

Stop 14

March 6, morning

Sigel's retreat.

N

1 mile

Bentonville Detour

Ryan Rd.

Little Sugar Creek Rd.

Sigel's Line

McIntosh attacks

Y Junction

Brush Creek

Branch of Brush Creek

Camp Stephens Marker

Spring Valley Rd.

Ridge

Blueberry Ln.

Site of Eagle Hotel

Little Sugar Creek

Little Sugar Creek Rd.

Town Square

Bentonville

SW. A St.

Osage Prairie

94

72

I540

71

72

102

STOP 14b   Bentonville

Directions   *Turn around* and *drive east* on ARKANSAS 102. Once in Benton-
                      ville *drive just past* the U.S. 71B intersection and *turn left* onto
                      SW A STREET (the old route of Highway 71 that heads due
                      north to the center of town). *Drive* to downtown, *turn right*
                      (east) onto WEST CENTRAL AVENUE, *continue* straight, and *stop*
                      at the town square.

Orientation   Get out of your car and note the appearance of the square.
                      In the center is a postwar monument to the Confederate sol-
                      dier, typical of the memorials erected in towns and cities all
                      across the South during the late nineteenth and early twen-
                      tieth centuries.

                      This square was occupied by a rear guard that Sigel kept
                      behind as the rest of his command moved toward Little
                      Sugar Creek on March 6. It consisted of eight companies of
                      the 12th Missouri, part of the 5th Missouri Cavalry, two cav-
                      alry companies of the 36th Illinois, and six guns of Elbert's
                      1st Missouri Flying Battery, a little more than 600 men. Sigel
                      intended for the 2nd Missouri, an additional 600 men, to be
                      part of this force, but due to a misunderstanding of orders,
                      it continued on toward the east. The remaining men stacked
                      arms and rested on the square as Sigel went to the Eagle Ho-
                      tel, a familiar hostelry in the area, for breakfast. (The site of
                      the hotel is on Central Avenue, a block west of the square,
                      where a historical marker is located.)

                      The general was unable to eat before Confederate forces
                      appeared south of town. When he visited the area in 1887,
                      Sigel returned to the Eagle Hotel and remarked that he had
                      come to finish his breakfast. Local legend has it that he or-
                      dered exactly the same food each morning during his stay.

                      Keep in mind that the little town of Bentonville had al-
                      ready been severely damaged by the time Sigel's rear guard
                      lolled about on the square. When Asboth left town following
                      his first raid there in late February, a member of the 5th Mis-
                      souri Cavalry broke from the column to refill his canteen
                      with whiskey. He never returned. A search party found his
                      body in an outhouse. It later came to light that a passing
                      Rebel paymaster found the man drunk on the side of the
                      road and killed him with a pistol shot to the head at such
                      close range that it shattered his skull. But the search party
                      believed the horrible wound was made by civilians who had
                      murdered the trooper. They went on a rampage and burned
                      many buildings in town before returning to the column.

Sigel's breakfast was interrupted by the sounds of gunfire to the south, indicating the early approach of *Van Dorn's* army. The Confederate commander had pushed his troops very hard. Starting from Strickler's Station and Cove Creek on March 4, the soldiers encountered a winter storm with howling winds and snow. They had only three days' rations in their haversacks, barely enough to reach Little Sugar Creek before running out of food. Their commander had a fever and was forced to ride northward in an ambulance, but he refused to allow that to interfere with his plans. The march was pressed with reckless speed. "We were being rushed upon the foe like a thunderbolt," recalled a Louisiana officer. "It seemed as if General *Van Dorn* imagined the men were made of cast-steel, with the strength and powers and endurance of a horse, whose mettle he was testing to its upmost capacity and tension. Scarcely time was given the men to prepare food and snatch a little rest." [25]

Van Dorn hoped to move swiftly enough to cut off Sigel's two divisions before they passed the road junction at Bentonville and destroy half of Curtis's army in one stroke. He bivouacked at Elm Springs, twelve miles south of town, on the cold night of March 5. The next day the army set out early, with *McIntosh's* Cavalry Brigade of *McCulloch's* Division in the lead. The horsemen entered a large open area, known as Osage Prairie, just south of town. The flat land gave *McIntosh* a clear view of Bentonville. Several plumes of smoke rising from the square seemed to indicate that a small detachment of Federals had been left behind to burn supplies while the main body had already departed eastward. Even though *Van Dorn* could not hope to cut off the two divisions now, *McIntosh* might be able to nab this detachment.

But his hastily formulated plan to do so was flawed. *McIntosh* circled around to the west and north of Bentonville to cut off the Federals before they escaped eastward. Why he did not simply ride northeastward across the open prairie was never explained. The troopers made their way northward in column, skirting the town's western edge. To *McIntosh's* surprise there was no crossroad leading eastward, thus forcing the brigade to continue north through dense woods. The column rode for several miles, removing itself from the coming scene of action, until it finally entered the valley of Little Sugar Creek and turned east on the LITTLE SUGAR CREEK ROAD.

With *McIntosh's* cavalry temporarily out of the picture, it was up to *Price's* small mounted force to cut off Sigel. The

Missouri troopers tried very hard to do so. *Gates's 1st Missouri Cavalry, Cearnal's Missouri Cavalry Battalion*, and Capt. Joseph *Shelby's Missouri State Guard Company* rode northeastward across the prairie and positioned themselves a couple of miles southeast of Bentonville to await developments. Fifteen minutes later they saw Sigel race out of town with his little column. *Gates* sent his command forward. The main road out of town crossed a shallow knoll and then turned northeastward into a wooded area. *Gates* wanted to position his cavalry in those trees to ambush Sigel. The stage was set for one of the most colorful episodes of the Pea Ridge campaign.

Brigadier-General
James McIntosh.
From a photograph.
BLCW 1:326

STOP 14c   The Ridge

Directions   Return to your car, *note* the mileage on your odometer, and
                          drive east on East CENTRAL STREET (ARKANSAS 72). The road
                          crosses a swale and continues due eastward. *Stop* at the
                          first rise of ground you encounter 1 mile from the square.
                          Park safely on the side of the highway and get out of your
                          vehicle.

Orientation   Face east and south. Unfortunately a number of commercial
                          buildings in the area obscures the commanding view to the
                          south that the ridge offered in 1862.

What Happened   This is the shallow ridge where Sigel halted to take in what
                          was happening. From here he saw the Missouri cavalry rid-
                          ing across the open prairie toward the woods in front of his
                          column, then prepared his little command for action. Sigel
                          sent skirmishers from the 12th Missouri to cover his front
                          and both flanks and ordered the rest of the infantry and four
                          of the guns to race eastward toward the trees. He kept two
                          guns and the cavalry on the ridge for a time and opened an
                          artillery fire on the Missouri cavalry, which scattered and
                          confused them. Then Sigel withdrew and rode eastward.

                          The Federal column entered the woods before the Rebels
                          could set up their ambush. It even freed a company of the
                          36th Illinois that had been detached to guard a broken-down
                          ammunition wagon in the wooded area earlier that morn-
                          ing. *Gates's 1st Missouri Cavalry* had ridden far enough ahead
                          of Sigel's column to capture this company, but the 12th Mis-
                          souri liberated most of the men a few minutes later, put-
                          ting the Rebel Missourians to flight. The rest of the enemy
                          horsemen were now regrouping on the prairie behind Sigel's
                          flying column. They were joined by *Gates's* troopers, and the
                          whole gave chase. In short order Sigel had gotten ahead of his
                          pursuers, but he had to push forward with speed and deter-
                          mination if he meant to avoid capture.

STOP 14d   The Y Junction

Directions   *Continue driving* east on ARKANSAS 72. About 0.5 mile east of
the ridge the road curves to the left; *stop* at BLUEBERRY LANE,
the first road to the right after that curve, about 0.75 mile
east of the ridge and 1.7 miles from the square in Bentonville. This paved road is the original Bentonville Road. In
1862 it entered a deep hollow that was a branch of Brush
Creek, which in turn entered Little Sugar Creek. The road
hugged the foot of the rugged, almost 150-foot-tall western
bluff of the branch as it drains northward into Brush Creek.
The branch enters the creek very near its junction with Little
Sugar Creek, and the road originally crossed the mouth of
Brush Creek and ran into the broad Little Sugar Creek valley
to join the LITTLE SUGAR CREEK ROAD at a junction that formed
the shape of a Y.

Today, however, a large chunk of the original Bentonville
Road is gone in the hollow and the branch. The road you are
on extends only 0.2 mile down the hollow and then ends.
(You can drive down this short spur but then will have to
return to the highway.) *Continue northward* on ARKANSAS 72
for about 2 miles to the southern edge of Little Sugar Creek
valley. *Continue* across the valley. The highway intersects with
LITTLE SUGAR CREEK ROAD (COUNTY 44) on the north side. *Turn
right* (east) and *stop* at this junction.

Orientation   The road system in Little Sugar Creek valley is a bit different
here than it was in 1862. Then, LITTLE SUGAR CREEK ROAD me-
andered back and forth across the wide valley floor, while today it hugs the foot of the northern bluff to minimize flood-
ing and road damage when the stream swells with rain. The
Y junction was about 300 yards east of ARKANSAS 72 and close
to the middle of the valley. Look in that direction, southeast
of your location.

What Happened   When Sigel entered the hollow leading to the branch of
Brush Creek, he was forced to call in his skirmishers and
move along the narrow road in a tight column. This took a
little time, allowing *Gates* to ride hard to the north and occupy the top of the bluff above his quarry. The dismounted
Rebels opened a harassing fire on the head of the column,
but Sigel was up to the challenge. He sent the infantry scram-
bling up the steep bluff and even ordered a gun to make its
way up a ravine to add even more firepower to the contest.
The gun made it up the difficult climb, but the ammunition
chest on the limber slid off and tumbled down the ravine.

On top of the bluff, the loyal Missourians engaged in a brief firefight with their Rebel counterparts as the rest of Sigel's column moved on. *Gates* ordered his frustrated troopers to disengage, and the Federals descended the bluff in time to catch up with their comrades.

This ended the hot pursuit by *Price's* cavalry, but Sigel was not yet out of trouble. He easily made it into the mouth of Brush Creek and gained the LITTLE SUGAR CREEK ROAD, turning east. Sigel's men moved on less than a mile when scouts brought word of a large Rebel column heading their way. This was *McIntosh's* brigade, coming onto the scene of action after a long and frustrating detour. Sigel quickly faced about and formed a line across the valley floor. His artillery and cavalry occupied a patch of woods while the infantry scaled the northern bluff to prevent a turning movement.

McIntosh impulsively ordered a charge as soon as the head of his column came within striking distance. A part of the *3rd Texas Cavalry* followed his lead and rode hard in column along the road, past the Y junction, and straight for Sigel's line. The rest of the regiment misunderstood *McIntosh's* hastily shouted order and deployed into line for a more conventional assault. Those who rode ahead were the unlucky ones. "We all raised the Texas war whoop," a trooper frankly recalled, "but soon a most galling fire of small arms, followed by the thunder of artillery, opened our eyes and closed our mouths."[26] The impromptu attack came to a dead halt sixty yards from the blazing Federal position. *McIntosh* waved the regimental flag and tried to rally the men for another try, but they all retreated in confusion. The rest of the regiment now rode up but veered to the right and stopped, to be followed by the rest of the brigade.

McIntosh was forced to pry Sigel from his position. He dismounted many of his units and sent them up the bluff to outflank the Yankees. But by this time Sigel received relief from Osterhaus and Asboth. The two divisions had nearly reached the fortifications when the sound of artillery fire echoed down the valley. Then a messenger from Sigel confirmed that help was needed. Both officers turned their columns around and raced back, reaching Sigel about 2:00 P.M. Four regiments and a battery of the 1st Division and two regiments of the 2nd Division strengthened the position so much that *McIntosh* gave up any hope of turning it. Sigel instructed Osterhaus to take charge of the troops so he could ride to Curtis's headquarters with Asboth to report. Osterhaus carefully withdrew, but the Rebel cavalry chose not to follow up. The retreat was over.

Analysis

This was the most spectacular episode of Sigel's military career, but it was wholly unnecessary. There was no reason for the German general to keep a rear guard behind at Bentonville, particularly when his two divisions had already left town. If he truly wanted to guard the crossroads and gather information on the location of *Van Dorn's* army, it would have been far better to do that with cavalry alone. Sigel burdened himself with a mixed force of all three arms, a legion that had heavy firepower but could not move too quickly. Most likely he tarried so long at Bentonville in hope that he could meet the enemy with his little band and exercise independent command without Curtis breathing down his neck.

Sigel did perform magnificently that day—he seems to have had a knack for conducting a desperate retreat. In fact he had initially made his military reputation by commanding such a retreat in the final days of the Baden Revolution in 1849. Public reaction to his American deed was enormous. Sigel had good rapport with the press, and Junius Henri Browne, a correspondent with the *New York Tribune*, wrote a colorful account of the affair, even though he was 280 miles away in Kentucky when it happened. "Sigel was at last cut off; but his energy and that of his men mowed a passage through the serried ranks of the Rebels. . . .The cavalry charged and re-charged upon the little band at Sigel's back, but each time the Union bayonets gleamed in their eyes, and the light drove them back." Browne pictured Sigel as a romantic hero. "Every loyal soldier kept his eye fixed upon his fearless leader, as did the followers of Murat or Henry of Navarre. Wherever they saw his streaming hair and his flashing sword, they knew all was safe." [27]

The home front read such drivel and believed it. Nathaniel Bacon of Niles, Michigan, wrote to Sigel and urged him not to allow his exploit to "be compressed by the historian into one single line." A detailed account was needed by the country to prove it was a "memorable event" in military history. "We compare it to the retreat of Xenophon—or that through the black forest—or that of Washington through New Jersey—let it stand side by side with them." [28]

Sigel's career as a self-promoter was well on its way. Curtis became so exasperated with the glowing and inaccurate press reports of Sigel's role in the battle of Pea Ridge that he described the newspapers as "a medium of false puffing and quack heroes to the disgust of honorable men." Curtis also complained to a superior that "for a long time after I had this command my brother in Ohio was puzzled to know from the papers whether I had even a subordinate position under General Sigel." [29] The army leader's thorn was removed soon after Pea Ridge when Sigel was promoted to major general of volunteers and transferred to Virginia, where he led a corps in Maj. Gen. John Pope's Army of Virginia and contributed to the Union disaster at Second Bull Run that August. Despite this he was retained in corps command until he resigned over imagined slights to his dignity in March 1863. Sigel rounded out his inglorious career by commanding a small Federal army in the Shenandoah Valley that was soundly defeated at the battle of New Market in May 1864.

The Eagle Hotel, Bentonville, Arkansas. Franz Sigel planned to eat breakfast here on the morning of March 6, 1862, before beginning his famous retreat to rejoin Curtis's army at Little Sugar Creek. This photograph was taken sometime after the war, probably in the 1880s, but appears here on a postcard that was postmarked in 1906. Courtesy Special Collections, University of Arkansas Libraries, Fayetteville.

Van Dorn's Flanking Movement, March 6–7

STOP 15a   Bentonville Detour

Directions   Notice the historical marker here at the junction of ARKANSAS
72 and LITTLE SUGAR CREEK ROAD for Camp Stephens. An ex-
pansive cantonment built by Brig. Gen. Nicholas B. *Pearce* of
the Arkansas State Troops in July 1861, it was named for the
Confederate vice president, Alexander Stephens. The huts
stretched from here for three miles to the east, as far as the
junction of Bentonville Detour and LITTLE SUGAR CREEK ROAD.
Some units of *Van Dorn's* army, including the wayward ammunition train, took refuge here on the evening of March 7
as the fighting at Leetown ended. Curtis also used the cantonment for his army, which he moved from the Pea Ridge
battlefield a few days after the fighting to escape the "stench
and filth."[30]

Continue driving east on LITTLE SUGAR CREEK ROAD for 2.3
miles and *stop* at the first public-access gravel road, RYAN
ROAD, to the left. This is the southern portion of the Bentonville Detour, stretching up a long, deep ravine from LITTLE
SUGAR CREEK ROAD. (If you miss it, keep in mind that 0.2
mile east of it, LITTLE SUGAR CREEK ROAD intersects ARKAN-
SAS 94 as it crosses the valley. If you reach that highway,
turn around and try again, stopping at the first gravel road
heading north.)

Orientation   Get out of your car and face north, looking up the deep ravine that allowed local road builders to take the detour out
of Little Sugar Creek valley. You are 4.1 miles west of Curtis's
fortifications.

What Happened   *Van Dorn's* risky scheme to completely outflank Curtis's strong
position at Little Sugar Creek was born at this junction on
the evening of March 6. Following his failed attempt to
cripple the Federal army that day by cutting off the 1st and
2nd Divisions, he was eager for a bold stroke that might en-
able him to have a decisive advantage over his opponent.
McCulloch pointed out that the Bentonville Detour offered
that opportunity, and *Van Dorn* immediately seized it. The
Texan preferred a short turning movement, however, while
his commander opted for a far grander move with a greater
potential for trapping and capturing Curtis's entire army. *Van
Dorn's* plan demanded a lot of his tired men, who had already
marched fifty miles in three days and had virtually no food

left. *Pike* joined the army that evening with two regiments of Cherokee troops, adding some fresh strength to the Rebels.

Van Dorn ordered a night march along the Bentonville Detour. When dusk descended, the Confederates built numerous campfires to fool the Yankees into believing they were bivouacking at Camp Stephens. The men were in marching column by 8:00 P.M. but encountered much confusion and delay. The winding nature of LITTLE SUGAR CREEK ROAD meant that the stream had to be crossed one last time before the army could take the detour, and it was particularly wide, deep, and cold here. A few logs had to be maneuvered into place so the men and the artillery could cross. The waiting troops suffered immensely due to the frigid night air. The surgeon of the *4th Arkansas Infantry* later wrote, "For my own part I shall retain a lively and an unpleasant recollection of my suffering on that wretched night, for my whole natural lifetime." [31]

The Confederate commander had hoped to have his men astride WIRE ROAD north of Elkhorn Tavern by daybreak. But *Price's* leading division did not start up the detour until midnight. *Hébert's* brigade followed and took three hours to cross the creek. *McIntosh's* large cavalry brigade took even longer, and *Pike's* tiny column crossed the wretched ford as the sun rose. The flanking movement was already in trouble.

Brigadier-General Albert Pike, C.S.A., commander of the Indian Forces at Pea Ridge. From a photograph.
BLCW 1:399

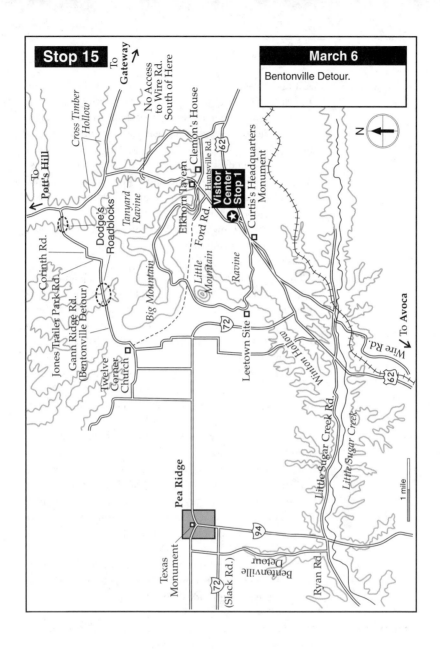

Stop 15

March 6

Bentonville Detour.

STOP 15b   Twelve Corner Church

Directions   Only about two-thirds of the original roadbed of the Bentonville Detour is intact today—the northwestern section of it has been replaced by a system of postwar roads and highways. Get in your car and *drive north* on RYAN ROAD through the long, deep ravine. After 1.5 miles you will reach the head of this hollow and 0.2 mile farther you will intersect ARKANSAS 72 (SLACK ROAD). *Turn right* and *drive* a short distance to intersect ARKANSAS 94. *Turn left* (north) and *drive* about 0.5 mile to the point where ARKANSAS 72 and 94 diverge. This is the center of the town of Pea Ridge(to your right front you will see the granite monument to Texas troops mentioned in Stop 8f).

Turn right and *drive east* on ARKANSAS 72, taking note of the mileage on your odometer. At 5.1 miles from the intersection, *turn left* on an UNMARKED PAVED ROAD. There is a sign directing you to Twelve Corner Baptist Church. Keep in mind that as you drive north, you are only a short distance west of Pea Ridge National Military Park.

Continue 1 mile and you will find that the paved road ends at a crossroad. *Turn right* (east) and very quickly the church will appear on your left just after you curve left. *Stop* here.

Orientation   This modern church building stands where the original log church stood in 1862. You have now regained the original roadbed of the Bentonville Detour. This is a strategic spot. Off to the southeast is the western end of Big Mountain. When the head of *Van Dorn's* army passed Twelve Corner Church in the middle of the night, the flanking movement became a viable maneuver. From this point eastward, the march was shielded by Big Mountain; WIRE ROAD lay only 3.2 miles to the northeast. A short distance to the east lies the junction of Ford Road and the Bentonville Detour, offering the Rebels access to the southern side of Big Mountain.

What Happened   All night long, from about midnight, a never-ending stream of exhausted soldiers passed this point on their dreary march to Curtis's rear. Because of the long delay in crossing Little Sugar Creek, though, the army was terribly strung out when it should have been concentrated for a rapid march. *Price's* Division was further delayed in the dark when it encountered two roadblocks of felled timber east of the church and west of WIRE ROAD. These had been created by industrious Federals under the charge of Grenville Dodge. The blockades forced *Price* to halt his weary men and send pioneers forward with axes to clear the road. His column halted for two hours at each one as this necessary but frustrating work was completed.

Many of the troops who dozed by the roadside while the trees were removed never bothered to return to their commands when the column resumed its progress. Stragglers lined the roadway. Brig. Gen. Daniel M. *Frost* estimated that one-third of the soldiers in his combined *7th and 9th Missouri State Guard Divisions* had dropped out, and many of them failed to catch up with their comrades in time for the coming battle.

It was 8:00 A.M. on March 7 before *Van Dorn* and the head of *Price's* infantry reached WIRE ROAD. His attempt to pounce on Curtis's rear at dawn had failed, but *Van Dorn* did not lose heart. He decided to partially compensate for the delay by splitting his army, instructing *McCulloch* to take Ford Road, march south of Big Mountain, and rejoin Price at Elkhorn Tavern for a united attack on the Federals. This would save hours of tedious plodding and bring the Army of the West into action by early afternoon.

The head of *McCulloch's* command had already passed Twelve Corner Church when the Texan received this order, forcing him to halt and retrace his steps. *McCulloch* tried to allay any doubts among the troops. While riding past the column he shouted, "We are going to take "'em on the other wing."[32] The tired soldiers turned south on Ford Road at midmorning and rounded the western end of Big Mountain a little before noon.

STOP 15c   Bentonville Detour Meets Wire Road

Directions   Before leaving Twelve Corner Church, note that the junction
of the Bentonville Detour and Ford Road is 0.2 mile east of
where you are parked. A gravel road joins the detour from
the right, all that remains of Ford Road. (Instead of following
the original road as it curves around Big Mountain to the
east, the modern road leads due south from this junction,
skirts the western edge of Pea Ridge National Military Park,
and joins ARKANSAS 72. It offers a slightly different perspective of the Leetown battlefield, visible off to the left as one
drives south, but the route is not a historic road.)

Continue driving east on the Bentonville Detour, which here
is called Gann Ridge Road, noting the mileage on your odometer. The location of the first roadblock *Price* encountered is
1 mile from the church. Here the road crosses a deep ravine,
making it impossible for the Rebels to simply march around
the felled trees. At 1.9 miles from the church, *turn left* onto
JONES TRAILER PARK ROAD. *Proceed* 0.3 mile and *turn right* onto
CORINTH ROAD. This gravel road is the continuation of the
original detour, approximately following its roadbed. At 2.6
miles from the church, the road begins to descend into Cross
Timber Hollow. Dodge placed the second roadblock here. At
3 miles from the church, the road hits the bottom of Cross
Timber Hollow, and at 3.2 miles it meets WIRE ROAD NORTH
OLD WIRE ROAD [COUNTY 67]).

Orientation   Stop at a safe spot, get out of your car, and scan the entire
area. You are about 3 miles north of Elkhorn Tavern and 1
mile south of the Missouri state line.

What Happened   The leading cavalrymen of *Price's* Division reached this junction at about 7:00 A.M. on March 7. They carefully explored
the area and found no Federal troops. *Van Dorn* and the head
of the Missouri infantry column arrived at 8:00 A.M. He
pondered the unraveling of his hastily conceived plan and
decided to split the army. Orders went out to *McCulloch* that
shaped the basic contour of the battle, with the powerful
Confederate army separated into wings incapable of supporting each other. With that fateful decision made, the Missourians pressed on, turning south onto WIRE ROAD and reaching
Tanyard Hollow late in the morning.

This road junction saw more activity associated with the
campaign than this pivotal moment. On February 16 *Price's*
harried command, alone and conducting a hasty retreat
from Springfield, fought a little skirmish as it left Missouri a
half mile north at Pott's Hill. The men continued streaming

past this junction that day until they had put some distance between themselves and their pursuers. The Federals moved south of Pott's Hill on February 17, their long column snaking past this point nearly all day.

This spot also saw action during the battle itself. Much of *McCulloch's* defeated division left the Leetown battlefield and completed the march east along the Bentonville Detour on the night of March 7, turning onto WIRE ROAD to rejoin *Van Dorn* and *Price* at the tavern. Then during the closing hours of the battle on March 8, many retreating units marched rapidly north on WIRE ROAD into Missouri, while others managed to turn left onto the detour, retreating along the same route the army had used to achieve the complete turning movement. A lot of history paraded by this key road junction in the early weeks of 1862.

Vignette

Grenville Dodge was a good self-promoter too. He filled the mail pouches with letters trumpeting his role in the victory following the battle. Unlike Sigel, however, there was a lot of truth to his self-important broadcasts. Dodge deserves enormous credit for suggesting to Curtis on the evening of March 6 that the Bentonville Detour should be obstructed in case the Rebels tried to use it for a flanking movement. The army commander had thought about this but was too busy all day planning the fortifications along Little Sugar Creek and worrying about Sigel's tardy command to do anything about it. He offhandedly told Dodge to "go and do it."

The colonel took six companies of his 4th Iowa Infantry and one company of the 3rd Illinois Cavalry along the roadway about dusk and went to work. Everyone expended their energies with "efficiency and dispatch" for two hours on the first roadblock, the same amount of time it took the Rebels to clear it.[33] The Yankees had just about finished the second obstruction when the sound of distant firing came across the night air. Some Union pickets left at the first one exchanged a few rounds with the head of *Price's* column before they fled. Dodge ordered his men to pick up their tools and march back to the army. He met Curtis at 2:00 A.M. to report the success of his mission but was surprised that the army leader took the news of picket firing along the detour nonchalantly. Curtis was convinced by the campfires at Camp Stephens that *Van Dorn* intended to spend the night there. All of the other commanders in the army assumed the same thing. Only a few enlisted men on the far right wing doubted this; they heard what seemed to be the rumbling of artillery to the west but had no authority to go out and investigate. For some reason no one ever brought convincing reports of this to army headquarters. If it was not for Dodge's felled timber, *Van Dorn* might have brought most of his army onto WIRE ROAD in time to give battle to an unwary Curtis early on the morning of March 7.

STOP 16   Pott's Hill, February 16, 1862

Directions   From the junction of the detour and WIRE ROAD, *turn left* (north) and *proceed* about 1.5 miles to the Missouri-Arkansas state line. A historical marker here refers to the fight at Pott's Hill. *Stop* at a safe place.

Orientation   Get out of your car and look north up the road.

What Happened   *Price's* fleeing Missouri army reached this spot at the state line after a trying ordeal. Having given up Springfield on February 13, the men had marched furiously for one hundred miles, hounded by the aggressive Colonel Ellis and his 1st Missouri Cavalry in the vanguard of Curtis's army. The WIRE ROAD came to Pott's Hill through Cross Timber Hollow, an eight-mile ravine starting three miles south of Keetsville, Missouri, and draining into the head of Big Sugar Creek. It then crossed the wide valley of that watercourse, passed the spot where you are standing, and continued up the southern arm of Cross Timber Hollow toward Elkhorn Tavern.

Ellis's troopers led the Union pursuit with spunk and determination. They had constantly skirmished with *Little's* brigade, *Price's* rear guard, long before the two armies reached Cross Timber Hollow. Both forces passed through the hollow on February 16. When Ellis emerged from its northern arm and entered the wide, open valley of Big Sugar Creek, he saw the tail of *Little's* column only a few hundred yards ahead. The colonel impulsively ordered a charge and led his regiment in a thundering gallop across the valley. He struck *Gates's* cavalry just south of the creek, and a running fight ensued that engulfed *Clark's Missouri Battery* as well. The gunners were forced to defend themselves against the sudden attack by swinging ramrods at lunging Union troopers. The melee spilled over the state line, where you are standing, and became the first combat to occur on Arkansas soil in the war. It ended when *Little*, farther down the column, realized what was afoot and ordered his infantry to hurry back. The men were exhausted and "could scarcely move one foot before the other," yet they retraced their steps.[34] Ellis wisely broke off the confused engagement before the reinforcements arrived. He lost one man killed and five wounded, while Confederate casualties amounted to sixteen killed and several wounded. The Federals retired to the north side of Big Sugar Creek valley as *Little* hurried south. It had been an inconclusive fight that merely served to hasten the Confederates on their way. The two sides would meet again the next day in the skirmish at Little Sugar Creek.

This ends your tour of the sites associated with the Pea Ridge campaign. You can *either retrace* your route back to the Bentonville Detour, *pass* Twelve Corner Church, and *return* to ARKANSAS 72, *or continue* to follow Van Dorn's route toward the battlefield by *passing* the intersection with the detour and *driving south* on NORTH OLD WIRE ROAD. Half a mile south of the detour, you can gain easy access to U.S. 62 by *turning left* (east) onto a postwar paved road (COUNTY 68) that intersects the highway at Gateway, about 7 miles from the entrance to Pea Ridge National Military Park.

If you want to follow *Van Dorn's* route as far as possible, *proceed south* on NORTH OLD WIRE ROAD another 0.5 mile beyond this paved road and *turn right* onto a gravel road that enters a narrow ravine. This is the continuation of the historical WIRE ROAD as it enters Williams Hollow and Tanyard Ravine. *Drive 0.6 mile and stop.* Here is the northern boundary of Pea Ridge National Military Park. The WIRE ROAD continues ahead, just to the left of a private road that leads straight to a residence. This section of WIRE ROAD is not used by traffic today and is overgrown with brush. After about 130 yards the road ends at a dry creek bed; on the other side is the end of the park trail that leads from Elkhorn Tavern into Williams Hollow. This is where *Price* began to deploy his division for battle at midday of March 7.

Return to your car and *continue driving* along the public-access road. It is a bit rugged but angles off to the southeast and intersects U.S. 62 about 2 miles away. This road needs to be driven with care, but it allows you to maximize your time on WIRE ROAD; it also joins the original roadbed of HUNTSVILLE ROAD for about the last 0.5 mile before you intersect U.S. 62. Remember that *Van Dorn's* defeated army marched along this stretch of HUNTSVILLE ROAD on its retreat from the battlefield.

The entrance to Pea Ridge National Military Park is about 2 miles to the right (west) of the junction with U.S. 62. You may move on to the Prairie Grove section of this book by driving west and south on this highway to Fayetteville.

Prairie Grove

Capture of a Confederate battery. BLCW 1:527

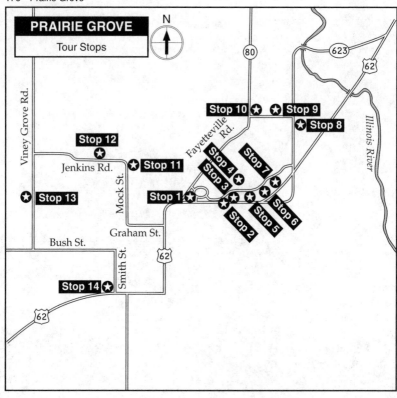

PRAIRIE GROVE
Tour Stops

N

Stop 10
Stop 9
Stop 8
Stop 12
Stop 11
Stop 4
Stop 7
Stop 3
Stop 1
Stop 13
Stop 6
Stop 2
Stop 5
Stop 14

Viney Grove Rd.
Jenkins Rd.
Mock St.
Graham St.
Bush St.
Smith St.
Fayetteville Rd.
Illinois River

80
623
62
62
62

Major-General T.C. Hindman, C.S.A.
From a photograph. BLCW 3:445

Overview

The forces hastily assembled to defend Little Rock from Samuel R. Curtis's campaign across northern Arkansas in the spring and summer of 1862 became the core of a new Confederate field army. In midsummer Lt. Gen. Theophilus H. *Holmes* took command of the newly created Trans-Mississippi Department. He placed Maj. Gen. Thomas C. *Hindman* in charge of Confederate military forces in the field, such as they were. Within a remarkably short time, *Hindman* cobbled together an embryonic army of about 12,000 men in the western part of the state. *Holmes* christened this new force the Trans-Mississippi Army.

Hindman selected Fort Smith on the Arkansas River as his base of operations. He hoped to recover northwest Arkansas and southwest Missouri as soon as possible. Only by boldly seizing the initiative, he believed, could the Confederates hope to reverse the disastrous outcome of the Pea Ridge campaign. By early fall *Hindman* and elements of his army were operating in Missouri.

Curtis, meanwhile, succeeded Maj. Gen. Henry W. Halleck as commander of the Department of the Missouri. Soon, reports of renewed Confederate activity in southwest Missouri reached his headquarters in St. Louis. Having previously driven the Confederates out of the state, Curtis was determined to keep them out. He instructed his principal subordinate, Brig. Gen. John M. Schofield, to take command of a new force, the Army of the Frontier, and push the Confederates back to the Arkansas River. Schofield did just that. Shrugging off an initial setback at Newtonia on September 30, he quickly had the Rebels on the run.

Schofield benefited from bad timing on the Confederate side. Just as the Union offensive got underway, *Holmes* recalled *Hindman* to Little Rock for a discussion about the wisdom of invading Missouri and stirring up the Federals. With *Hindman* absent, the Confederates made only feeble efforts to halt the Union juggernaut. The only noteworthy engagement took place on October 22, when Brig. Gen. James G. Blunt, commanding one of Schofield's three divisions, routed a small Confederate force in the Indian Territory near Maysville, Arkansas.

Now it was Schofield's turn to err. From his position near the Arkansas border, he led two divisions of the Army of the Frontier back to the Wilson's Creek battlefield south of Springfield. Inexplicably, he kept Blunt's division near Maysville, about seventy-five miles away. To make matters worse, Schofield became ill and departed for St. Louis. Nominal command of the army passed to Blunt, though Brig. Gen. Francis J. Herron assumed operational control of the two divisions near Springfield. Neither man had any idea what Schofield expected them to do in his absence, and the two wings of the Union army remained dangerously separated.

When *Hindman* returned to Fort Smith from Little Rock, he discovered the inviting disposition of Union forces. He sent Brig. Gen. John S. *Marmaduke's* cavalry force across the Boston Mountains to strike at Blunt's isolated command. Blunt unexpectedly advanced and repulsed *Marmaduke* at Cane Hill on November 28. The Federal commander secured a tactical victory, but his division was thirty-five miles deeper inside Arkansas. Blunt now was more than one hundred miles south of Herron's two divisions near Springfield but barely thirty miles north of *Hindman's* army in Fort Smith. Only the Boston Mountains separated the two opposing forces. Despite the obvious danger, Blunt chose to stay at Cane Hill and await developments. He cautioned Herron to be ready to come to his support at once.

Hindman could not resist the opportunity to defeat the Army of the Frontier in detail. His plan for a full-scale attack was simple. The infantry would attack Cane Hill from the south. With Blunt distracted, the cavalry would pass around the east side of Cane Hill and get into the Federal rear. Cut off from his base, Blunt would have to surrender or flee. The Trans-Mississippi Army left Van Buren on December 3 and headed north. Success depended on speed and surprise, but *Hindman's* malnourished men and animals needed three days to struggle across the Boston Mountains.

Blunt was no fool. He knew that his advanced position at Cane Hill was precarious, so he kept a close eye on the Confederates. On December 2 he sensed that something was up and ordered Herron to come at once. Herron responded in heroic fashion. He put his command on Wire Road on December 4 and headed south. During the next three and a half days, the two Union divisions completed one of the most extraordinary marches of the war—an average of thirty-five miles per day on a primitive road atop the Ozark Plateau. Thousands of blue-clad soldiers fell by the wayside, but by nightfall on December 6, the hardiest of Herron's men were approaching Fayetteville, only six miles from Cane Hill.

Hindman did not learn of Herron's astonishingly rapid approach until the night of December 6. Caught off guard by this unexpected development, he was forced to improvise in what had suddenly become a fluid tactical situation. *Hindman* abandoned his attempt to envelop Blunt and turned north to intercept Herron. He apparently hoped to drive off

Herron, then turn back and destroy Blunt at Cane Hill. The Confederate commander deployed his army about halfway between Fayetteville and Cane Hill on a wooded hill overlooking a broad valley. The hill was crowned by a simple structure called Prairie Grove Church.

On the morning of Sunday, December 7, Herron reached Prairie Grove. He seems to have believed that he had encountered a Confederate blocking force; he almost certainly did not realize that he was facing *Hindman's* entire army. Herron deployed his artillery and pounded the Confederate position, then sent his exhausted infantry across the valley against the Confederate right. Heavy fighting raged along the slope and on top of the hill. The Union attackers were overwhelmed and driven back by superior numbers. The Confederates launched disorganized counterattacks, but they were broken up by a storm of Union artillery fire. By midafternoon Herron realized that he could not fight his way through to Cane Hill. Blunt would have to come to him, and he would have to come quickly or else Herron's depleted force would be crushed.

Six miles away at Cane Hill, Blunt waited all morning for *Hindman* to attack him. When he heard the roar of battle to his rear at Prairie Grove, he realized what had happened and immediately put his command in motion to rescue Herron. After securing his trains and forward supply depot at Rhea's Mill, Blunt marched toward the sound of the guns in the best military tradition. In midafternoon his division made contact with Herron's beleaguered force.

With the Army of the Frontier reunited on the battlefield, all hope of a decisive Confederate victory was gone, but the bloodletting continued. Blunt sent his division across the valley against the Confederate left. *Hindman's* men again held their ground, and when they left the cover of the woods to launch a counterattack, they were again decimated by Union artillery. The battle sputtered to a close as darkness fell. During the night, the Confederates slipped away and trudged back across the Boston Mountains to the Arkansas River.

Prairie Grove was a tactical draw, with a slight advantage to the Confederates for holding their position. In strategic terms, however, it was another major Union victory. *Hindman* failed to destroy Blunt's isolated division, which was the immediate objective of his campaign. He also failed to achieve his ultimate strategic goal of recovering northwest Arkansas and southwest Missouri. The heavy loss of men and equipment meant that Prairie Grove was the last serious Confederate attempt to regain control of Missouri until *Price's* Raid in September 1864. After December 7, 1862, the effective northern border of the Trans-Mississippi Confederacy was the Arkansas River.

The Union side of the campaign was not quite over. Blunt and Herron were concerned that *Hindman* would rebuild his army south of the Boston Mountains and threaten Missouri in the spring. They decided on a daring move to knock their opponent off balance and cripple his fragile logistical system. On December 27–30 Blunt and Herron led most of the Army of the Frontier on a rapid raid across the Boston Mountains to Van Buren on the north bank of the Arkansas River. The Federals surprised and scattered the Confederate defenders, captured and burned five steamboats (the Confederates panicked and burned two more), seized or destroyed a large amount of stores, and liberated hundreds of slaves. The Federals then returned over the mountains to Prairie Grove without the loss of a single man. It was one of the most successful raids of the war.

Hindman was safe on the south side of the Arkansas River in Fort Smith, but he lost his head and withdrew eastward in considerable haste. Thousands of men were left behind in hospitals, and hundreds more deserted during the chaotic retreat. By the time the Trans-Mississippi Army reached Little Rock in January 1863, it was a shadow of the force that had set out across the Boston Mountains a month earlier. *Hindman* was reassigned east of the Mississippi River, and the ill-starred army he had labored so hard to create was merged with other Confederate forces.

Blunt and Herron received little recognition for their hard-won victories at Cane Hill, Prairie Grove, and Van Buren. The huge battles of Fredericksburg, Virginia, and Murfreesboro (Stones River), Tennessee, were fought at about the same time and crowded news from Arkansas off the pages of most newspapers—and off the pages of most history books as well.

Schofield resumed command of the Army of the Frontier shortly after the Van Buren raid. Within a few months, though, the army ceased to exist. Herron's two divisions were sent to Vicksburg, but Blunt's division continued to operate in the Trans-Mississippi. One by one the important towns along Wire Road—Springfield, Fayetteville, Van Buren, and even Fort Smith—fell into Union hands. For the rest of the war, southwest Missouri and northwest Arkansas were crisscrossed by cavalry raids and plagued by guerrillas and outlaws. But after 1862 the grim spectacles of marching armies and thundering battles were seen and heard no more.

Battle for the Wooded Ridge

STOP 1a   Visitor Center

Directions   *Proceed* on U.S. 62 from Fayetteville 8 miles to Prairie Grove
Battlefield State Historic Park.

Orientation   The core of the park is the wooded ridge just outside the postwar town of Prairie Grove. Confederate veterans from north-
west Arkansas held annual reunions here in the shade of the
trees from 1886 to 1924. The United Daughters of the Confederacy purchased ten acres of the ridge in 1908 and established
a Confederate memorial park, but they gave little thought to
preserving or marking the battlefield. Public memory of the
battle, and of the reason for the park, faded as the decades
rolled by. The site gradually became cluttered with picnic
facilities and historic pioneer buildings. Meanwhile, more
and more of the battlefield was lost to the growth of the
nearby town.

The state of Arkansas acquired the property in 1971, but
nearly two decades passed before the state, with the support
of Federal and private funds, began a sustained campaign to
acquire additional land and interpret the park as a battlefield. During the 1990s, the park grew by leaps and bounds.
It now encompasses over 840 acres, or about one-fourth of
the original battlefield. Additional acquisitions are planned.

You should begin your visit at the Visitor Center, which
is a story in itself. Biscoe Hindman, the son of Maj. Gen.
Thomas C. *Hindman*, the Confederate commander at Prairie
Grove, bequeathed $100,000 to the UDC for the creation of a
"suitable memorial" to his father on the battlefield. The result is Hindman Hall, probably the only Visitor Center in the
country with such a direct link to the Civil War, and surely
the only one dedicated to a Confederate general. Inside the
boxy building is a diorama of the battle and an unusual ar-
ray of exhibits about the Civil War in northwest Arkansas.
Also on display is a painting of a key moment in the battle by
Andy Thomas (an artist mentioned elsewhere in the pages of
this guide).

After leaving the Visitor Center, walk across the drive to the
circular enclosure with the tower in the center. Stroll around
the enclosure and read the plaques and memorials. The sandstone tower is not a rustic obelisk but a smokestack. It was
once part of a steam-powered mill owned by William Rhea
(pronounced "ray"). The tiny settlement of Rhea's Mill, which
also included an older water-powered mill, was located six

miles northwest of the battlefield. It served as an important Union supply depot during he campaign and played a role in the battle. When the mill was demolished in the 1950s, the smokestack was moved here to serve as a monument. It is fifty-four feet high and weighs 225,000 pounds. (The site of Rhea's Mill is included in the campaign driving tour).

A few steps away from the tower is the John Morrow House. This modest frame dwelling was originally located on Cove Creek Road nine miles south of Prairie Grove. The Morrow House has the unique distinction of being associated with *two* Civil War campaigns and *three* Confederate commanders. No other building west of the Mississippi River, and few if any east of it, have such an outstanding pedigree. On March 2, 1862, Maj. Gens. Earl *Van Dorn* and Sterling *Price* stayed in the house and planned the offensive that ended in disaster at Pea Ridge. Nine months later *Hindman* spent the night of December 6 in the Morrow House and made the fateful decision to march to Prairie Grove the next morning. All three generals used the bedroom to the left of the front door. (It was the north bedroom in 1862, but due to the present alignment of the house, it is now the west bedroom.) The fabric of the structure is largely original except for the porch, which was added in the 1890s. (The original site of the Morrow House in Cove Creek valley is also included in the campaign driving tour.)

The best way to experience Prairie Grove is to take *both* the walking tour and the driving tour that is outlined in this guide. For the walking tour, obtain a brochure at the Visitor Center, then look for the colorful "Battlefield Trail" sign beyond the Morrow House. The trail is a self-guiding one-mile loop. It runs eastward along Battle Ridge to the Borden farm, where the heaviest fighting took place, then returns along the valley floor. The trail provides outstanding views of the battlefield and includes a number of informative markers. Allow one hour, and be advised that portions of the trail are steep. Stay on the path to avoid ticks.

The walking tour is being revised in phases over the next several years. Thus any detailed description of it in this guide would soon become outdated. Be assured, though, that the area covered by the walking tour is visible from the driving tour; the former covers a small area in a largely open landscape around which the latter circles.

The battlefield driving tour is a six-mile loop that follows a mix of park roads, highways, county roads, and city streets. Traffic may be heavy and turnouts are rare, so drive carefully and stop even more carefully. To begin the driving tour, return to the Visitor Center parking lot.

STOP 1b   The Confederate Center

Orientation   Stand in the Visitor Center parking lot facing north with u.s.
                         62 to your rear. You are located atop Battle Ridge near the cen-
                         ter of the Confederate position. Notice how the ground falls
                         away in front of you. The commanding ridge descends into a
                         broad valley about two hundred yards north of your location.
                         The valley and the opposite heights were occupied by Union
                         forces. Unfortunately, the current growth of trees makes it
                         impossible to see the valley from the parking lot. The narrow
                         incised road to your left is Fayetteville Road, a well-traveled
                         thoroughfare that ran diagonally northeast-southwest across
                         the battlefield and bisected the Confederate position.

What Happened   On the morning of December 7, 1862, *Hindman's* Trans-Missis-
                         sippi Army, 12,000 strong, emerged from the Boston Moun-
                         tains on Cove Creek Road. In the van was Brig. Gen. Francis
                         A. *Shoup's* infantry division. Cove Creek Road intersected Fay-
                         etteville Road a half mile southwest of your present location
                         atop Battle Ridge. When *Shoup* reached the intersection, he
                         turned northeast onto Fayetteville Road and marched over
                         the ridge.

                         The division halted near the Visitor Center between nine
                         and ten o'clock in the morning. From the high ground where
                         you are located, *Shoup* saw Brig. Gen. John S. *Marmaduke's* cav-
                         alry division falling back across the Illinois River in the valley
                         below. The Confederate horsemen were retiring before the
                         steady advance of Brig. Gen. Francis J. Herron's two Union
                         divisions, which were en route to reinforce Brig. Gen. James
                         G. Blunt's isolated Union division at Cane Hill, six miles to
                         the southwest.

                         Shoup's assignment was to intercept Herron and prevent
                         him from reaching Blunt. The Confederate general faced a
                         difficult decision. Should he continue to advance down into
                         the valley and collide head on with the Federals near the Il-
                         linois River, or should he establish a blocking position atop
                         this commanding height and wait for the Federals to come
                         to him? After learning that the Union force was only about
                         two miles away, *Shoup* decided to stay where he was and hold
                         the high ground.

                         The general placed his division in line of battle on the east
                         side of Fayetteville Road. His left flank rested on the road
                         near the Visitor Center, while his right flank extended along
                         the ridge to the Archibald Borden farm, a quarter mile to the
                         east. Col. Dandridge *McRae's* 1,600-man brigade was on the
                         left; it consisted of the *26th, 28th, 30th,* and *32nd Arkansas.*
                         Brig. Gen. James F. *Fagan's* Brigade of 1,500 men was on the

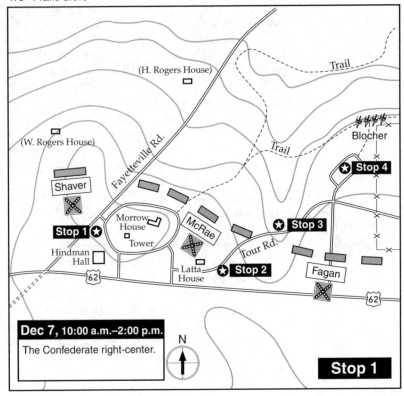

(H. Rogers House)

(W. Rogers House)

Fayetteville Rd.

Trail

Trail

Blocher

Shaver

Stop 4

Morrow House

Tower

McRae

Stop 3

Stop 1

Hindman Hall

Latta House

Tour Rd.

Stop 2

Fagan

62

62

Dec 7, 10:00 a.m.–2:00 p.m.

The Confederate right-center.

N

Stop 1

right; it was composed of the *34th, 35th, 37th,* and *39th Arkansas,* and *Chew's Arkansas Battalion. Blocher's Arkansas Battery* provided artillery support.

Later in the day more Confederate infantry arrived atop this part of Battle Ridge, filing into line on the west side of Fayetteville Road. The regiments nearest the road belonged to Col. Robert G. *Shaver's* Brigade of Brig. Gen. Daniel M. *Frost's* infantry division. The *Shaver* monument adjacent to the parking lot is the only surviving marker placed on the battlefield by veterans. Unfortunately, it is not accurate—*Shaver* and his command remained on the west side of Fayetteville Road throughout the battle.

Analysis

Shoup believed that Battle Ridge offered an excellent defensive position. In addition to the obvious tactical advantages of occupying high ground with a clear field of fire in front, it commanded the main ford on the Illinois River. This meant that Herron had to either cross the stream under artillery fire or find an alternate ford. (Herron ultimately did both.) Delaying the Federals at the river allowed time for additional Confederate forces to come up. This was no minor consideration, for when *Shoup* arrived on Battle Ridge, the rest of the Confederate army was strung out for miles to the south on Cove Creek Road.

Hindman reached Prairie Grove around midmorning. He approved of *Shoup's* choice of ground and later described the Confederate position as "an exceedingly strong one."[1] *Hindman* apparently intended to defeat Herron at Prairie Grove, then turn around and deal with Blunt at Cane Hill. In order for this improbable scenario to unfold, Blunt had to remain inert at Cane Hill. But as the morning wore on, he began to stir.

The Army of the Trans-Mississippi was squarely between two converging Union forces. Every passing hour made the high ground at Prairie Grove a more attractive place to fight. The terrain allowed *Hindman* to confront Herron with half of his army and await Blunt with the other half, while Cove Creek Road provided a secure line of retreat into the Boston Mountains. Nonetheless, he must have been chagrined at the way things had turned out. Because of Herron's rapid march from Missouri, *Hindman's* promising plan to envelop Blunt was foiled, and his bold offensive campaign to rid northwest Arkansas of the Federals culminated in a defensive battle.

Major-General
James G. Blunt.
From a photograph.
BLCW 3:447

STOP 2   Latta Homestead (The Lord's Vineyard)

Directions   Leave the Visitor Center parking lot and *proceed* around the
circular drive in a clockwise direction. *Turn left* onto the TOUR
ROAD and follow the signs. *Proceed* east about 0.1 mile and
stop in the parking area on the right. This is one of only three
parking areas along the road. As you continue on this driving
tour, carefully pull over at each stop in order to allow traffic
to pass. Watch for bicyclists and pedestrians as well as other
vehicles.

What Happened   The 1834 John Latta homestead (called the Lord's Vineyard)
has no direct connection with the battle; the house and outbuildings were moved here because of their historic value as
pioneer structures. By the time of the Civil War, many buildings in northwest Arkansas were made of brick or frame
construction, but a large number of log structures dating
from the pioneer era of the 1830s and 1840s still existed. You
may wish to explore the Latta homestead before continuing
the tour. Keep in mind that this portion of Battle Ridge was
covered with trees at the time of the battle and that *McRae's
Brigade* was deployed in this vicinity.

Major-General John
S. Marmaduke, C.S.A.
From a photograph.
BLCW 3:446

STOP 3   The Ravine

Directions   *Proceed* east on the TOUR ROAD about 0.1 mile and carefully
                         stop in the ravine.

What Happened   This ravine marks the approximate boundary between
                         McRae's and *Fagan's* brigades. No fighting took place in this
                         wooded area near the upper end of the cut, but the South-
                         erners posted here and elsewhere on Battle Ridge endured a
                         barrage of Union artillery fire from late morning until late
                         afternoon. During each of Herron's attacks, the Confederates
                         moved forward to meet the Federals, then returned to their
                         positions in the woods.

Vignette   The Confederate position atop Battle Ridge was a strong one,
                         but it offered little protection against artillery fire. Union
                         long-range rifled guns rained shot and shell on the Rebels
                         throughout the day. Most of the ridge was covered with a
                         forest of oak, hickory, elm, and other hardwood trees. Con-
                         federate troops suffered casualties from the artillery projec-
                         tiles and from the shower of splintered wood that erupted
                         whenever a projectile struck a tree. Sgt. Benjamin F. McIntyre
                         of the 19th Iowa explored this area after the battle and made
                         the following observation: "For the space of a mile there is
                         scarce a tree or even a bush but bears upon it the marks of a
                         ball. Large trees have been cut entirely off, limbs torn from
                         the trunks, and many huge trees split and splintered as if
                         struck by a thunderbolt while bushes and underbrush seem
                         to have been cut and clipped to pieces by small shot. I have
                         been an eye witness to the battlefields of Wilson Creek and
                         Pea Ridge but the devastation and destruction visible there
                         are nothing in comparison to that which the woods at Prairie
                         Grove today present." [2]

STOP 4   Borden House

Directions   *Proceed* east on the TOUR ROAD 0.1 mile and *turn left* into the parking lot and stop. *Follow* the trail to the front of the Borden House and enjoy the superb view of the battlefield. This is the only place at Prairie Grove where the driving and walking tours intersect. If you have not taken the park's walking tour, you may wish to do so at this time.

Orientation   You have moved from the center to the right-center of the Confederate position. The building near the parking lot is the Archibald Borden House. The original structure was burned during the war but rebuilt on the original foundations. A barn was located about one hundred yards east of the house, but it no longer exists. Also gone is the clutter of outbuildings and the maze of fences that once surrounded the house and barn. The Borden House was located on the western edge of the farm, which was the only significant open area on Battle Ridge in 1862. The farm was square in shape and about a half mile wide. It sprawled over the ridge, down the slope, and partway across the valley. The Borden farm was the scene of the most intense fighting at Prairie Grove—the carnage in the orchard behind the house was particularly gruesome.

The fence between the parking lot and the orchard marks the western boundary of the Borden farm. At the time of the battle, the parking lot was part of the forest that covered most of Battle Ridge. The park planted trees around the parking lot and on the east side of the orchard in 2000; eventually this area will take on a more historically accurate wooded appearance. The southern boundary of the Borden farm is approximated by U.S. 62. The Confederate line of battle was located behind a fence there. Note that this area, currently blighted by a busy highway and a commercial strip, is a swale or depression that leads down to the Illinois River. Confederate soldiers deployed in the swale could not be seen by Union forces in the valley. From Herron's limited perspective, the short Confederate line of battle was located between Fayetteville Road and the Borden House. In reality the Confederate line extended nearly a half mile farther east.

What Happened   After skirmishing with Herron's force east of the Illinois River for most of the morning, *Marmaduke* fell back to Battle Ridge around eleven o'clock. He placed his cavalry division to *Shoup's* right in the swale. Col. Joseph O. *Shelby's* "Iron Brigade" was deployed southeast of the orchard. This force of about 1,000 troopers was composed of the *5th, 6th,* and *12th Missouri*

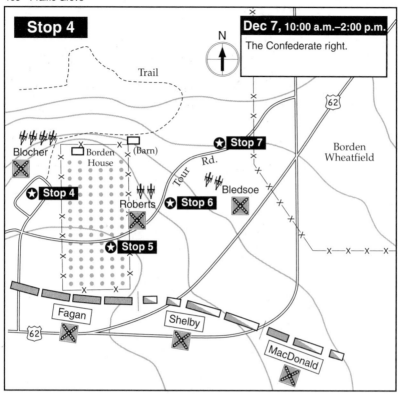

Cavalry and *Elliot's Missouri Cavalry Battalion.* Loosely attached to *Shelby's* brigade was William *Quantrill's* band of Missouri guerrillas. *Quantrill* was absent during this campaign, and the band was led by William *Gregg.* The guerillas were armed primarily with revolvers, so it is doubtful that they were of much use in the battle. Col. Emmett *MacDonald's* Brigade of about 700 Missouri horsemen was deployed on *Shelby's* right, closer to the Illinois River. It consisted of *MacDonald's Missouri Cavalry* and Lt. Col. R. Philip *Crump's First Texas Partisan Rangers.* *MacDonald's* Brigade was the right flank of the Confederate army. The Rebel cavalrymen fought dismounted, which meant that one of every four soldiers had to look after the horses. Four Confederate guns occupied the relatively open brow of the ridge east of the Borden House: two 14-pounder James rifles of Capt. Westley *Roberts's Missouri Battery* (the only rifled cannons in the Confederate army at Prairie Grove) and two 6-pounder smoothbores of Capt. Joseph *Bledsoe's Missouri Battery.* The guns moved frequently to avoid the barrage of Union artillery fire. At the height of the fighting, *Hindman* detached the 23rd and 38th *Arkansas* from *Shaver's* Brigade

near Fayetteville Road and sent them to support *Marmaduke.*
The reinforcements added another 600 men to the Confederate right flank and extended the line down the swale toward
the river. *Shoup's* and *Marmaduke's* divisions endured a Union
artillery cannonade until about two o'clock, when Herron's
first infantry attack commenced.

STOP 5   Carnage in the Orchard (Herron's First Attack)

Directions   Return to your car, *proceed* east 0.1 mile on the TOUR ROAD,
                            and *stop*.

What Happened   While Union artillery hammered Battle Ridge, Herron formed
                            a line of battle in the valley. He was determined to drive the
                            Confederates off the ridge and hurry on to join Blunt at Cane
                            Hill. Around two o'clock Herron directed Col. William W.
                            Orme to take his brigade and gain the high ground. The Fed-
                            eral ranks had been thinned by the arduous three-day march
                            from Wilson's Creek. To make matters worse, Orme kept the
                            94th Illinois in reserve to cover his exposed left flank and
                            went forward with only two understrength regiments: Lt.
                            Col. Henry Bertram's 20th Wisconsin consisted of just over
                            400 men; Lt. Col. Samuel McFarland's 19th Iowa about 350.

                            The focal point of the Union attack was the Borden House
                            and *Blocher's Arkansas Battery*, which was located immediately
                            west of the house. Herron hoped to overrun the exposed bat-
                            tery and roll up the enemy's right flank. He did not realize
                            that he faced a Confederate force several times larger than
                            his own and that the Borden House was near the right-center
                            of that force, not the flank.

                            The imposing terrain of Battle Ridge favored the Federals
                            in one important respect. In order to take advantage of the
                            cover provided by the woods, the Confederates were posi-
                            tioned well back from the brow, or "military crest," of the
                            ridge. This meant that Union soldiers were safe from Con-
                            federate fire as long as they remained in the "shadow" of the
                            slope below the brow of the ridge. Only when the attackers
                            ascended the ridge and reached the elevation of the Borden
                            House did they come into full view of the defenders.

                            After reaching the foot of the ridge in relative safety, the
                            men of the 20th Wisconsin and 19th Iowa surged up the
                            steep slope toward the house. The 20th Wisconsin, on the
                            Union right, overran *Blocher's* battery without any difficulty.
                            The regiment halted while excited troops cheered the easy
                            capture of the Rebel artillery. A moment later, however, the
                            cheers turned to cries of alarm as regiment after regiment of
                            Arkansas infantry from *McRae's* and *Fagan's* brigades emerged
                            from the woods behind the battery and opened fire. The 20th
                            Wisconsin disintegrated under the hail of bullets. Bertram
                            was wounded and knocked off his horse. He and other sur-
                            vivors fled down the slope in disorder. The regiment's losses
                            were extremely heavy: 50 killed, 154 wounded, and 13 miss-
                            ing, a casualty rate of over 50 percent.

While this was happening on the Union right, the 19th Iowa, on the left, swept past the east side of the Borden House and advanced across the orchard where you are located. Unknown to McFarland, his regiment was advancing into a deadly trap. When the Iowans reached the area between the TOUR ROAD and U.S. 62, *Fagan's* infantrymen and *Shelby's* dismounted cavalrymen opened fire with rifles and shotguns. Fighting raged at extremely close range, and the carnage was terrific. "The rebels all at once rose out of their hiding place and began to fire at us," recalled William H. H. Clayton. "We were ordered to retreat which each one did as best he could. The balls fell like hail on all sides of me. If we had remained in the orchard but a few minutes longer we would all have been killed, wounded or taken prisoners."[3] The outnumbered Federals broke and ran for their lives. Losses in the 19th Iowa were appalling: 45 killed, 145 wounded, and 3 missing, a casualty rate of about 55 percent, the highest at Prairie Grove. McFarland was one of the fatalities. He fell in the orchard along with dozens of his men.

Hundreds of Rebels also were struck down during the intense fighting. Among the dead and mortally wounded of *Shoup's* Division were Col. Joseph C. *Pleasants* of the *37th Arkansas* and Maj. Robert E. *Chew* of *Chew's Arkansas Battalion*. When the survivors of the two shattered Union regiments fled to the safety of their own lines, several regiments of cheering Confederates followed down the slope in pursuit. In the Borden wheat field on the valley floor, the Rebels were halted by Union artillery and driven back to their original positions atop Battle Ridge.

Vignette

An unidentified officer related the story of the 20th Wisconsin and *Blocher's Arkansas Battery*. "We came out nearly at the crest . . . and there, a few feet off, so that we were looking into their muzzles, were the guns, and near by the horses standing quietly attached to the caissons. The guns which had been belching flame and smoke all the morning stood there still and cold, and the horses as if waiting for us. We could have taken the horses away, but some officer called out to shoot the horses. Men and officers called out in reply: 'Save the horses.' Again the order was repeated, and this time obeyed. The beautiful horses were piled in a bloody heap, and the men swarmed over and around the guns, and a great cheer went up."

A few minutes later the 20th Wisconsin was overwhelmed by *Shoup's* Division. The heaviest fighting took place in the mouth of the ravine a short distance west of *Blocher's* battery. The Union officer continued: "The line in the ravine began

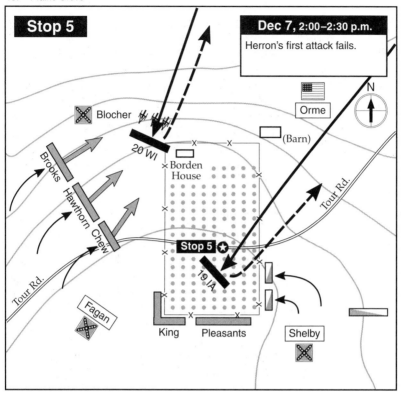

to thin out; wounded men dragged themselves back out of the fire, and occasionally an unhurt man arose and made a dash for the rear. . . . After awhile I felt a pain in the foot, and a feeling as if one leg had died. Then I took a dead man's gun for a crutch, and limped back; there were no more men alive and unwounded in the ravine by that time. I passed the battery we had taken. The guns stood as we had left them. I saw our Colonel's horse stagger riderless down the slope and fall dead; the Colonel limped after, using his sabre as a support; he was covered with blood. The Major was forming the men as they came back from the ravine down the slope below the guns, but our fight for that day was done."[4]

STOP 6   Confederate Right Flank (Herron's Second Attack)

Directions   *Proceed* east on the TOUR ROAD 0.1 mile and *stop.*

Orientation   Take a moment to look around and try to imagine the scene
                             following the first spasm of fighting on the ridge and in
                             the valley. Hundreds of dead and wounded soldiers of both
                             armies covered the ground around the Borden House, many
                             of them in the orchard. Hundreds of other unfortunate men,
                             mostly Confederates, littered the slope and the wheat field in
                             the valley.

What Happened   Around two-thirty, immediately after the failure of the first
                             Union attack, Col. Daniel Huston sent two of the three regi-
                             ments in his brigade toward Battle Ridge in an attempt to re-
                             trieve the situation. Col. John G. Clark's 26th Indiana Infantry
                             was composed of 450 men, while Lt. Col. John C. Black's 37th
                             Illinois Infantry consisted of 400 men. Both regiments were
                             understrength and exhausted because of the long march
                             from Missouri, but Huston apparently was inspired by the
                             sight of the pursuing Confederates being mowed down by
                             artillery fire in the Borden wheat field a quarter mile to the
                             east of his position.

                             The second Union assault was a reprise of the first. Both
                             regiments advanced up the open slope east of the Borden
                             House. When the blue lines reached the area around the
                             TOUR ROAD, the Confederates again produced a hail of bullets
                             and buckshot. On the Union left the 26th Indiana stumbled
                             to a halt and then fell back in disarray. "As we came off the
                             field the bullets were flying seemingly as thick as hail and
                             nearly every one was struck either in his person or clothing,"
                             wrote Robert F. Braden. "I was one of three in my company
                             who did not receive a mark of a bullet."[5] Survivors tumbled
                             down the slope and fled to the safety of the Union artillery
                             line midway across the valley. Losses were extremely serious:
                             25 killed, 175 wounded, and 1 missing, a casualty rate of
                             nearly 45 percent.

                             When the Hoosiers gave way, the men of the 37th Illinois
                             found themselves alone in the Borden orchard facing the
                             same Arkansas and Missouri troops who had overwhelmed
                             the 19th Iowa a short time earlier. The 37th Illinois was a vet-
                             eran regiment that had made a name for itself at Pea Ridge,
                             and two of its companies were equipped with Colt revolving
                             rifles, which took a heavy toll of the defenders, but the odds
                             were too great. "We let them have all that we had but it did
                             not faize them," reported Alcander O. Morse, a member of
                             the Illinois unit.[6]

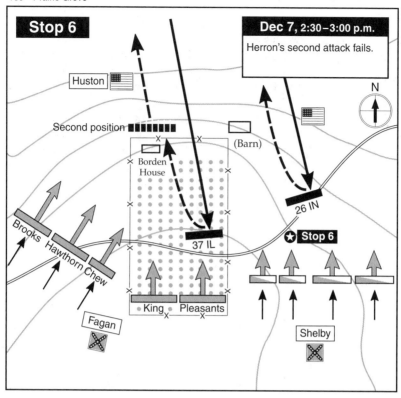

Stop 6

Dec 7, 2:30–3:00 p.m.

Herron's second attack fails.

Huston

N

Second position

(Barn)

Borden
House

26 IN

Brooks

Hawthorn

Chew

37 IL

★ Stop 6

Fagan

King   Pleasants

Shelby

Black ordered a withdrawal to the Borden House to prevent his regiment from being overwhelmed. The Confederates followed through the orchard. (The painting by Andy Thomas in the Visitor Center depicts the final moments before the Federals fell back into the valley.) The 37th Illinois lost 8 men killed, 58 wounded, and 8 missing, or about 18 percent. The mounting number of casualties among the Confederates and the daunting firepower of the Colt repeaters probably were responsible for these relatively moderate losses.

Vignette

Black had been severely wounded at Pea Ridge nine months earlier, and he carried his right arm in a sling at Prairie Grove. During the fighting near the Borden House, a bullet struck the lieutenant colonel in his upper left arm and shattered the bone. When the 37th Illinois retreated, Black and his horse were carried along with the tide of fleeing soldiers. "As I went up the hill I met Col. Black coming down," reported Colonel Huston. "I said to him, 'Great God, Colonel Black, can't you do something to stop this.' He replied, 'Colonel, my arm is broken all to pieces, and I cannot hold my horse.' I then said to him, 'Colonel, go at once to the rear if you are wounded.'"[7]

Surgeon Benoni O. Reynolds of the 3rd Wisconsin Cavalry resectioned Black's mangled arm instead of amputating it, a daring and dangerous procedure in 1862. He removed several inches of splintered bone and rejoined the undamaged sections. Black survived both the wound and the operation and received the only Medal of Honor awarded at Prairie Grove. In a remarkable coincidence, his younger brother, Capt. William P. Black of the same regiment, had received the Medal of Honor for his actions at Pea Ridge.

Union Cavalryman—the water-call. BLCW 3:441

STOP 7   Borden Wheatfield

Directions   *Proceed* east on the TOUR ROAD 0.1 mile and *stop.*

Orientation   You are located near the center of the Borden farm. The
                             Borden wheat field covered the slope straight ahead and ex-
                             tended well out onto the valley floor to your left and left
                             front. At the time of the battle, most of the valley floor was
                             cropland, pasturage, or prairie and was largely clear of trees,
                             much like it is today. The slope on the north, or opposite,
                             side of the valley is Crawford's Hill, site of Samuel Crawford's
                             farm. Union artillery opened the battle from Crawford's Hill,
                             and Herron established his headquarters there. At the time
                             of the battle, Crawford's Hill was a mix of fields and forest
                             and was not as open as it is today.

What Happened   On the morning of December 7, Herron's two Union divisions
                             approached the Illinois River on Fayetteville Road. A quick re-
                             connaissance revealed that the road was blocked by a Confed-
                             erate force of unknown strength atop Battle Ridge. Despite
                             the exhausted condition of his troops, Herron decided to
                             break through and reach Blunt, who was only six miles away
                             at Cane Hill. He accompanied two guns across the river via
                             the main ford but was compelled to return to the east bank
                             by a hail of Confederate artillery fire. Herron then learned
                             of another ford about one-third mile downstream (that is,
                             to the north) that was beyond the range of the Confederate
                             guns. He had a road cut through the timber to the down-
                             stream ford and sent Capt. David Murphy's Missouri Battery
                             across the river at that point. Murphy planted his six rifled
                             guns on Crawford's Hill and opened fire. With the Confeder-
                             ate batteries distracted by Murphy, Herron rushed his infan-
                             try and remaining artillery across the river without suffer-
                             ing any casualties. The 2nd Division used the downstream
                             ford (now called Taylor's Ford); the 3rd Division used the
                             main ford.

                                With the 3rd Division were Lt. Joseph Foust's Missouri Bat-
                             tery, Capt. Frank Backof's Missouri Battery, and a section of
                             Lt. Herman Borris's 2nd Illinois Battery. The three batteries
                             were equipped with fourteen guns, ten of them rifled. Just
                             before noon the Union artillery emerged from the woods
                             along the Illinois River and went into action about halfway
                             across the valley floor. For the next hour they joined with
                             Murphy's battery in silencing the lighter and less accurate
                             Confederate guns atop Battle Ridge. When that was accom-
                             plished, the Union gunners fired into the trees where the
                             Confederate infantry and dismounted cavalry were located.

Around two o'clock the cannonade ended, and Herron launched his first attack. As discussed earlier, the Federals were repulsed with heavy losses and tumbled down the hill in disorder. Several Arkansas regiments from *Shoup's* Division followed in pursuit.

As soon as the Union infantry reached the safety of their artillery line on the valley floor, the gunners swept the wheat field with canister. An Iowa officer reported that when the first salvo ripped into the oncoming Confederates, "it seemed to lift them up in the air and hurl them back into the forest."[8] The men were knocked down in squads, and the pursuit ground to a halt. Meanwhile, Union soldiers rallied around the guns and added their musketry to the fight. Surviving Confederates returned to the relative safety of the ridge. More than 100 mangled gray-clad bodies remained behind in the wheat field.

Vignette

About one-fourth of the 400 men in the *34th Arkansas* were volunteers and conscripts from farms and villages around Prairie Grove. Enthusiasm for the Confederate cause was not widespread in northwest Arkansas, and the *34th Arkansas* reflected this situation. Some of the men in the regiment literally were defending their hearths and homes against an invader, but others had little interest in slavery or secession and were primarily concerned with personal survival. The unit was in the thick of the fighting around the Borden House atop the ridge and in the wheat field on the valley floor. At least 15 men were killed outright and several others were mortally wounded. The day after the battle, relatives converged on Prairie Grove to search for their loved ones. "All the women and children of that section of the country were there hunting up their dead fathers, brothers, and friends," recalled Sgt. George W. Sommerville of the 19th Iowa, "and whenever they found one of their kindred such a cry of anguish and sorrow never was heard before; nor do we want to hear it again. Gathering up loads of their dead they hauled them home for burial." Benjamin F. McIntyre of the same unit described a young woman accompanied by two small children who found the bodies of her husband and two of her brothers. The woman emitted a "wild unearthly shriek," then turned to the Union medical and burial details nearby and screamed, "The death of thousands of your number cannot revenge my wrongs or bring my brothers and husband back!"[9]

The Borden House as viewed
from the walking trail.
Courtesy William L. Shea.

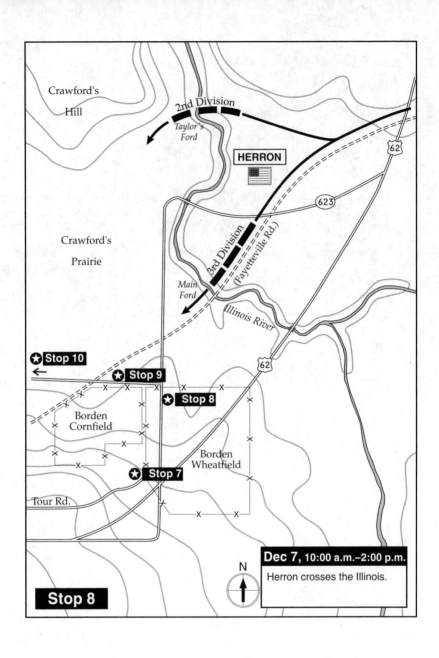

Crawford's
Hill

2nd Division

*Taylor's
Ford*

HERRON

Crawford's

Prairie

3rd Division

(Fayetteville Rd.)

62

623

*Main
Ford*

Illinois River

62

★ Stop 10

★ Stop 9

★ Stop 8

Borden
Cornfield

Borden
Wheatfield

★ Stop 7

Tour Rd.

N

Dec 7, 10:00 a.m.–2:00 p.m.

Herron crosses the Illinois.

Stop 8

STOP 8   Illinois River Ford

Directions   *Proceed* on the TOUR ROAD to the intersection and *turn left. Proceed* 0.2 mile and *stop.*

Orientation   You are located near the northern edge of the Borden wheat field, about 100 yards south of Fayetteville Road. The road ran diagonally northeast-southwest across the valley floor and crossed the Illinois River about a quarter mile northeast of your location. In 1862 the low-lying area along the river was wooded, which provided a degree of cover for Herron's troops as they forded the stream.

What Happened   After crossing the Illinois River, the 3rd Division moved onto the valley floor and formed a line of battle near Fayetteville Road. Around two o'clock, Confederate artillery fire from Battle Ridge sputtered out, and the 94th Illinois, 19th Iowa, and 20th Wisconsin advanced south of the road into the Borden wheat field. From this vicinity Herron launched the first of two ill-fated assaults against the Confederate position.

STOP 9	Borden Cornfield

Directions   *Turn left, proceed* on the TOUR ROAD 0.1 mile, and *stop.*

Orientation   You are located near the northern edge of the Borden cornfield. You are also near the route of Fayetteville Road where it cut across the northeast corner of the Borden farm.

What Happened   Between one and two o'clock, the Confederate guns on Battle Ridge were wrecked or compelled to withdraw by the intense Union artillery fire from the valley floor and Crawford's Hill. Encouraged by this development, Herron ordered the 2nd Division to advance from the base of Crawford's Hill to Fayetteville Road on the right of the 3rd Division. The 26th Indiana and 37th Illinois halted in this vicinity along the north side of the road. The 20th Iowa stopped several hundred yards to the northwest to guard the exposed right flank. This movement brought all six of Herron's infantry regiments into an irregular and attenuated line across the middle of the valley floor.

From here Huston watched the 20th Wisconsin and 19th Iowa retreat in disarray across the wheat field. After the Confederates were driven back by Union artillery, Huston sent the 26th Indiana and 37th Illinois to attack Battle Ridge. This second attack failed as well, and the survivors retreated across the cornfield toward the safety of the Union artillery line. Arkansas regiments from *Shoup's* Division again surged after the retreating Federals. "The rebels came down like a cloud into the valley in pursuit," reported Capt. William P. Black of the 37th Illinois. "But we had the rebels now, just where we had always wanted them, on level clear ground, and we felt now was an hour of vengeance." [10]

As soon as the fleeing Indiana and Illinois infantrymen cleared the muzzles of the guns along Fayetteville Road, the Federal artillerymen swept the cornfield with blasts of canister at ranges of less than 100 yards. Black's Illinoisans rallied and supported the batteries with their Colt revolving rifles. Rushing forward into a storm of bullets and canister balls, the Arkansans faltered and then retreated back up Battle Ridge. Here, as in the adjacent wheat field a short time earlier, 100 or more bodies littered the ground in front of the smoking Union guns.

Vignette   The horror of death or serious injury on any Civil War battlefield was magnified at Prairie Grove by the presence of hogs. Farmers had allowed their hogs to forage in the woods for many generations. By the time of the Civil War, the countryside was swarming with feral hogs. The Confederates were aware of the danger posed by these powerful animals. When the fighting sputtered out after sunset, Arkansas and Missouri soldiers fanned out across the battlefield. They stripped the dead of both sides of everything useful, then dragged the bodies into piles and surrounded them with fence rails to ward off the hogs. Union soldiers discovered the crudely enclosed burial heaps the next morning. Not realizing their true purpose, the Federals termed them "slaughter pens." The Confederates also recovered as many of the wounded as possible, placing them in groups for mutual protection against the hogs and providing them with loaded pistols.

Unfortunately the Confederates were unable to locate all of the dead and wounded before they decamped around midnight. The day after the battle, Albert R. Greene of the 9th Kansas Cavalry chanced upon a particularly grisly scene. "I found a man lying flat on his back, his arms extended their full length on either side. In one [hand] was clenched a lot of parched corn and the other was gnawing convulsively into the ground. A shell had torn away a part of his abdomen, and his bowels were protruding. At these wild hogs were chewing. I drove them away and shouted for the guards, who came and bore the dying man away."[11] Many Union and Confederate corpses were partially devoured by hogs. For the next few days, disgusted Union soldiers shot the animals on sight but refused to eat them.

The well-known mascot of the nearby University of Arkansas at Fayetteville is a feral hog of the type present at Prairie Grove. It is known as a "razorback" because of the stiff bristles along its spine. Feral hogs no longer exist in the Prairie Grove area but there are occasional sightings in less-settled parts of the Ozark Plateau.

STOP 10   Position of 20th Iowa

Directions   *Proceed* on the TOUR ROAD 0.1 mile to the intersection and
                        stop.

Orientation   You are located near the right flank of Herron's command. To
                        your left front is the only surviving fragment of Fayetteville
                        Road on the battlefield. To your right front is a distant hill
                        topped with a grove of trees. The hill is West's Knoll.

What Happened   The repulse of the Confederate counterattack in the Borden
                        cornfield marked the end of fighting on the eastern half
                        of the battlefield. Around three o'clock in the afternoon,
                        an unidentified artillery battery fired two shots from atop
                        West's Knoll. The Federals feared that the Confederates were
                        moving around their right flank, but they soon spotted U.S.
                        flags flying atop the rise. Herron's attempt to break through
                        Hindman's army had failed, but his battered command was
                        safe. Blunt had arrived with the rest of the Army of the
                        Frontier.

Analysis   Herron simply did not have the manpower to push *Hindman*
                        out of the way. The Federals had demonstrated great skill
                        and gallantry, but the Confederates had the high ground
                        and an insurmountable advantage in numbers. Although
                        Herron engaged only half of *Hindman's* army (*Shoup's* and
                        Marmaduke's divisions), he was still outnumbered nearly two
                        to one.

                        With the advantage of hindsight, it is easy to censure Her-
                        ron for sending four regiments to their doom, but there is no
                        evidence that he realized how many Rebels were blocking his
                        path. *Shoup's* Division was vaguely visible in the woods west
                        of the Borden House, but *Marmaduke's* Division was out of
                        sight in the swale south and east of it. Herron's attacks were
                        directed at what he apparently thought was the unsupported
                        Confederate left flank.

                        Herron can be legitimately criticized, however, for two
                        questionable decisions. The first was his failure to seek a way
                        around the Confederate roadblock at Prairie Grove. After
                        all, the purpose of his forced march from Missouri was to
                        reunite the Army of the Frontier *before* taking on the Rebels.
                        Herron could have detoured to Cane Hill via Rhea's Mill on
                        the same route that Blunt followed to Prairie Grove later that
                        day. Apparently he never considered such a move, despite the
                        presence of the 1st Arkansas Cavalry (U.S.), which had in its
                        ranks many men familiar with local roads and byways. Hav-

ing decided to slug it out, Herron erred again by making two
weak attacks instead of a single assault with all of his limited
manpower. He was too quick to come to grips with the enemy
at Prairie Grove, and his men paid the price. Had it not been
for the superiority of Union artillery, the battle might have
turned out differently.

On the skirmish line. BLCW 1:465

STOP 11   Confederate Left (West Overlook)

Directions   *Turn left* and *proceed* on the TOUR ROAD up Battle Ridge to the intersection with U.S. 62. Notice the Visitor Center on your left. *Turn right* onto the highway. After negotiating the sharp curve, *turn right* onto GRAHAM STREET (the second street on your right). *Proceed* west for two blocks, then *turn right* onto MOCK STREET. *Proceed* north 0.3 mile over the crest of Battle Ridge (which roughly corresponds with DOUGLAS STREET). *Turn right* into the West Overlook parking lot and *stop*. *Walk* to the overlook.

Orientation   The West Overlook is located roughly a quarter mile west of Fayetteville Road and about 200 yards in front of the left-center of the Confederate line of battle. The town of Prairie Grove has spread across this section of Battle Ridge and obliterated the Confederate position, but most of the valley and the opposite slope remain in cultivation, and it is still possible to visualize the terrain and the tactics employed on this part of the battlefield. Remember that the Union position straight ahead across the valley floor is north; the Confederate position atop the ridge to your rear is south. In 1862 the area around the overlook and to your rear was wooded; the area to your front was open, much as it is now.

The William Morton farm was the focal point of the fighting on the western half of the battlefield during the late afternoon. The Morton hayfield, dotted with several haystacks, occupied the valley floor directly in front of the overlook. The Morton cornfield was located west of the hayfield to your left front. About twice as large as the hayfield, it extended a half mile out onto the valley floor.

On the opposite side of the valley, due north of the overlook, is a prominent round hill topped by a grove of trees. This is West's Knoll. In 1862 the Robert West House crowned the knoll. Blunt established his headquarters and his primary hospital there. The knoll provided the general a panoramic view of the entire battlefield all the way to the Illinois River, one of the best views afforded any army commander in the Civil War.

What Happened   While Herron assaulted the Confederate right wing during the early afternoon, most of General *Frost's* infantry division remained a half mile south of this location facing southwest toward Cane Hill. *Hindman* was concerned that Blunt might take the most direct route and approach Prairie Grove from that direction on Fayetteville Road. Blunt was indeed on the move, but he took a more roundabout course via his supply depot at Rhea's Mill and approached Prairie Grove from the northwest. When *Hindman* learned of this, he ordered *Frost* to move to Battle Ridge and connect with the left flank of *Shoup's* Division. This extended the Confederate line of battle a half mile west of Fayetteville Road.

The left-center of the Confederate position was held by Brig. Gen. Mosby M. *Parsons's* large 3,000-man brigade, which was composed of the *8th, 10th, 11th, 12th,* and *16th Missouri.* Colonel *Shaver's* smaller brigade was stationed on the right near Fayetteville Road, as noted earlier, though now represented by only the 300 men of the *33rd Arkansas;* the *23rd* and *38th Arkansas* had been detached to support *Marmaduke* during Herron's assaults on Borden's farm.

When the sound of Herron's artillery reached Blunt at Cane Hill in the early afternoon, he led his 1st Division north to Rhea's Mill, where his supply trains were parked. After leaving a brigade-size force of infantry, cavalry, and artillery behind to protect the wagons, he then hurried eastward toward Prairie Grove with about 4,900 men. The Confederates on Battle Ridge saw the first Union troops appear on the horizon just west of West's Knoll around three o'clock in the afternoon.

To announce his arrival on the field, Blunt fired two cannon shots in the direction of Herron's embattled command a half mile to the southeast. He then prepared to assault the Confederate left. Blunt's four artillery batteries initially went into action on the slope below the knoll before moving forward to the middle of the valley floor. For about an hour eighteen Union cannons, ten of them rifled guns, showered the western half of Battle Ridge with shot and shell. The Union artillery consisted of Capt. Marcus D. Tenney's 1st Kansas Battery, Capt. Henry Hopkins's 3rd Kansas Battery, Lt. Elias Stover's 2nd Kansas Battery, and Capt. John W. Rabb's 2nd Indiana Battery.

Under cover of the barrage, about 2,400 Union infantry and dismounted cavalry formed a line of battle on the valley floor. Col. William Weer's brigade on the Union right consisted of the 10th Kansas, 13th Kansas, and the 3rd Indian Home Guard; Col. William F. Cloud's brigade on the left was composed of the 11th Kansas, 2nd Kansas Cavalry, 1st Indian Home Guard, and 20th Iowa (borrowed from Herron's command). When the 1st Indian Home Guard, on Blunt's left flank, made contact with the 20th Iowa on Herron's right flank, *Hindman's* hope of defeating the two wings of the Army of the Frontier in detail flickered out.

Around four o'clock Blunt's line of battle advanced across the valley floor and up the forested slopes to either side of the overlook where you are located. *Frost's* 3,300 Missouri and Arkansas infantry moved partway down the slope to meet them. The result was a confused clash—a sort of enormous skirmish—amid a tangle of trees, vines, briars, and fallen branches. Thousands of balls and bullets tore through the smoky woods and produced an unceasing shower of leaves and bark as the ragged lines surged back and forth. While the infantry fight raged, the Union artillery moved to a new position on the valley floor.

Vincent B. Osborne of the 2nd Kansas Cavalry described how the dismounted troopers of his regiment "rushed forward sheltering themselves as much as possible behind trees and opened a brisk fire on them and kept it up some time. We did not fire by volleys but each man fired when he saw some enemy to shoot at and the enemy fired in the same manner." Confederate soldiers also sought protection in the woods. "I lay down behind a bush about the size of my arm," recalled Spencer H. *Mitchell* of the *10th Missouri*. "That bush saved my life several times for several bullets struck it right before my head." [12]

Unable to drive off the numerically superior Confederates, Weer and Cloud ordered their men to fall back to the artillery line on the valley floor around five o'clock. Believing that the Federals were on the run, *Frost* followed with his entire division. What happened next was a repeat of the two earlier Confederate repulses on the Borden farm. Missouri and Arkansas troops emerged from the woods in the twilight and advanced across the Morton farm in front of the overlook.

As the Rebels closed to within 100 yards, the massed Union batteries sprayed canister into the gloom. Capt. John W. Rabb described the damage wrought by his flaming guns: "For fifteen minutes my men stood firm, firing their pieces with terrible precision, making roads in the ranks of the enemy, which were quickly filled by fresh men from the rear." Standing alongside the cannons, Lt. Henry E. Palmer of the 11th Kansas watched the horrible effect of the first salvo of artillery fire on the oncoming Confederates. "They staggered back like drunken men, then rallied and pushed on again." *Parsons's* Missourians were unable to withstand the continuous storm of metal and retreated back up Battle Ridge, leaving Morton's fields littered with dead and wounded. Among the fatalities was Col. Alexander A. *Steen* of the *10th Missouri*. This grim affair marked the end of serious fighting at Prairie Grove. [13]

Nearly 500 Union Indians fought in the 1st and 3rd Indian Home Guard regiments at Prairie Grove. The Cherokees, Creeks, Chickasaws, Seminoles, and other Native American

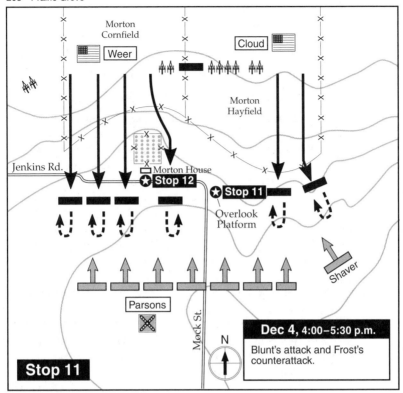

Morton
Cornfield

Cloud

Weer

Morton
Hayfield

Jenkins Rd.

Morton House

Stop 12

Stop 11

Overlook
Platform

Shaver

Parsons

Mock St.

N

Dec 4, 4:00–5:30 p.m.

Blunt's attack and Frost's
counterattack.

Stop 11

soldiers were better trained, better equipped, and better mo-
tivated than Albert *Pike's* hapless Confederate Cherokees at
Pea Ridge, and they fought well. The 1st Indian Home Guard
was engaged in the woods about 200 yards east of the overlook; the 3rd Indian Home Guard about a quarter mile to
the west.

Analysis

Hindman was a first-rate administrator but a cautious field
commander. Blunt was a heads-down slugger whose well-de-
served reputation for aggressiveness proved to be *Hindman's*
undoing. *Hindman* feared that as soon as Blunt heard the
sounds of battle, he would come storming directly toward
Prairie Grove on Fayetteville Road. Uneasy about being
caught between two converging Union forces, the Rebel commander kept half of his army facing southwest toward Cane
Hill for much of the day. While the fighting on the Borden
farm reached a crescendo in the early afternoon, 5,000 idle
Confederate soldiers watched an empty road.

As the hours crept by without any sign of a Union advance from Cane Hill, *Hindman* wondered where Blunt had
gone. The mystery was solved when Federal troops appeared

near West's Knoll in midafternoon. It was a bitter moment for *Hindman*, who recognized that by holding back so many men to counter a threat that never materialized, he had missed his only opportunity to win a resounding victory over Herron.

Blunt was fooled by *Hindman's* snap decision to bypass Cane Hill and intercept Herron at Prairie Grove, but he recovered quickly. *Hindman's* assessment of Blunt's personality was correct: the Union general was indeed spoiling for a fight. But his appraisal did not take into account his counterpart's anxiety about the fragility of Union logistics on the frontier. Blunt's concern for his supply depot and trains at Rhea's Mill overcame his natural inclination to march directly toward the sound of the guns. His dogleg route via Rhea's Mill delayed his arrival at Prairie Grove by two or three hours, but he still arrived in time to rescue Herron and save the day.

Vignette

The 20th Iowa was on the extreme left of Blunt's line of battle. The regiment struggled up the slope toward the William Rogers House, located about 300 yards east of the overlook. Just behind the infantry was Maj. William G. Thompson, a conspicuous target on horseback. "The balls were going and coming so fast and thick, and my whole attention was on the enemy who were not twenty yards from us. At last I heard some of the boys say 'for God's sake Major get off your horse' or you will be killed, for they [are] shooting at you out of the house."

Thompson stayed in the saddle, but his luck finally ran out. As the 20th Iowa withdrew down the slope, Thompson took a look back at the bullet-riddled Rogers home. While he watched, "one of the cowardly curs raised the window and took good aim, and I was hit that time." The bullet struck him in the hip and exited through the groin, but he managed to ride to the field hospital on West's Knoll. Thompson survived his grievous wound. His description of his Iowa troops at Prairie Grove also applied to himself. "Our boys fought nobly, every man of them done their duty." [14]

STOP 12   Morton House

Directions   Return to your vehicle and *proceed* west 0.1 mile on JENKINS
                  ROAD and *stop* in front of a narrow empty lot on your right.

Orientation   The William Morton House was located about fifty yards
                  north of JENKINS ROAD. It was surrounded by the usual as-
                  sortment of outbuildings, sheds, cribs, and fences. No trace
                  of the house or the other structures remain.

Vignette   When fighting erupted east of Fayetteville Road around
                  noon, the Archibald Borden, Hugh Rogers, and William
                  Rogers families fled westward to the apparent safety of the
                  Morton House. They were trapped here when Blunt's division
                  reached the field in midafternoon. The Mortons and their
                  neighbors, a total of at least twenty adults and children, hud-
                  dled in the shallow basement for three hours while the battle
                  raged above. "They fought through and around the house,"
                  recalled Nancy Morton Staples, "the shots flying like hail in
                  every direction, only a few cannon balls striking close."[15] No
                  one was hurt. A pony belonging to the Borden family was
                  hitched outside the house and somehow survived the battle
                  untouched. When the firing stopped after sunset, Mrs. Bor-
                  den placed her three small children on the frazzled pony and
                  set off in search of a quieter place to spend the night.

The Morton House in
the early 1900s. Nancy
Morton Staples stands
at the gate. Courtesy
Prairie Grove Battlefield
State Park and Shiloh
Museum of Ozark
History, Springdale AR.

STOP 13   Confederate Left Flank

Directions   *Proceed* west on JENKINS ROAD 0.5 mile and *turn left* onto VINEY
                          GROVE ROAD. *Proceed* south 0.3 mile and *stop* across the street
                          from the Prairie Grove Upper Elementary School.

Orientation   You are located about 100 yards below the crest of the west-
                          ernmost portion of Battle Ridge. In this vicinity the ridge is
                          little more than a gentle rise. The trees along the crest are a
                          reminder of the forest that covered this area in 1862.

What Happened   The Confederate position extended a quarter mile west of
                          this road. The left flank was held by Brig. Gen. John S. *Roane's*
                          Brigade, consisting of the *20th, 22nd, 31st,* and *34th Texas Cav-*
                          alry (all dismounted) and the *9th Missouri,* a total of about
                          2,000 men. The artillery consisted of Capt. James G. *Reid's*
                          and Capt. John C. *Shoup's* Arkansas batteries. *Roane's* Brigade
                          was temporarily attached to *Frost's* Division and spent the
                          late morning and early afternoon waiting for Blunt to attack
                          from Cane Hill. After moving to this position, *Roane* detached
                          the *9th Missouri* (his only true infantry regiment) to fight
                          with *Parsons's* Brigade. The Texans remained in this vicinity
                          and skirmished with Union cavalry but were not otherwise
                          engaged. This may have been a good thing, for the Texans
                          were poorly armed and intensely disgruntled about being
                          demoted to pedestrians. Hundreds deserted in the weeks
                          following the battle. After the fighting near the Borden
                          House ended, *Hindman* moved most of *MacDonald's* cavalry
                          brigade from the Confederate right flank to the left flank to
                          support *Roane.*

STOP 14	Prairie Grove Church

Directions   *Proceed* south on VINEY GROVE ROAD over the crest of Battle Ridge. The Boston Mountains are visible straight ahead. At the T-shaped intersection, *turn left* onto BUSH STREET. *Proceed* east 0.5 mile, then *turn right* onto KATE SMITH STREET Street. *Proceed* south two blocks and *stop* at the white frame church. You may wish to walk over to the churchyard and view the modest UDC marker.

Orientation   The modern church is located on the site of the wartime Prairie Grove Church. The original church was a simple log structure located inside the Y-shaped angle formed by the intersection of Fayetteville Road and Cove Creek Road. The intersection itself was located about two blocks to the northeast near the crossing of KATE SMITH STREET and Parks streets. Remember that Prairie Grove is a postwar town and that this area was forested in 1862; the churchyard and the nearby Buchanan House, a short distance to the east on the west side of Cove Creek Road, were among the few open areas in the vicinity.

What Happened   *Hindman* established his headquarters in the church and stayed here for most of the battle, for the building stood between the half of the Trans-Mississippi Army facing north atop Battle Ridge and the half facing southwest toward Cane Hill. Late in the day the general and his staff moved out so that the church could be used as a hospital. During the evening of December 7, *Hindman* concluded that his army was too badly battered and too low on ammunition to fight another day; there was nothing left to do but return to Fort Smith. Around midnight the Confederates slipped away to the south on Cove Creek Road, the wheels of the artillery vehicles wrapped with blankets to minimize noise.

The next morning, December 8, *Hindman* and *Marmaduke* met with Blunt and Herron near the Aday Post Office on Fayetteville Road. The generals arranged a truce in order to care for the wounded and bury the dead of both sides. The Federal commanders did not realize that the truce was a ruse to allow the Confederates to make good their escape. Around noon *Hindman*, *Marmaduke*, and a rear guard of Rebel cavalrymen trotted past the church and headed south toward the Boston Mountains in the wake of the retreating army.

Prairie Grove was a costly battle. The Trans-Mississippi Army lost 1,483 men: 204 killed, 872 wounded, and 407 missing, the latter mostly unhappy conscripts who deserted. The Army of the Frontier lost 1,233 men: 175 killed, 808 wounded, and 250 missing, the latter mostly cavalrymen captured in an early morning skirmish. The most intense fighting and the highest casualty rates occurred on the Borden farm. Roughly one out of ten soldiers in each army was killed or wounded during the battle. Wounded Federals were moved to Fayette-ville, Confederates to Cane Hill. Doctors and medical supplies were in short supply on the frontier, and the wounded of both sides suffered grievously.

Vignette   Following the departure of the Confederate generals on December 8, Capt. Chester Barney of the 20th Iowa visited the Buchanan House next to the church: "The floors were strewn with [Confederate] wounded, and the large yard surrounding it was also covered by them. They were lying in the hot sun, moaning piteously, while at a large table in the principal room the surgeons were busily engaged dressing wounds and amputating limbs. After amputation the limbs were thrown out the back door, and I observed a number of hogs feeding on them. The sight was so disgusting that I hastened away." [16] The scene at the nearby church, and all other field hospitals, was similar.

This concludes the driving tour of the battle. To return to Prairie Grove Battlefield State Historic Park, *turn left* onto u.s. 62 and follow it through town.

After completing the battlefield driving tour, you may wish to take the Prairie Grove campaign driving tour, which follows. This is a fifty-mile loop that includes many important sites, including Cane Hill, Reed's Mountain, Cove Creek Road, and Rhea's Mill.

OPTIONAL EXCURSION: Driving Tour of Prairie Grove Campaign, November–December 1862

This excursion will introduce you to roads and sites associated with the Prairie Grove campaign that are not included in the battlefield driving tour. The campaign driving tour is about fifty miles in length and can be completed in less than half a day.

Prairie Grove is located near the southern edge of the Springfield Plain, a relatively level subsection of the Ozark Plateau that encompasses the southwest corner of Missouri and the northwest corner of Arkansas. Large-scale military operations were possible in this area because the rolling terrain permitted relatively easy movement and provided a surprising amount of food. In 1862 the Springfield Plain was a mix of farms, grasslands, and forested hills. Today the region still retains some of its nineteenth-century character, though the prairie grasses have been replaced by cultivated fields and pastures and the forests have been greatly diminished.

The forbidding landscape south of Prairie Grove is an altogether different place. The southern edge of the Ozark Plateau is known as the Boston Mountains, a significant barrier that separates the upland Springfield Plain from the lowland Arkansas River valley. Five north-south roads wound through the Boston Mountains in 1862. They connected the settlers and settlements of northwest Arkansas, principally Fayetteville and Cane Hill, with the booming towns along the Arkansas River, principally Fort Smith and Van Buren. From east to west the five roads (and their modern designations) were Ozark Road (ARKANSAS 16/23), Frog Bayou Road (approximated by U.S. 71/ARKANSAS 282), Wire Road (ARKANSAS 265/220), Cove Creek Road (COUNTY 21/285), and the Line Road, or Military Road (ARKANSAS 59). Wire Road and Cove Creek Road figured prominently in both the Pea Ridge and Prairie Grove campaigns and are featured in this guide. Moving men, animals, wagons, and artillery through the Boston Mountains on primitive roads was a major undertaking. After completing the campaign driving tour, you may conclude that negotiating the modern versions of these roads in an automobile still requires a certain amount of grit.

Nearly all of the roads used by Union and Confederate armies during the Prairie Grove campaign survive in some form. Most are paved, at least in part, but some are only graded; a few stretches of the latter may be difficult in wet weather, especially for low-slung automobiles. Use caution when driving on graded roads, especially in creek bottoms prone to floods and washouts, and use common sense when traveling in isolated areas. No turnouts are available along the campaign driving tour. Watch for local traffic and look for safe places to stop.

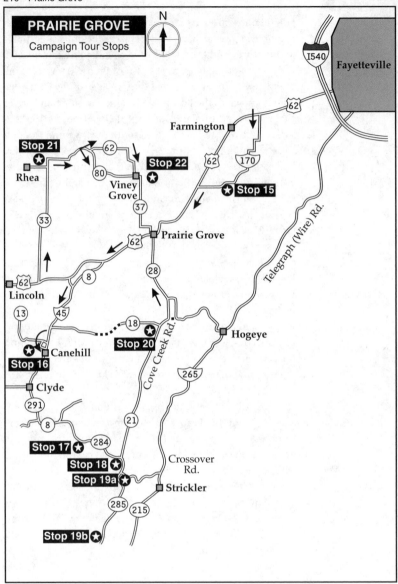

STOP 15   Herron's Approach on Fayetteville Road, December 7, 1862

Directions   *Begin* the campaign driving tour 8 miles east of Prairie Grove
                    at the intersection of U.S. 62 and I-540 on the west side of Fay-
                    etteville. *Proceed* west 2.5 miles on U.S. 62, then *turn left* onto
                    ARKANSAS 170. *Proceed* 2.7 miles and *stop* in the Walnut Grove
                    Church parking lot.

Orientation

The wartime Walnut Grove Church was a log structure; the handsome brick church on the site today was built in 1903. In the mid-nineteenth century, Fayetteville Road connected Fayetteville, Prairie Grove, Cane Hill, and the Cherokee Nation in the Indian Territory. ARKANSAS 170 includes all of the surviving fragments of Fayetteville Road between Fayetteville and Prairie Grove. The winding sections of the road (including the section in front of the church) are original; the straight sections and right-angle turns are modern. The country on both sides of ARKANSAS 170 is open today, but at the time of the Civil War, it was a patchwork of farms, prairies, and woods.

ARKANSAS 170, or Fayetteville Road, runs along the southern edge of the Springfield Plain. The outlying ranges of the Boston Mountains rise only a short distance to the south. The mountains in this vicinity are about 1,800 feet above sea level. During the war a Confederate cavalry force or even an entire Confederate army could emerge from the mountains with little or no warning. The only way for Union commanders to prevent this was to maintain strong mounted pickets on all five of the mountain roads across a fifty-mile front. This was an impossible task in a theater where Union cavalry was stretched to the limit guarding lines of communication that extended hundreds of miles northward to Springfield, Missouri, and Fort Scott, Kansas.

What Happened

After receiving Brig. Gen. James G. Blunt's call for help, Brig. Gen. Francis J. Herron set his two Union divisions in motion. Following a forced march of over 110 miles in three days from the vicinity of Springfield, they reached Fayetteville during the night of December 6, 1862. At dawn the next morning, December 7, the exhausted Federals arose and trudged west on Fayetteville Road. Their objective was Cane Hill, about six miles ahead, where Blunt was expecting an attack at any time. A short distance west of Fayetteville, the Federals encountered fleeing horsemen belonging to the 1st Arkansas Cavalry (U.S.) and the 7th Missouri Cavalry. This mounted force had been surprised and routed by Brig. Gen. John S. *Marmaduke's* cavalry near Prairie Grove Church. Herron shot one panic-stricken Federal cavalryman out of the saddle, but even this drastic action failed to deter the horsemen, who disappeared in the direction of Fayetteville.

Herron pressed on, worried that Maj. Gen. Thomas C. *Hindman* had gotten between him and Blunt at Cane Hill. His fears were confirmed when the head of the Union column reached Walnut Grove Church, where you are parked. On the rolling terrain just to the west, the Federals encountered a line of dismounted cavalry belonging to Col. Joseph O. *Shelby's* Iron Brigade. After skirmishing for thirty minutes, the Confederates fell back across the Illinois River toward Prairie Grove.

Analysis

Herron's extraordinary march from Springfield to Prairie Grove was the key event in the campaign. The unexpected arrival of Union reinforcements in northwest Arkansas forced *Hindman* to alter his plans just as he was on the verge of enveloping Blunt at Cane Hill. Instead of following through against Blunt, *Hindman* turned away from Cane Hill and intercepted Herron at Prairie Grove. Despite *Hindman's* best efforts, the two Union commands joined forces on the battlefield and fought the Confederates to a draw. Little wonder, then, that veterans of Herron's march were enormously proud of what they had accomplished and always regarded their epic of endurance as the greatest march of the Civil War.

Major-General
John M. Schofield.
From a photograph.
BLCW 1:293

STOP 16   Battle of Cane Hill, November 28, 1862

Directions   *Proceed* west on ARKANSAS 170 to the intersection with U.S. 62
                            and *turn left*. *Proceed* west through the town of Prairie Grove.
                            Do not stop at Prairie Grove Battlefield State Park at this
                            time.

                            About 2 miles west of Prairie Grove, *turn left* onto COUNTY
                            8. *Proceed* south a short distance, then *turn right* onto COUNTY
                            287. You are now back on Fayetteville Road. *Proceed* west 1.2
                            miles until you reach a stop sign, then *turn left* onto ARKANSAS
                            45. You are still on Fayetteville Road.

                            Proceed south 2.6 miles on ARKANSAS 45 to Cane Hill. Slow
                            down as you approach the town and *turn right* onto COUNTY
                            13. *Proceed* west 0.3 mile, then *turn left* onto COUNTY 440. Stop
                            in front of the Cane Hill Cemetery. Take a few moments to
                            look around and perhaps stroll through the graveyard. The
                            opening round of the battle of Cane Hill, a prelude to Prairie
                            Grove, began here on November 28, 1862.

Orientation   The term "Cane Hill" has meant different things at differ-
                            ent times. Early settlers referred to this entire area as Cane
                            Hill. The settlements of Boonsboro and Newburg developed
                            a mile apart along Fayetteville Road in the narrow valley of
                            Jordan Creek. The towns boasted pleasant homes, shops and
                            mills, and colleges for both men and women. The schools
                            were among the westernmost institutions of higher learning
                            in the United States in the 1850s, and Cane Hill was widely
                            regarded as the educational and cultural center of northwest
                            Arkansas. Despite the calamity of the Civil War, Cane Hill
                            was not fully eclipsed until the 1870s, when nearby Fayette-
                            ville gained a railroad line and was selected as the site of the
                            state's land grant university. One of the earliest presidents
                            of the new University of Arkansas was a former Confeder-
                            ate general from North Carolina named Daniel Harvey Hill.

                            To confuse the unwary traveler, Boonsboro is now known
                            as Cane Hill, and Newburg is now called Clyde. For our pur-
                            poses Cane Hill means the mile-long valley occupied by Cane
                            Hill (Boonsboro) and Clyde (Newburg) and traversed by AR-
                            KANSAS 45 (Fayetteville Road). The cemetery where you are
                            located is on the northern edge of Cane Hill (Boonsboro).

What Happened   After the Army of the Frontier completed its mission of driv-
                            ing Confederate forces out of southwest Missouri, two of
                            the three divisions withdrew to the vicinity of Springfield
                            in November. Blunt's division remained in an advanced posi-
                            tion in Arkansas, about thirty-five miles north of Cane Hill.
                            Hindman, only thirty miles to the south in Fort Smith, be-

lieved he had an opportunity to defeat this isolated division. He dispatched *Marmaduke's* cavalry division to disrupt Union foraging operations and to learn as much as possible about the size and composition of the enemy force. *Hindman* also directed him to gather supplies from the fertile Cane Hill region. As a result, the Confederate cavalry was encumbered with a slow-moving train.

Marmaduke led about 2,000 horsemen across the Boston Mountains to Cane Hill, where he halted to allow the troops to forage in accordance with his somewhat contradictory instructions. When Blunt learned that *Marmaduke* was on the north side of the mountains, he took 5,000 men on a rapid march south toward Cane Hill. On the morning of November 28, the van of Blunt's division, led by the general himself, approached Cane Hill on Fayetteville Road.

Surprised by the unexpected appearance of the Union army, *Marmaduke* fought a delaying action while his train retired into the Boston Mountains with tons of badly needed supplies for the army in Fort Smith. He directed *Shelby* to form his brigade into a line of battle along Cincinnati Road (COUNTY 13) facing north. *Shelby* anchored his right flank in this cemetery. Two guns of Capt. Hiram *Bledsoe's Missouri Battery* went into action amid the headstones. Union infantry, cavalry, and artillery formed a line of battle across Fayetteville Road (ARKANSAS 45) about a quarter mile north of the cemetery.

Shelby soon was forced to withdraw. For about four hours fighting swirled southward through Jordan Creek valley from Cane Hill (Boonsboro) to Clyde (Newburg). In midafternoon *Marmaduke* fell back about two miles on Van Buren Road to Reed's Mountain, where both sides skirmished in heavy woods. Late in the day the Confederates withdrew from Reed's Mountain and turned south on Cove Creek Road. (The latter stages of the battle beyond the Cane Hill region are discussed below.)

When fighting sputtered out at dusk, the leading Union forces were twelve miles south of the cemetery where the battle had opened. Like most clashes between mounted forces, casualties were relatively light for the numbers engaged. Blunt's losses were 6 men killed and 35 wounded. *Marmaduke* lost 10 killed, 66 wounded, and 6 missing. Following the battle, Blunt occupied Cane Hill and established a supply depot at Rhea's Mill, about eight miles to the north. Then he sat back to await developments.

Analysis

The battle of Cane Hill was a tactical Union victory. Blunt drove *Marmaduke* back across the Boston Mountains, but in doing so he plunged his own command another thirty-five miles deeper into Arkansas. Blunt's division now was over one hundred miles south of Herron's two divisions near Springfield but only thirty miles north of *Hindman's* army in Fort Smith. *Hindman* believed that Blunt had played into his hands. He shrugged off *Marmaduke's* setback and prepared to take advantage of this extraordinary opportunity to attack an isolated and apparently unsupported Union force. The result was the Prairie Grove campaign.

STOP 17   Skirmishes on Reed's Mountain, November 28 and December 5–6, 1862

Directions   *Proceed* 0.3 mile on COUNTY 440 around Cane Hill Cemetery to ARKANSAS 45. The road is narrow but passable for all but the largest vehicles. *Turn right* onto the highway. One block south you will see a sign pointing out the location of Cane Hill College. If you wish, make a brief side trip to visit the site. A postwar brick building survives, but nothing remains of the antebellum school that produced many prominent nineteenth-century Arkansans.

Proceed south 1.6 miles on ARKANSAS 45 to the nearly extinct hamlet of Clyde (Newburg). The road forks here, but the intersection is easy to miss, so be alert. *Turn left* onto COUNTY 291 and *stop*. You have left historic Fayetteville Road and are now on historic Van Buren Road, an east-west route that connected Fayetteville Road with Cove Creek Road. Notice the small marker at the fork of the road commemorating the Cane Hill Female Seminary, which was located in Clyde. It was a smaller feminine counterpart to Cane Hill College. No trace of the school remains.

Proceed east 1.2 miles, then *turn left* onto COUNTY 8. *Proceed* east 0.8 mile, then *turn right* onto COUNTY 284. Despite the turns and changes in numbers, you are still on Van Buren Road. *Proceed* east to the intersection with COUNTY 299 on the crest of Reed's Mountain and *stop* if conditions permit. Watch for local traffic.

Orientation   Reed's Mountain is an outlier of the Boston Mountains. The rounded crest is about 1,700 feet above sea level, the highest point on the campaign driving tour. From the east slope (straight ahead) there is a nice view of Cove Creek valley and the heart of the Boston Mountains. Panoramas of the Boston Mountains are rare because most roads snake through valleys and canyons. The highest ridges in the Boston Mountains are between 2,400 and 2,500 feet in elevation.

What Happened   Reed's Mountain was the scene of two separate engagements during the Prairie Grove campaign. The fighting that erupted at Cane Hill during the morning of November 28 reached this area by midafternoon. The Confederates dismounted and scattered through the woods on the west slope. Pursuing Union forces also dismounted and ascended the mountain. Skirmishing flared for two hours before the Confederates withdrew on Van Buren Road into Cove Creek valley.

A week later, on December 6, Reed's Mountain was the scene of another prolonged skirmish as *Hindman's* advance clashed with Blunt's outposts. From Morrow's the Confederates turned west onto Van Buren Road and slowly pushed the Union defenders over the crest of the mountain and down the west slope. That night *Hindman* learned of Herron's approach and hurried north on Cove Creek Road. A single cavalry regiment remained behind on Reed's Mountain to maintain the pretense that the principal Confederate attack would come from the south.

STOP 18   Morrow House, March 2 and December 6, 1862

Directions   *Proceed* east to the intersection with COUNTY 21/285 and *stop* if
                     conditions permit. Watch for local traffic.

Orientation   You are at the intersection of Van Buren and Cove Creek
                     roads, a crucial point in the Prairie Grove campaign. COUNTY
                     21 north of the intersection is Cove Creek Road, but COUNTY
                     285 south of the intersection is an approximation of Cove
                     Creek Road. In the mid-nineteenth century, the old road wan-
                     dered back and forth across the creek about forty times be-
                     tween this point and the junction with Wire Road at Oliver's
                     Store. Because of severe flooding in the valley, little of the old
                     road remains. COUNTY 285 south of this point is cut into the
                     hillside well above the creek to minimize flooding.

                     Notice the terrace on the east side of the intersection. In
                     1862 the John Morrow House was located there. Morrow was
                     one of only a handful of settlers in Cove Creek valley. Travel-
                     ers often stopped at the home for a meal or a night's lodging.
                     The Morrow House is preserved at Prairie Grove Battlefield
                     State Historic Site (see Stop 1a).

What Happened   During the Pea Ridge campaign, Maj. Gens. Earl *Van Dorn* and
                     Sterling *Price* stayed in the Morrow House on March 2, 1862.
                     Between February 22 and March 4, Cove Creek valley south
                     of the house was filled with thousands of soldiers of *Price's*
                     Missouri State Guard. Because a great many men transferred
                     from the State Guard to Confederate service here, this nar-
                     row valley is the birthplace of the Missouri Confederate units
                     that distinguished themselves on so many battlefields in the
                     West. It also is the place where the soldiers of the *1st Missouri
                     Brigade* received their unusual white uniforms. (These same
                     uniforms, somewhat the worse for wear, are depicted in the
                     painting by Andy Thomas in the Visitor Center at Pea Ridge
                     National Military Park.)

                     Hindman spent the night of December 6 in the Morrow
                     House; his men camped on the grounds occupied by *Price's*
                     army the previous spring. The Missourians in *Marmaduke's* Di-
                     vision and Brig. Gen. Mosby M. *Parsons's* infantry brigade rec-
                     ognized the place and observed wryly that after nine months
                     of arduous service, they were back where they had started.

                     While *Hindman* plotted the destruction of Blunt's division
                     at Cane Hill, a courier galloped up with the stunning news
                     that Herron's two divisions, last reported to be camped over
                     one hundred miles to the north near Springfield, were fast
                     approaching Fayetteville. Herron obviously was hurrying
                     south to join forces with Blunt at Cane Hill.

Hindman had not expected Union reinforcements to arrive so quickly. Faced with a suddenly altered tactical situation, he improvised a new plan. Instead of assaulting Blunt at Cane Hill, he decided to intercept Herron. The only possible place to do this was the junction of Cove Creek Road and Fayetteville Road nine miles to the north at Prairie Grove.

Shortly after midnight on the morning of December 7, the Trans-Mississippi Army moved north toward Prairie Grove on Cove Creek Road. Men and animals were tired after the arduous trek through the Boston Mountains, and progress was slow. *Marmaduke's* cavalry (minus one brigade left behind at Reed's Mountain to distract Blunt) led the way, with instructions to reach Fayetteville Road and delay Herron until the infantry could reach the scene. *Hindman* thanked the Morrow family for their hospitality, then mounted his horse and rode north toward Prairie Grove.

The Morrow House as it appears today. The porch was added in the 1890s. Courtesy William L. Shea.

STOP 19a   Cove Creek Road

Directions   *Turn right* onto COUNTY 285. *Proceed* south 0.6 mile. *Turn left* onto COUNTY 215 and *stop* if conditions permit.

Orientation   COUNTY 215 is Crossover Road. This route played a role in the Pea Ridge campaign because it connects Cove Creek Road with Wire Road 1.5 miles to the east. The Missouri State Guard used Crossover Road to enter Cove Creek valley on February 22 and to leave their camps on March 4. After spending the night at the Morrow House on March 2, *Price* and *Van Dorn* used the road the next day to journey to Strickler's Station on Wire Road, where they met with Brig. Gen. Benjamin *Mc-Culloch* and made final preparations for the Pea Ridge campaign. If you wish, make a brief side trip to Wire Road and the hamlet of Strickler.

In the van. BLCW 3:1

STOP 19b   Cove Creek Road

Directions   *Proceed* south 1.4 miles on COUNTY 285. Carefully slow where
                      the road crosses over Cove Creek. It is not recommended that
                      you attempt to drive much beyond this point. *Turn around* at
                      the first suitable opportunity.

Orientation   The creek crossing is about 2 miles south of the site of the
                      Morrow House and the intersection of the Van Buren and
                      Cove Creek roads. This is where the battle of Cane Hill came
                      to an end. Remember that the historic road ran along the
                      bottom of the narrow valley.

What Happened   Cove Creek valley was gloomy as sunset approached on No-
                      vember 28, 1862. Arkansas and Missouri cavalrymen from
                      Marmaduke's Division waited here in ambush on either side
                      of the road. A battalion of the 6th Kansas Cavalry, in the van
                      of the pursuing Union force, rode directly into the trap. Lt.
                      Col. Lewis R. Jewell was mortally wounded, and several other
                      Kansans were wounded or captured. With darkness falling,
                      Blunt halted his pursuit and returned to Cane Hill (as dis-
                      cussed above).
                          Cove Creek Road, between the Morrow House and the junc-
                      tion with Wire Road at Oliver's Store on the south side of the
                      Boston Mountains, was busy in the fall and winter of 1862.
                      Marmaduke's Division used the road before and after the fight
                      at Cane Hill in late November. A week later *Hindman's* army
                      advanced to and retreated from Prairie Grove on it. Finally,
                      in late December Blunt's army used the road during its Van
                      Buren raid.

STOP 20   Hog Eye Road Intersection, December 7, 1862

Directions   *Return* to the intersection with COUNTY 284. *Continue* north
                               5.2 miles on COUNTY 21. *Turn left* onto COUNTY 18 and *stop* as
                               close as possible to the intersection. Watch for local traffic,
                               as always.

Orientation   You are at the intersection of Cove Creek and Hog Eye roads,
                               another important point in the campaign. Cove Creek Road
                               is the route followed by *Hindman's* Trans-Mississippi Army on
                               the morning of December 7 as it marched north toward Prai-
                               rie Grove. COUNTY 18 is historic Hog Eye Road, which once
                               connected Cane Hill to the west with Hog Eye to the east on
                               Wire Road. In 1862 this was a true crossroads, but the road
                               east of the intersection was abandoned long ago—only faint
                               traces remain today.

What Happened   Blunt was concerned, and properly so, that the skirmishing
                               on Reed's Mountain on December 5–6 was a diversion. He
                               feared that *Hindman* would bypass Cane Hill by moving north
                               on Cove Creek Road. While the Confederate commander was
                               at the Morrow House making preparations to do exactly that,
                               Blunt sent a cavalry detachment to picket this crossroads and
                               watch for any Confederate movement on Cove Creek Road.
                               Unfortunately for the Federals, the reconnaissance effort was
                               a fiasco.

                               A Union force led by Col. John M. Richardson, a Missouri
                               militia officer, left Cane Hill and rode east on Hog Eye Road.
                               What happened next is murky, but it seems that when the
                               Missourians approached this crossroads from the west, they
                               encountered a screen of Confederate horsemen. Instead of at-
                               tempting to push the Rebels out of the way, or at least inform
                               Blunt that he could not carry out his mission, Richardson
                               simply stopped a quarter mile west of the crossroads and
                               did nothing. On the morning of December 7, after the Rebel
                               horsemen had departed, the Federals finally reached the
                               crossroads where you are located. They belatedly discovered
                               that the Trans-Mississippi Army had already passed by on its
                               way to Prairie Grove.

STOP 21   Blunt Reaches Rhea's Mill, December 7, 1862

Directions   *Proceed* north 1.4 miles on COUNTY 21 to the intersection. *Turn left* onto COUNTY 28 and *proceed* north to Prairie Grove. You are still on Cove Creek Road. When you reach the traffic light in downtown Prairie Grove, *turn left* onto U.S. 62 and *proceed* west 5 miles to the outskirts of Lincoln. *Turn right* onto COUNTY 33 and *proceed* north 4.7 miles. Notice the sign for Rhea, the site of Rhea's Mill. If you wish, take a brief side trip to the site, which is 0.5 mile west of the highway.

Orientation   William Rhea's water-powered mill is gone, and the smoke-stack at Prairie Grove Battlefield State Historic Park is all that survives of the steam-powered mill.

What Happened   Blunt chose Rhea's Mill as the location of his forward supply depot after his lunge southward to Cane Hill in late November. During the ten days between the battles of Cane Hill and Prairie Grove, a substantial force of Union infantry, cavalry, and artillery was stationed here to protect the Army of the Frontier's irreplaceable trains and stores. Well-protected trains of up to two hundred wagons constantly rumbled back and forth between this point and Fort Scott, Kansas.

Late on the morning of December 7, Blunt belatedly realized that *Hindman* had gotten around his flank and engaged Herron in the vicinity of Prairie Grove. Instead of marching directly from Cane Hill to Prairie Grove on Fayetteville Road, which is what *Hindman* expected him to do, Blunt marched north from Cane Hill to Rhea's Mill to secure his vital supply depot. After adding additional troops to the strong detachment already here, Blunt hurried toward Prairie Grove, about five miles to the east.

Vignette   Albert R. Greene, 9th Kansas Cavalry, was part of an escort for a train of two hundred wagons from Fort Scott that arrived on December 4. He described the scene: "Rhea's Mills was a beautiful spot. A gently sloping hillside facing the east, with scattering great oaks loaded with mistletoe, a sparkling rivulet issuing from a ledge of moss-grown rocks, trained to the flume of an overshot water wheel thirty feet high; a weather-beaten mill with a sagging roof, the cottage of the miller hard by . . . another venerable gray-brown shack which served the purposes of post office, country store and loafers' headquarters combined—and you have the hamlet as it was when our regiment first saw it." For some reason Greene neglected to mention the adjacent steam-powered mill and its towering smokestack.

Despite this curious omission, Greene's account illuminates the tenuous overland supply situation in the Trans-Mississippi, where quartermaster and commissary officers operated without the benefit of railroads or steamboats. "Our arrival was hailed with shouts all along the line . . . because we had brought 'grub' to a half-famished army. They had been subsisting on hard-tack and scenery, and wanted a change of diet." The soldiers in Blunt's main body had to wait another twenty-four hours for the "grub" to reach Cane Hill, but when they marched to Prairie Grove two days later, their haversacks were full.[17]

Rhea's Mill in the 1890s. The smokestack was moved to the Prairie Grove Battlefield when the structure was demolished. Courtesy David A. Huff, Bob's Studio of Photography, Fayetteville.

STOP 22   Blunt's Approach to Prairie Grove, December 7, 1862

Directions   From the sign for Rhea, *proceed* north 0.2 mile on COUNTY 33,
                         then *turn right* onto COUNTY 62. *Proceed* east 1.9 miles, then
                         turn right onto COUNTY 80. *Proceed* east 2.7 miles. At the vil-
                         lage of Viney Grove, *turn right* onto COUNTY 37 (VINEY GROVE
                         ROAD) and *stop*. None of these roads are historic, but they
                         approximate the route of Blunt's approach to Prairie Grove.
                         COUNTY 80 is a one-lane gravel road suitable only for cars and
                         light trucks. Buses and recreational vehicles should stay on
                         COUNTY 62 for 3.3 miles, then *turn right* onto COUNTY 37 and
                         return to Prairie Grove.

Orientation   You are traversing an agricultural landscape that has changed
                         little in appearance since the late nineteenth century. The
                         fertile soils of the Springfield Plain attracted thousands of
                         settlers to northwest Arkansas and southwest Missouri be-
                         fore the Civil War. Many came from the Midwest, which
                         partly accounts for the widespread Unionist sentiment in
                         this region during the war. The entire Ozark Plateau was a
                         recruiting ground for "Mountain Feds," white Arkansans and
                         Missourians who volunteered for service in Union regiments
                         such as the 1st Arkansas Cavalry. Although the horrors of the
                         war in this region led to the death or flight of thousands,
                         within two decades the population had rebounded and the
                         present bucolic landscape had appeared.

What Happened   Spurred on by the roar of artillery fire, Blunt's division
                         covered the five miles from Rhea's Mill to Prairie Grove
                         in less than ninety minutes. He arrived on the battlefield
                         around midafternoon and immediately began an artillery
                         bombardment of the Confederate left while his infantry
                         prepared for an assault.

                         Follow COUNTY 37 (VINEY GROVE ROAD) into Prairie Grove. This
                         concludes the Campaign Driving Tour. *Turn left* onto BUSH
                         STREET, then *turn right* onto MOCK STREET. At the traffic light
                         turn left onto U.S. 62 and *proceed* to Prairie Grove Battlefield
                         State Historic Park.

Advancing under difficulties. BLCW 4:681

Wire Road

Overview

The connecting link between the battles of Wilson's Creek, Pea Ridge, and Prairie Grove was Wire Road, also known as Telegraph Road, which ran from Springfield, Missouri, to Fort Smith, Arkansas. Wire Road was the main transportation artery of southwest Missouri and northwest Arkansas. It brought the armies to the battlefields, serving as a readymade invasion route for the Federals and a convenient avenue of concentration for the defending Confederates. All Civil War armies were dependent on logistical support and thus had to orient their campaigns around available transportation routes. There were no convenient rivers in Missouri or northern Arkansas for the Federals to use, and there were no railroads extending onto the Ozark Plateau, which dominated this region. Although rocky and poorly maintained in many places, Wire Road was the only way for the armies of both sides to extend their power into the area.

The road was built in 1838 by the U.S. government to offer logistical support for several frontier forts constructed on the western borders of Missouri and Arkansas, following the removal of thousands of Native Americans from the southeastern states to the Indian Territory, now known as Oklahoma. It became part of the Trail of Tears when many Cherokees and members of other tribes trudged along its way toward their new homes, having endured intense suffering along the way. Several taverns, inns, and small towns prospered from the traffic that utilized the road over the next two decades as this frontier region slowly grew. Springfield, Missouri, and Fayetteville, Arkansas, developed into major commercial points because of this growing traffic.

A significant boost took place when John Butterfield chose this road as part of a route to deliver mail twice per week from St. Louis to San Francisco in 1858. His enterprise caught the imagination of the country. The Butterfield Overland Mail Company sent a fleet of stagecoaches along the route, carrying passengers as well as mail, until the Civil War brought its operations to an end. Wire Road took these coaches along a portion of the rolling landscape of the Ozark Plateau, from Springfield toward the Arkansas state line. South of Fayetteville it entered the rugged Boston Mountains, which fringe the southern border of the plateau, until it crossed the Arkansas River at Van Buren and reached Fort Smith. Here, on the border between Arkansas and the Indian Territory, the road truly entered the frontier to continue southwesterly to Texas, the New Mexico Territory, and California. A number of new hostelries, including Elkhorn Tavern on the future Pea Ridge battlefield, sprang up to serve the needs of travelers on the route.

Conditions on the road were good at least until the Boston Mountains; from that point the ride on a Butterfield Overland Mail coach became a harrowing experience. Hiram S. Rumfield, who hired on as an agent of the company and traveled to his post out west in June 1860, described it in a letter to his wife. "No one who has never passed over this road can form any idea of its bold and rugged aspect. It winds along the mountain sides over a surface covered with masses of broken rock, and frequently runs in fearful proximity to precipitous ravines of unknown depth. Over such a route as this the coaches of the mail company are driven with fearful rapidity. The horses are seldom permitted to walk even when traversing the steepest and most tortuous hills, and when drove at their utmost speed, which is generally the case, the stage reels from side to side like a storm tossed bark, and the din of the heavily ironed wheels in constant contact with the flinty rock, is truly appalling. The man who can pass over this route a passenger in one of the Overland Mail Coaches, without experiencing feelings of mingled terror and astonishment, must certainly be oblivious to every consideration of personal safety." [1]

The road gained its Civil War–era name when a telegraph line was strung alongside it in 1860. The line was taken down south of Springfield soon after Federal forces occupied the town in the summer of 1861. Southern Missouri became Rebel territory when the Unionists evacuated Springfield in August, giving prominence to Wire Road as the natural route of invasion for future military campaigns.

Noble Prentis, who had a lot of experience marching along Wire Road as a member of a Kansas regiment, later remembered it with jaded accuracy. It "was a very natural road, and the soldiers whose painful duty it was to march up and down it, declared that not a tree had been felled in making it. Winding along, up and down, guiltless of art, or fill, or bridge; mere hard and beaten path, or prolonged dust-heap, or lengthened quagmire, according to the sun or the rain, the shifting and uncertain elements, stretched the 'Wire road,' a *Via Dolorosa*." [2]

The road lost its prominent role in the region's development when a railroad was built connecting Springfield with Fort Smith after the war. The telegraph line was transferred from Wire Road to the railroad grade, and fewer people used the historic transportation route. By 1888, when Prentis revisited the area, portions of Wire Road were not used at all, while the rest of it carried only local traffic. Most of the modern highways built in the region beginning in the 1920s also bypassed the roadbed.

Crude as it was, Wire Road made possible three major campaigns during the Civil War. Each one saw Union and Confederate armies use the road as a primary route of invasion or defense. The battles that resulted from these campaigns were among the most dramatic and bloody of the Trans-Mississippi war, and they played a significant role in determining the course of the conflict on the frontier.

Driving Tour of Wire Road:
Springfield Missouri to Fort Smith Arkansas

It is possible to drive along the route of WIRE ROAD and get the full flavor of the countryside that was marched on and fought over in this part of the Civil War. There are sections of the route, mostly in the area south of Springfield, where the original roadbed no longer exists or is inaccessible. But the original route can be closely followed from a point almost midway between Springfield and the Arkansas line down to the Arkansas River. In fact, in some places the only modern road is the original roadbed used by the Union and Confederate armies during their campaigns.

The length of time needed to complete this driving tour will vary according to how deeply you wish to experience the trip. If you drive entirely along modern highways, it would take you three or four hours to travel from Springfield to Fort Smith. But a leisurely drive, following the historic route as closely as possible, will take one or two days. Be prepared to drive over some stretches of gravel road as well as some rugged terrain. Caution is urged at all times.

An awkward squad. BLCW 1:84

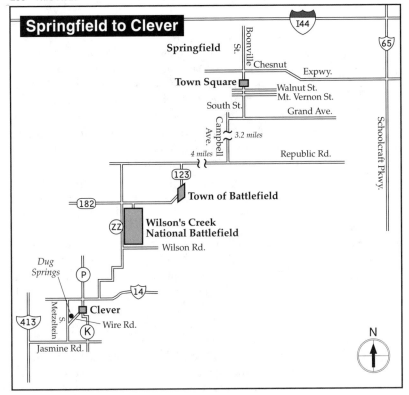

SECTION 1   Springfield, Missouri, to Wilson's Creek National Battlefield

Directions   Park Central Square in Springfield, which encompasses the original town square, is a good place to start your exploration of WIRE ROAD. If you are approaching from the north side of Springfield, *take* the U.S. 65/SCHOOLCRAFT PARKWAY EXIT from INTERSTATE 44. *Go south* to CHESTNUT EXPRESSWAY and *turn right*. From the south of Springfield, *take* U.S. 65/SCHOOLCRAFT PARKWAY north to CHESTNUT EXPRESSWAY and *turn left*. *Drive west* on the expressway to BOONVILLE AVENUE and *turn left*. *Proceed* four blocks and *park* in the public parking lot on your right. Leaving your car, *walk* south on Boonville one block to Park Central Square. WIRE ROAD entered town from the north via Boonville and passed directly through the square.

What Happened   Springfield was an important supply depot and base of operations during the war. While a majority of its 3,000 citizens held to the Union, the town supplied companies of soldiers for both sides. During the course of the war, it changed hands five times, and commanders such as Sterling *Price*, Benjamin

McCulloch, Nathaniel Lyon, and Samuel Curtis established headquarters here.

No Civil War–era buildings survive on or near Park Central Square. The Greene County Court House, a new three-story building on the west side of the square, was used as a hospital for much of the war. Thousands of Northern and Southern soldiers marched through the square between 1861 and 1865. One man who knew Springfield was James Butler Hickock, whose national reputation as "Wild Bill" got its start in July 1865 when he shot a man on the town square. This was one of the few gunfights of the Old West that actually followed the "showdown in the street" pattern popularized by Hollywood.

Directions

To begin your tour of Wire Road, *return* to your car, *drive* around the square, and *head* south on SOUTH STREET. Two blocks from the square, just after crossing WALNUT STREET, a historical marker notes the location of a Methodist church that the Federals used as an arsenal during the war. Two blocks farther a marker on your right at the corner of SOUTH STREET and MT. VERNON STREET denotes the location of Fort No. 4. Built in 1862, this earthwork played a key role in the repulse of an attack by Confederate general John S. *Marmaduke's* cavalry on January 8, 1863.

Near Fort No. 4 Wire Road curved off to the right, running 9 miles southwest to its crossing of Wilson Creek. The only portion now remaining is in the modern town of Battlefield, which is nearly adjacent to Wilson's Creek National Battlefield. To reach this remnant, *continue* along SOUTH STREET until it ends at GRAND AVENUE and *turn right. Follow* GRAND for several blocks to CAMPBELL AVENUE and *turn left. Proceed* south for 3.25 miles to REPUBLIC ROAD and *turn right.* Follow REPUBLIC approximately 4 miles to FARM ROAD 123 and *turn left. Follow* FARM ROAD 123 into the town of Battlefield, *turning right* onto OLD WIRE ROAD. *Follow* OLD WIRE ROAD for about 1 mile to the intersection of ELM STREET on your right. Wire Road continues south past this point for only about 100 yards. You will have to turn around if you continue straight, so it is best to *turn right* on ELM STREET. After leaving the Battlefield, ELM STREET becomes FARM ROAD 182. About 2 miles farther on you will see the entrance to Wilson's Creek National Battlefield on your left.

What Happened

Wire Road was very important in relation to the battle of Wilson's Creek. For details and an opportunity to walk the surviving portions of the road within the park, see the Wilson's Creek tour.

SECTION 2   Wilson's Creek to Madry, Missouri

Outside of Wilson's Creek National Battlefield, the next large intact section of Wire Road is at Clever. As you follow modern highways to this town, the route of Wire Road lies generally to your right, though a few short stretches of modern roads follow the original roadbed.

Directions   From the battlefield entrance *turn left* onto FARM ROAD 182, *proceed* 0.1 mile to the intersection of MISSOURI ZZ, and *turn left*. After you have gone 4 miles, keep a lookout on your right. *En route*, just past MAPLES LANE, right before the road makes a sharp left turn at the bottom of a hill, is a low historical marker denoting Ashmore Station, an early WIRE ROAD stop on the Butterfield Overland Mail route. The marker is on the right side of the road.

From the marker *proceed* another 2.7 miles to MISSOURI 14 and *turn right* toward Clever. After 1.4 miles *turn left* on MISSOURI K and *drive* 0.4 mile to the point where the highway doglegs to the left. Instead of following this turn, *continue straight* on PUBLIC AVENUE. *Turn right* onto INMAN STREET and set your odometer. At 0.1 mile INMAN becomes OLD WIRE ROAD. At 1.4 miles water from Dug Springs crosses under the road. The springs are to your right rear, out of sight, in a pasture. During the strategic maneuvering prior to Wilson's Creek, forces under Lyon and *McCulloch* clashed briefly just south of Dug Springs on August 3, 1861.

A short distance beyond Dug Springs, the intact portion of Wire Road ends at SOUTH WETZELTEIN ROAD, and it is necessary to follow modern roads for several miles. *Turn left* onto METZELTEIN and *proceed* 1.6 miles to JASMINE ROAD. *Turn right* and *drive* 3.9 miles to MISSOURI 13. *Turn left* (south) and *go* 4.4 miles to the junction with MISSOURI A. Here, instead of turning left onto MISSOURI A, *turn right* onto OLD WIRE ROAD. There is also a sign pointing the way to the Wire Road Conservation Area to the west.

In about 1 mile *turn left* onto an unmarked gravel road. Just past the intersection of OLD WIRE ROAD and ARLISS ROAD, you will descend into the valley of Crane Creek, a little past the entrance to the Wire Road Conservation Area. *Cross* the stream and *pull over* to the side of the road. You will notice that a postwar railroad now lies in the valley.

What Happened   This wide and spacious valley was the scene of a pivotal incident during Curtis's pursuit of *Price* following the evacuation of Springfield on February 13, 1862. While the Missouri Rebels bivouacked at McCullah's Spring, about eight miles to the northeast of Crane Creek, the Federals slept snugly

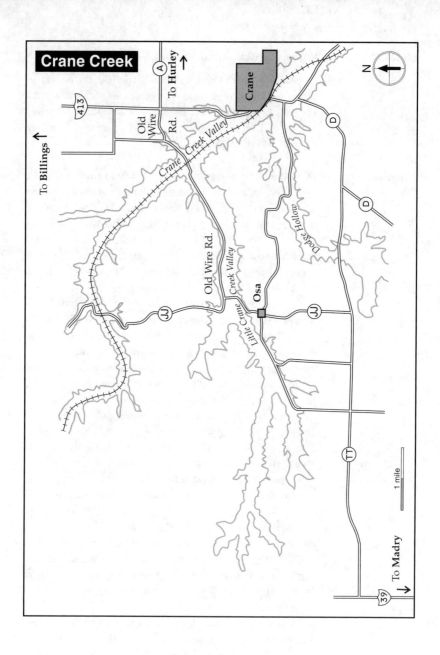

in Springfield, some thirty miles from the creek. A winter storm lashed the area that night with sleet, snow, and chilling winds. But the sky cleared the next morning to let the sun shine on the white, rolling landscape.

Curtis set out by dividing his army into two columns, based on Brig. Gen. Franz Sigel's recommendation. While the army leader took the 3rd and 4th Divisions along WIRE ROAD, Sigel led the 1st and 2nd Divisions on a system of country roads to the west. He wanted to reach McDowell, about twenty-five miles southwest of Crane Creek, to cut off *Price* and capture his Missouri army. It was essential that Curtis delay the Rebels to give Sigel an opportunity to pull off this coup.

Price had no idea that Curtis would pursue in this cold weather. He moved his command from McCullah's Spring to Crane Creek that day, intending to encamp there for several days and await Curtis's next move. The camps stretched off to the southwest along Little Crane Creek valley, which intersects the main valley at a right angle. Brig. Gen. Henry *Little's* 1st Missouri Brigade was the rear guard and thus became the target of a small attack by Curtis's advance just as night was falling on February 14. Col. Calvin M. Ellis's 1st Missouri Cavalry and Maj. William D. Bowen's Missouri Cavalry Battalion came up to Crane Creek that evening. Ellis had the idea that Curtis wanted him to harass the Rebels as much as possible, so he ordered Bowen's mountain howitzers to fire a few salvos at *Little's* camp in the valley. The Confederates were startled, the entire command was aroused, and *Little* hurried his men into a battle line atop the bluffs northeast of the creek, straddling WIRE ROAD. But there was no further action. Ellis contented himself with merely disturbing the Missourians' sleep and then retired to Curtis's column, which had halted at McCullah's Spring.

This small affair had a big influence on the rest of the campaign. *Price* was astonished that the Yankees were after him in such force, and he completely altered his plans. That night his men hastily repacked their gear and set out in the darkness. They had to reach Arkansas and the supporting troops of *McCulloch's* command as quickly as possible. *Price* set his large wagon train, loaded with supplies, ahead of the infantry column. Crane Creek was empty by dawn of February 15.

Curtis was angry with Ellis for scaring the Confederates, and he even considered placing the colonel under arrest. But he needed the aggressive Missourian even more now that *Price* was racing to the south. Curtis set out early on the morning of February 15 determined to catch and hold his opponent. *Price* made it to McDowell before Sigel did; in fact Curtis also reached the town before Sigel. The German had at least ten miles more to march than either *Price* or Curtis, but he did not push his command as vigorously as needed. His two divisions finally reached McDowell on February 16 and raced along to catch up with Curtis. As a result of the little fracas at Crane Creek, the Pea Ridge campaign turned into a race for Arkansas.

Directions

Continue along OLD WIRE ROAD, going under the railroad bridge to the stop sign. *Turn right* onto ROUNDHOUSE ROAD, which is unmarked, but you need *drive* only 0.1 mile and *turn left* onto OLD WIRE ROAD again. The pavement ends after 1.1 miles; *follow* the left fork here onto an unmarked gravel road. This road will later be labeled as FARM ROAD 2005, but it is not marked as such here. *Follow* it another 1 mile to the intersection with COUNTY JJ. *Turn left* and *drive* due south, quickly leaving the original Wire Road and climbing the bluffs out of Little Crane Creek valley. You will *pass through* the tiny postwar village of Osa and *continue south* for about 1.5 miles to the intersection of COUNTY TT. *Turn right* and *drive* due west on this road for 4.8 miles and *turn left* (south) on MISSOURI 39. The postwar town of Madry is 0.5 mile away.

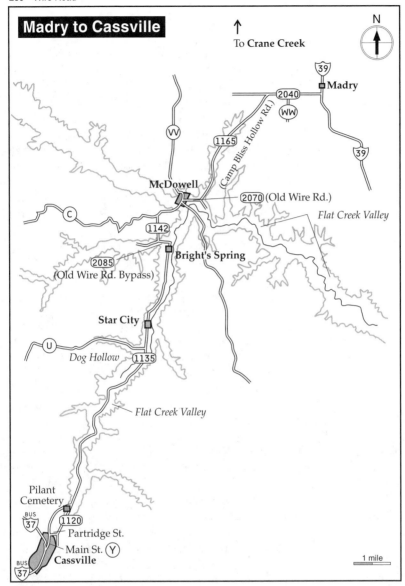

Madry to Cassville

↑
To **Crane Creek**

N

To **Crane Creek**

Madry

2040

WW

1165

Camp Bliss Hollow Rd.)

VV

39

39

McDowell

2070 (Old Wire Rd.)

C

Flat Creek Valley

1142

Bright's Spring

2085

(Old Wire Rd. Bypass)

Star City

U

Dog Hollow   1135

Flat Creek Valley

Pilant
Cemetery

BUS
37

1120

Partridge St.

Main St. Y

BUS
37

Cassville

1 mile

SECTION 3   Madry to Missouri-Arkansas state line

Directions   *Continue* through Madry and *turn right* (west) onto COUNTY WW
just south of town. After 1 mile the road makes a ninety-
degree turn to the south; leave it here and *turn right* onto
FARM ROAD 2040; *go* 0.5 mile and *turn left* onto FARM ROAD
1165 (CAMP BLISS HOLLOW ROAD). This is the original roadbed
of Wire Road. From this point on, you will be able to drive on

the original roadbed or very near it all the way to Van Buren, Arkansas.

The road goes through this shallow hollow for about 4 miles to McDowell.

Vignette

Camp Bliss Hollow derives its name from a camp established here by Unionists at the midpoint of the war. About two miles into the hollow you will find a pleasant glade with a spring. This was the site of the encampment. A piece of graffiti was still visible here when Roscoe P. Conkling and Margaret B. Conkling drove through during the 1930s, exploring the route of the Butterfield Overland Mail coaches. Scrawled on the limestone face of a little ridge on the north side of the road was the inscription "Camp Bliss, Feb. 1863."

The modern historian is indebted to the Conklings for this and many other bits of information about the Overland Mail route and WIRE ROAD. They were indefatigable researchers and field investigators. It was a labor of love for the couple to research all available information about the route from one end to the other, and they spent months on the road driving along every stretch of it. They located every station, recorded the remains of all buildings, and even interviewed the very few people still alive who had worked on the route. Their work was made arduous by the comparatively primitive state of the road system in the 1930s, and it is a monument to their dedication.

Directions

Continue southwestward. When you reach the mouth of Camp Bliss Hollow, the road will reach a fork. *Turn right* here. You are now on FARM ROAD 2070 (OLD WIRE ROAD). *Drive* along the edge of Flat Creek valley for 0.5 mile to McDowell. *Turn left* at the stop sign onto COUNTY VV, which is located on the northern side of the valley of Flat Creek. Sigel's two divisions reached McDowell by marching from the north along this stretch of road. *Drive* a short distance south, and you will soon encounter another intersection in the valley of Flat Creek. Here COUNTY C comes up from the southeast. *Continue driving straight* onto the continuation of COUNTY C as it curves to the southwest.

Now you have reached a point where the original roadbed of Wire Road, from McDowell to Brights Spring, is gone. You will have to bypass this 1.5-mile break by driving on the modern road system.

COUNTY C leaves Flat Creek valley and heads due west. At 0.8 mile after crossing the bridge over Flat Creek, *turn left* onto FARM ROAD 1142, which heads due south. After 0.7 mile

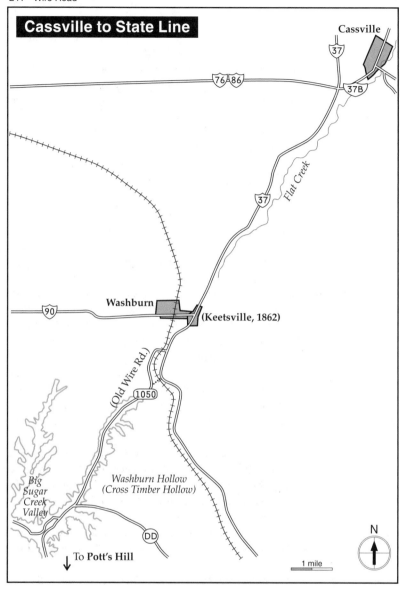

Cassville to State Line

Cassville

76 86

37B

Flat Creek

37

90

Washburn

(Keetsville, 1862)

(Old Wire Rd.)

1050

Big
Sugar
Creek
Valley

Washburn Hollow
(Cross Timber Hollow)

DD

↓ To **Pott's Hill**

1 mile

N

the gravel road descends into a branch of Flat Creek valley. Here you will encounter yet another intersection. *Turn left* onto FARM ROAD 2085 (OLD WIRE ROAD BYPASS) and *drive* another 0.5 mile to a very sharp turn to the right in the middle of the valley.

You have now rejoined the original roadbed of WIRE ROAD. To the left it stretches for a few hundred yards as a private road. *Turn right* to continue on FARM ROAD 2085, and you will quickly enter the hamlet of Brights Spring.

As you *continue driving south* of Brights Spring, you will encounter another village, named Star City, after about 2.5 miles. Here the road briefly joins COUNTY U, and there is a 0.75-mile stretch of pavement. COUNTY U then makes a ninety-degree turn to the right into Dog Hollow. *Turn left* onto FARM ROAD 1135, continuing along the valley of Flat Creek, but reset your odometer when you leave the county road.

As you drive the remaining 7 miles to Cassville (the road soon becomes paved), note the topography of Flat Creek valley. It is a wide and spacious landscape with an irregular line of bluffs to either side that are deeply cut by numerous ravines. There was no good place along Flat Creek for *Price* to make a stand. A more-narrow valley with steep and difficult bluffs would have been ideal for a delaying action by the rear guard.

Continue driving in the valley, avoiding the numerous side roads that lead to right and left. At 5.5 miles from COUNTY U, you will encounter a major fork in the road at Pilant Cemetery. *Bear left* onto FARM ROAD 1120, which continues along the valley of Flat Creek, and reset your odometer. At 0.9 mile from Pilant Cemetery, you will enter Cassville on PARTRIDGE STREET. At a stop sign 0.1 mile farther on, *turn left* onto MAIN STREET (COUNTY Y). Another 0.1 mile farther on you will see MISSOURI 37B join MAIN STREET. *Turn left* and follow it into downtown, passing the Barry County Courthouse in Cassville. Markers concerning the Civil War and Cassville are on the courthouse lawn.

Reset your odometer at the courthouse. MISSOURI 37 joins MISSOURI 37 1.3 miles away. *Turn left* here and *continue* through the valley of Flat Creek, noticing that it is even wider and more shallow here than north of Cassville. Also note that the highway hugs the northern edge of the valley and thus does not conform exactly to the original roadbed of WIRE ROAD, which meandered back and forth across the valley floor.

Vignette

At 7.9 miles from the courthouse in Cassville, you will enter the north side of Washburn. This is the original site of the Civil War–era town named Keetsville. It had been settled by a man named Washburn about 1828 and originally named after him. But the name was changed to Keetsville, after Thomas and James Keets, about 1846. The Keets brothers later moved to Springfield, opening up the opportunity for yet another name change for this little town. The place was known as O'Day for a few months in 1860 when surveyors plotted the route of the St. Louis and San Francisco Railroad through the area. Yet it was widely known as Keetsville by the armies that marched through it during the Civil War.

The railroad was not built before the war broke out, and Wire Road remained the town's only link with the outside world.

This collection of buildings along MISSOURI 37 marks the original site of the village. After the war, when the railroad was finally constructed, it bypassed the town about three quarters of a mile to the west. The residents built along the railroad track and once again called their community Washburn. Today the town is located in both spots, along the two major transportation arteries that existed in the nineteenth century.

Directions

The valley of Flat Creek ends just before you reach the site of Keetsville. South of town Wire Road entered Cross Timber Hollow, today known as Washburn Hollow. *Continue* on MISSOURI 37 out of old Keetsville. At 9.9 miles south of the Cassville courthouse, *turn right* onto FARM ROAD 1050 (OLD WIRE ROAD). This crosses the railroad about 1 mile north of the original Wire Road crossing of the track, but that crossing is no longer accessible. Driving across the railroad, you will soon join the original roadbed of Wire Road and enter the head of Cross Timber Hollow about 1.3 miles from MISSOURI 37.

What Happened

This is the most pristine stretch of Wire Road. The roadbed is exactly the same as it was in 1862, winding from one side of the narrow valley to the other, fording the stream about eight times in two miles. The only improvement is that it is graveled. The road is one lane wide so you are urged to drive with extra caution. Also, be particularly careful when driving over the fords as any recent rains may have raised the water level.

The Conklings found this portion of Wire Road to be as primitive as possible in the 1930s. They described it as "a narrow country lane traversing a sparsely settled region, . . . a picturesque and pleasing country that appears to have undergone but little change since the days of the mail coach. Some sections of the road here are almost hidden in a dense and impenetrable jungle-like growth of rushes, cane, alders and willow, quite sub-tropical in character, and that assumes a height in places, twice that of an automobile."[3]

This was a good place for *Price* to have his rear guard make a delaying stand. Not only is the hollow narrow but also the road often runs between the bluff and the creek, where the two come close together. Since the creek is deep enough to prevent wheeled vehicles and cannon from crossing it anywhere except along the road, this was an ideal place for an ambush. The natural strength of the location was enhanced by a timber blockade that *McCulloch* had constructed in November 1861, when he prepared for a possible invasion of Arkansas by Maj. Gen. John C. Frémont after the latter occupied Springfield. His men cut thousands of trees along the road for about four miles inside the hollow. When Maj. Gen. David Hunter replaced Frémont and the Federals retreated to Rolla, the Confederates cut a narrow, winding passage through the blockade to open up the road for wagon traffic. Thus Cross Timber Hollow gained its local name.

Price had no intention of making a stand here with his whole army, though it would have been a good place for one, because he was intent on joining *McCulloch* in Arkansas. His Missourians marched swiftly through the hollow on February 16. Col. Elijah *Gates's 1st Missouri Cavalry* and two guns of Capt. Churchill *Clark's Missouri Battery* were left at a bend in the valley to keep watch for the pursuing enemy. You will notice such a sharp bend about two and a half miles inside the hollow, which is the possible site of this position. Ellis's 1st Missouri Cavalry, still the vanguard of Curtis's army, came on this contingent and halted. When the head of the first infantry unit, Col. Jefferson C. Davis's 3rd Division, arrived on the scene, the Rebels evacuated.

Still, the Yankees were wary. There were too many possibilities for a deadly ambush in this hollow. Davis and Ellis worked out a plan. The cavalrymen would gallop ahead and hope to clear the timber blockade before the Rebels could establish another strong position. Taking a deep breath, hundreds of Federal horsemen thundered behind the impetuous Ellis and soon found themselves out of the wilderness and into the broad open valley of Big Sugar Creek. Cross Timber Hollow had been cleared.

Directions

Stay on FARM ROAD 1050, driving carefully through the hollow. Near its mouth you will encounter an intersection with COUNTY DD, a paved road joining Wire Road from the left, at 14.5 miles from the courthouse in Cassville. *Turn right* at the stop sign and *continue* driving down the hollow on the continuation southwestward of COUNTY DD. You will enter the head of Big Sugar Creek valley, an expansive feature that stretches off to the west. The road hugs the eastern bluffs and curves southward into the southern arm of Cross Timber Hollow, leading toward Elkhorn Tavern. At 16 miles from the courthouse in Cassville the paved road ends at the state line. Here on February 16 was fought the first engagement on Arkansas soil in the Civil War, the skirmish at Pott's Hill. (This action is described in Pea Ridge Stop 16).

SECTION 4	State line to Cross Hollow, Arkansas

Directions

The route of Wire Road from the MISSOURI-ARKANSAS STATE LINE southward to Cross Hollow has already been described in Part 2. This sixteen-mile stretch of the road was closely involved in the final movements that led to the battle of Pea Ridge. For information on the road and events here, refer to Pea Ridge Stop 16, which deals with the skirmish at Pott's Hill.

The directions at the end of Stop 16 will tell you how to drive from here around the east side of Pea Ridge National Military Park and reach the park's entrance on U.S. 62.

From the park entrance, you can follow the directions in Stops 11–13 to drive along the route of Wire Road across Little Sugar Creek, visit the site of the battle at Little Sugar Creek (Dunagin's Farm) on February 17, drive through the postwar towns of Avoca and Rogers, and reach the site of the Confederate winter encampment at Cross Hollow.

After reading about its route in Stops 11–13, you can resume the Wire Road driving tour south from Cross Hollow.

A very raw recruit. BLCW 1:262

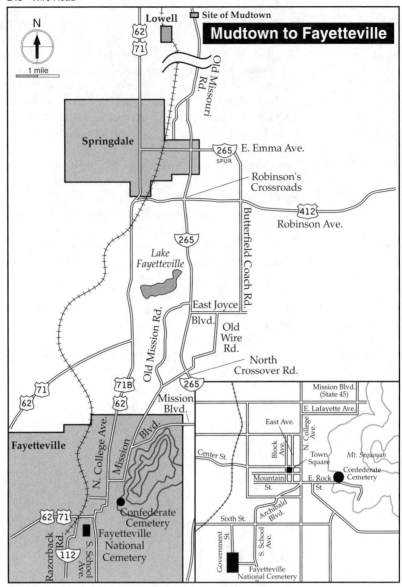

SECTION 5 Cross Hollow to Strickler's Station, Arkansas

Directions Be careful as you *drive* south on SOUTH OLD WIRE ROAD from
the crossroads in Cross Hollow; the road is roughly paved in
gravel. Reset your odometer at the crossroads, for you will
need it to find your way along the road system, part of which
is not thoroughly marked. After *driving* south 1.1 miles from
Cross Hollow, you will reach the level upland and enter a

paved segment of the road. At a three-way stop 1.6 miles from the crossroads, *bear left*. At 2 miles from the crossroad, you will see a granite marker on the right (west) of the road at the Lowell city limits.

What Happened

This marker, which is fenced in, indicates the site of a village officially named Bloomington, which was more popularly known as Mudtown during the Civil War. Here some of Brig. Gen. Alexander Asboth's troopers drank what they thought was liquor and died soon after Curtis's capture of Cross Hollow, an incident that infuriated many Union soldiers. Asboth later launched his cavalry reconnaissance toward Fayetteville from Mudtown on February 22. The settlement was destroyed by a tornado after the war. Rather than rebuild it, residents simply moved the village a couple of miles west to be near the new railroad that was built through the area in 1881. They named their new town Lowell, adding yet a third name to the little collection of houses.

As you continue south from the site of Mudtown, keep in mind that the modern road system often incorporates the original roadbed of WIRE ROAD. In other places it bypasses the original, and at other places it is impossible to tell for certain whether you are on the original roadbed or not.

Directions

Drive south from Mudtown. At 5.3 miles from the crossroads in Cross Hollow, the road widens into four lanes and is called OLD MISSOURI ROAD. You will come to a stoplight at 6.2 miles. *Continue south* to a second stoplight at 6.7 miles. Here ARKANSAS 265 SPUR (EAST EMMA AVENUE) crosses OLD MISSOURI ROAD east to west. As YOU *continue south* the road is now labeled ARKANSAS 265. You will follow this highway for the most part all the way from here to Strickler's Station. This second stoplight is just east of the post–Civil War town of Springdale.

At 9 miles from the crossroads in Cross Hollow, you will intersect U.S. 412 (Robinson Avenue), which crosses ARKANSAS 265 east to west. This junction is known as Robinson's Crossroads. U.S. 412 follows the Civil War–era road that connected Huntsville to the east with the Robinson settlement in the western part of Benton County. The settlement was founded by Revolutionary War veteran John Robinson about 1837.

Reset your odometer and *turn left* onto ROBINSON AVENUE. *Go* 1.3 miles and *turn right* at the stoplight onto BUTTERFIELD COACH ROAD. *Follow* this south; it becomes OLD WIRE ROAD. At Oakland Cemetery, approximately 3 miles, *turn right* onto EAST JOYCE BOULEVARD. *Drive* 0.4 mile, *turn left* onto OLD WIRE ROAD, and *proceed* to the intersection with ARKANSAS 265 (NORTH CROSSOVER ROAD). *Continue through* the intersection on

OLD WIRE ROAD; it will soon merge with ARKANSAS 45 (MISSION BOULEVARD).

Turn right onto MISSION and continue to its junction with EAST LAFAYETTE STREET. Turn right (west) and go a short distance to NORTH COLLEGE AVENUE (U.S. 71B). You are now in the downtown area of Fayetteville. Turn left onto COLLEGE and drive south one block, then turn left onto EAST DICKSON STREET. Drive a short distance to the Tebbetts House at 118 EAST DICKSON STREET.

Vignette

This house was owned by Jonas M. Tebbetts, an outspoken Unionist. The first Union troops to enter Fayetteville were Asboth's cavalrymen, who rode into town on February 22, 1862. Tebbetts invited the general to use his house as headquarters. An eccentric Hungarian, Asboth and his pet dog, a huge St. Bernard named York, ate dinner with the family. The youngest child, Marion Tebbetts, remembered that her mother became very angry when the general ate the family's last jar of jelly by himself. Asboth's cavalry evacuated Fayetteville on February 26, leaving the town unoccupied by either army for a while. The Tebbetts home is maintained by the Washington County Historical Society, which has named it the Headquarters House.

Directions

Leaving the Headquarters House, drive back to NORTH COLLEGE AVENUE and turn left. Drive three blocks south and turn right onto CENTER STREET. Drive west to the town square.

What Happened

The original Wire Road entered Fayetteville from the northeast and snaked its way to the center of town. Read the description of the Confederate evacuation of Fayetteville just before the battle of Pea Ridge at Pea Ridge Stop 13. This square was the scene of chaotic destruction as the retreating Rebels of McCulloch's and Price's commands ransacked government stores and set fire to a number of buildings in town. Fayetteville was briefly visited by Asboth's cavalry force soon afterward and then again evacuated. The town lay in the no-man's land between the armies for several days before Van Dorn's advancing army once again passed through on its way to attack Curtis. Finally, a portion of the defeated Confederate army retreated through town after Pea Ridge. A semblance of peace once again settled over the community after both Van Dorn and Curtis moved their forces eastward, only to once again become the focal point of major operations when the Prairie Grove campaign occurred later in 1862. Brig. Gen. Francis J. Herron's two Union divisions rested in Fayetteville on the night of December 6 after a three-day forced march on Wire Road from the vicinity of Wilson Creek. The next morning they hurried on to Prairie Grove, ten miles to the southwest. For several weeks after the battle, every church, school, and large private dwelling in Fayetteville was filled with wounded Union soldiers.

Directions

It is impossible to drive directly along the original Wire Road south from the town square, for the modern street system in south Fayetteville does not conform to it. The road left the square by way of MOUNTAIN AVENUE, but that street does not continue out of town. *Circle* the square counterclockwise, taking MOUNTAIN AVENUE back to NORTH COLLEGE AVENUE. *Turn right* and drive south. There are two cemeteries of Civil War interest on your way out of town. *Turn left* almost immediately onto EAST ROCK STREET and drive a short distance until you come to the Confederate Cemetery. There are 622 Rebel soldiers buried here—only 121 are known. Several of them died as a result of the battle of Pea Ridge, but records are far too scanty to accurately estimate how many. William Y. *Slack*, who was mortally wounded on March 7 while leading his Missouri brigade into action near Elkhorn Tavern, is buried here. His remains were removed from their original resting place and reinterred here on May 27, 1880, with his widow, sister, and two sons in attendance. The youngest son had been born six months before Pea Ridge; *Slack* never saw him.

Drive back to COLLEGE and *turn left*. The street soon curves and is renamed ARCHIBALD YELL AVENUE. *Turn right* onto SIXTH STREET and look for the sign for Fayetteville National Cemetery. *Turn left* at the sign onto GOVERNMENT STREET. The cemetery was created in 1867 and contains 810 unknown dead. Of the identified bodies, 110 died as a result of the Pea Ridge campaign, 20 died at the battle of Cane Hill, and 144 lost their lives because of the battle of Prairie Grove.

Leave the cemetery the way you came and *turn left* onto SIXTH STREET. *Proceed* west 0.6 mile and *turn left* onto RAZORBACK ROAD (ARKANSAS 112). You are now heading south on the original roadbed of Wire Road. RAZORBACK ROAD becomes ARKANSAS 265. *Drive* straight through the INTERSTATE 540 overpass, but reset your odometer at the overpass. The rest of the drive to Strickler's Station is easy. When you have gone 16.3 miles south of the overpass, you will find COUNTY 215 extending to the right (west). This is the crossroad that connected *McCulloch's* camps at Strickler's with *Price's* camps at Cove Creek. You can drive along the county road, which is rather rugged and steep, over the spiny ridge separating the

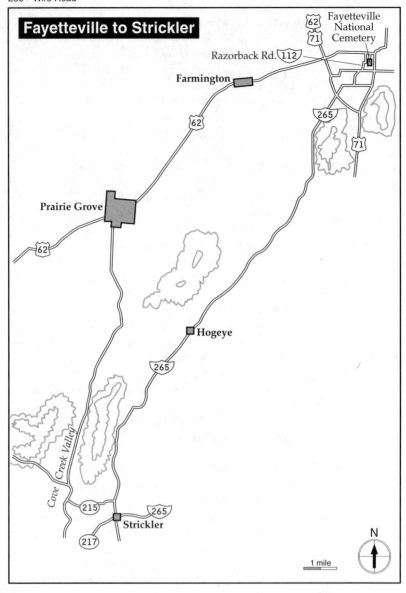

Fayetteville to Strickler

Fayetteville
National
Cemetery
62
71

Razorback Rd. 112

Farmington

62

265

71

Prairie Grove

62

Hogeye

265

Cove Creek Valley

215   265

Strickler

217

N

1 mile

two encampments; the distance is about 1.5 miles. When you reach the bottom of Cove Creek, note the rugged but secure valley, then *drive back* to ARKANSAS 265. Additional information about Cove Creek valley may be found in the "Driving Tour of the Prairie Grove Campaign" in Part 3, especially Stops 18, 19a, and 19b.

Turn right and *continue south* on the highway for about 0.5 mile to Strickler's Station, now known simply as Strickler.

There is no marker here, but at 1,560 feet in elevation, it is the highest point on Wire Road in either Missouri or Arkansas. You will notice that the road forks. COUNTY 217, which is the continuation of Wire Road, goes to the right; ARKANSAS 265 makes a ninety-degree turn to the left (east).

Union Camp—a quiet game.
From a war-time sketch. BLCW 3:148

SECTION 6   Strickler's Station to Fort Smith, Arkansas

This section of Wire Road was the most rugged of all, and it quickly became almost legendary for the hair-raising journeys it offered travelers. The postmaster general's report for 1858 stated that it was "impossible that any road could be worse." A newspaper reporter for the *New York Herald*, who rode over the Boston Mountains that same year, agreed. "I had thought that before we reached this point that the rough roads of Missouri and Arkansas could not be equalled; but here, Arkansas fairly beats itself. I might say our road was steep, rugged, jagged, rough and mountainous—and then wish for more impressive words in the language." Another traveler named William Talleck, who rode the stagecoach in July 1860, was fearful of accidents. "Our principle danger was the extreme liability to an overset; but, though often apparently within a hair's breadth, we escaped the unpleasantness also, and here again we were better off than our predecessors[sic] by the same route a month afterwards, who were overturned in the night whilst going down a hill near Fort Smith, in Arkansas. One passenger was killed on the spot, and several others seriously injured."[4]

The road between Strickler's Station and Fort Smith was hardly improved for many decades. When the Conklings drove their car along it seventy years later, they felt lucky to have escaped from the wilderness. "South from Strickler's the country road, which is much the same as the old mail road, becomes increasingly rough and treacherous, especially in bad weather. Winding down through the Boston mountains and crossing the boundary line of Washington and Crawford counties, the road narrows down to a torturous one-way trail, almost impassable in places, where there is scarcely enough clearance for the wheel hubs of an automobile between the tree trunks and the boulders that strew the way, and though the distance is relatively short, each mile covered seems ten in reality. Not until the old ford on Lee creek, now spanned by an iron bridge, is reached, is this roughest of rides over."[5]

You need not worry about encountering such perilous difficulties. The way has been graded, widened, and paved with gravel since the 1930s. But you should exercise caution, for there are places where numerous rocks still poke out of the roadbed and erosion has created unauthorized grading. In wet weather parts of the road can become all but impassable except for off-road vehicles. Drive slowly and carefully, and enjoy the ride.

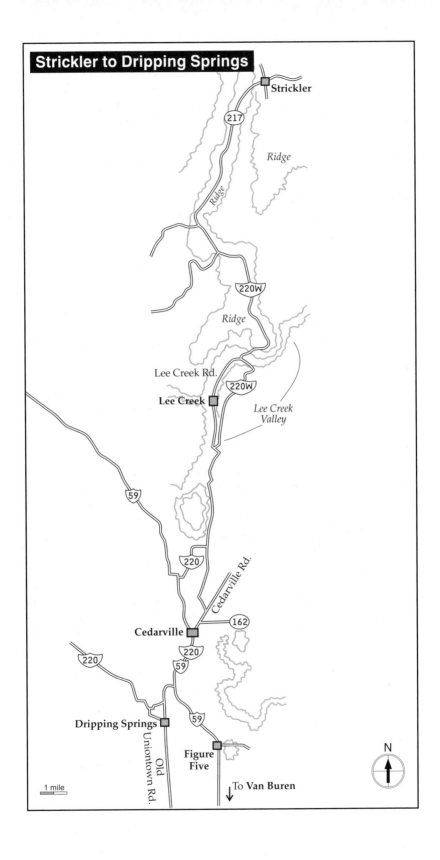

Strickler to Dripping Springs

Strickler

217

Ridge

Ridge

220W

Ridge

Lee Creek Rd.

220W

Lee Creek

*Lee Creek
Valley*

59

220

Cedarville Rd.

162

Cedarville

220

220

59

59

Dripping Springs

**Figure
Five**

Old
Uniontown Rd.

To **Van Buren**

1 mile

N

Directions Reset your odometer before starting from Strickler's Station. *Proceed* on COUNTY 217, which is paved for 3.2 miles, at which point it begins to enter the Boston Mountains. Note as you drive along that you may see the remnants of an unimproved roadbed to the side of COUNTY 217, which was the earlier version of Wire Road.

You will also see several road junctions along the route, but always *continue straight ahead*, going south. About 7 miles from Strickler's *turn right* onto ARKANSAS 220W, which also is unpaved.

Continue south for 3.3 miles to the valley of Lee Creek, the major watercourse in this part of the Boston Mountains. It has a wide, deep valley and was forded by the Butterfield stages. The road becomes paved just before you cross the bridge, but it is still marked as ARKANSAS 220W. It runs along the bottomland for 0.8 mile before leaving the valley to the left (east). Before you leave the valley, *turn right* onto LEE CREEK ROAD. This gravel road is the continuation of Wire Road. You will rejoin the highway 3.2 miles farther south, but for now *continue* along LEE CREEK ROAD. You will pass through a string of houses, the modern village of Lee Creek, along the way. The road will leave the valley and quickly rejoin ARKANSAS 220W.

The broad valley of Lee Creek was the staging area for *Hindman's* army prior to the battle of Prairie Grove. After their defeat the Confederates returned here to regroup before falling back to Van Buren and Fort Smith. Lee Creek was the junction of Wire Road and Cove Creek Road.

Turn right and *drive* south on ARKANSAS 220W. At 4.3 miles from the intersection, the highway makes a ninety-degree turn to the right (west), but you will *continue driving south* on an unmarked gravel road, the original roadbed of Wire Road. After 2.2 miles *turn right* onto CEDARVILLE ROAD. *Proceed* another 0.7 mile and *turn right* again onto COUNTY 162, then almost immediately *turn left* onto ARKANSAS 59. This intersection is in a village named Cedarville. *Continue south* on ARKANSAS 59, a modern road, for 1.9 miles, then *turn right* onto ARKANSAS 220, which puts you back on Wire Road. After 1 mile the highway makes a ninety-degree turn to the right (west), but you will *continue south* on an unmarked gravel road. This is another section of the original roadbed of Wire Road. After 0.4 mile *stop* at the intersection with a paved road. This is Dripping Springs, and the paved road is Old Uniontown Road.

What Happened The field in the northwest angle of the intersection (to your right rear) was the site of a sharp engagement between Lt.

Col. Owen A. Bassett's 2nd Kansas Cavalry and Lt. Col. Phillip *Crump's 1st Texas Partisan Rangers* on December 28, 1862, as Blunt's army dashed toward Van Buren. The Confederates were routed, abandoned their train, and fled south, with the Federals in hot pursuit.

You may wish to walk across the paved road to the house in the southwest angle of the intersection. Stand at the gate and look into the yard. Barely visible (but clearly audible) to your right front is Dripping Springs, a famous landmark and stopping place. *Hindman's* army camped below the spring going to and coming from Prairie Grove, and Blunt's army did the same a few weeks later on the way back from Van Buren.

Directions

Drive south through the intersection and onto Old Uniontown Road, the route of Wire Road, for 4.2 miles, then *turn right* onto ARKANSAS 59. Continue south through Van Buren. After passing Interstate 40 you will ascend a steep hill called Mount Vista. At the top, if conditions permit, *pull over* and enjoy the panoramic view of Van Buren, the Arkansas River, and the Ouachita Mountains in the distance. Blunt and Herron halted here for a few minutes before storming down the hill into Van Buren.

What Happened

As you descend from the Boston Mountains and enter the wide valley of the Arkansas River, keep in mind that Van Buren was the end point of the Pea Ridge campaign for *Van Dorn's* Army of the West. It encamped in the bottomland near the town after its harrowing adventure and spent a few days recuperating before starting out on a long eastward march to join the Confederate concentration at Corinth, Mississippi. Van Buren also was both the beginning point and the end point of the Prairie Grove campaign for *Hindman's* Army of the Trans-Mississippi.

Throughout the war, 433 unknown Confederate dead were buried at Van Buren, the victims of illnesses and wounds received at Wilson's Creek, Pea Ridge, and Prairie Grove. Missourians made up half this total. The remains of Capt. Churchill *Clark*, who was killed leading his Missouri battery on March 8 at Pea Ridge, were placed in the foundation of a monument erected on the Crawford County Courthouse lawn in 1899. The monument honors the memory of these Confederate dead, but *Clark's* is the only name chiseled on its face. The courthouse is at the corner of MAIN STREET and THIRD STREET. You will pass by it when you reach downtown.

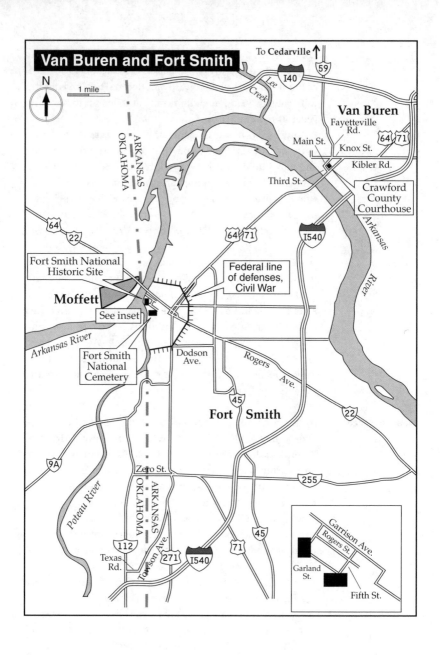

Directions

As you near downtown Van Buren, ARKANSAS 59 becomes MAIN STREET. The Old District of town, with many late-nineteenth-century buildings, stretches along a section of the street, giving it something of a Civil War–era flavor. The Butterfield stages had to cross the Arkansas River by using a ferry at the end of MAIN. Today, though, you will *turn left* onto FOURTH STREET and intersect with U.S. 64/71, then *turn right* and *drive* across a modern bridge over the river. The elevation here on the river bank is a mere 400 feet, more than 1,100 feet lower than Strickler's Station.

You are now entering the inside of a large projection of land formed by a graceful curve of the Arkansas River to the north. In 1862 there were no houses here; Fort Smith and a small collection of civilian homes around it was four miles to the southwest on the shoulder of the curve. Today this entire area is filled up with the expansive city of Fort Smith. *Continue* along U.S. 64/71 toward downtown, where the original fort was located. *Follow* U.S. 64 as it separates from U.S. 71, *turns right* onto GARRISON AVENUE, and *passes* through downtown. *Follow* the signs to Fort Smith National Historic Site, before the highway crosses the river, by *turning left* onto FIFTH STREET, then *right* onto ROGERS AVENUE.

What Happened

Fort Smith has a rich frontier history as well as a significant role in the story of the Civil War. Built by the U.S. government in 1817 to keep peace in the Indian Territory, it is located at the junction of the Arkansas River and the much smaller Poteau River. The army temporarily abandoned it in 1824 in favor of another post, Fort Gibson, built inside the territory. But the flood of Native Americans and white settlers coming to the region during Indian Removal prompted authorities to construct a new post on the site in 1838. Originally designed as a masonry fortification, the plans were later modified to turn the post into a supply depot. A masonry wall with bastions enclosed the compound, located about 500 feet northeast of the original fort.

The Confederates held Fort Smith from the beginning of the war until they abandoned it to Federal forces on September 1, 1863. The Yankees built an outer line of defense, consisting of a trench with two blockhouses, that protected both the compound and the small town to the northwest of it. The line extended about a mile from the fort and the town in a semicircle from the Poteau River on the right to the Arkansas River on the left.

The army again abandoned the post in 1871 with the shifting of the frontier farther west, but the Federal Court for the

Western District of Arkansas took over the compound the next year. This court had jurisdiction over the Indian Territory as well as western Arkansas, and Judge Isaac C. Parker presided over it from 1875 to 1896. Gaining a reputation for toughness, Parker worked in one of the most difficult judicial arenas in America, for the Indian Territory became a refuge for white outlaws who understood that Indian laws did not apply to them. Only Judge Parker and his handful of marshals could find, arrest, and try white lawbreakers in the Indian Territory. With the growth of white settlements and the creation of judicial systems in the territory, Judge Parker's jurisdiction over it was progressively reduced until Congress eliminated it entirely in 1896. Harried by the strenuous workload of twenty years, Parker died a few weeks later.

Today you can see only a trace of the Civil War–era facilities at Fort Smith. The outer line of entrenchments is gone, destroyed by the rapid growth of the city. Only the foundations of one bastion of the masonry wall that was built in 1838 remains intact. The historic site mainly highlights the postwar history of Fort Smith, with buildings and a jail associated with Judge Parker's court open to visitors and a reconstructed gallows on the grounds.

Fort Smith National Cemetery is near the compound, only two blocks away along Garland Street. Brig. Gen. James *McIntosh*, who was killed at Leetown on March 7 after he took command of *McCulloch's* Division, and Col. Alexander A. *Steen*, killed in the final Confederate charge at Prairie Grove, are buried here.

You have completed the driving tour of Wire Road from Springfield to Fort Smith. The Butterfield stages continued to travel south from here on what was popularly known as the Texas Road, also known as the Fort Towson Trail. It was surveyed by the army in 1827 to connect Fort Smith with Fort Towson in the Indian Territory. When later extended to Texas, the road developed its more popular name. This section *began* at the intersection of Garrison Avenue and Towson Avenue, where U.S. 64 and 71 separate, and *went south* along Towson. This is also the route of U.S. 71. South of DODSON AVENUE, the southern boundary of Fort Smith until 1890, the road wound through the countryside. *Follow* Towson a couple of miles. U.S. 71 will then branch off to the left, but *continue south* on Towson, which is now marked U.S. 271. Shortly after this, *turn right* again onto TEXAS ROAD, leaving both TOWSON and U.S. 271. TEXAS ROAD becomes unpaved, crosses the state line into Oklahoma, and intersects OKLAHOMA 112. This is as far as you can go in tracing the route of the Butterfield stages out of Fort Smith. *Turn left* onto OKLAHOMA 112 and *enter* IN-TERSTATE 540 0.5 mile south. From here you may go in any direction to your next destination.

Union cavalry scouting in front of
Confederate advance. BLCW 3:244

Appendix: Orders of Battle

WILSON'S CREEK

Union Forces

Abbreviations:

BDE: brigade

BN: battalion

S.S.: sharpshooters

CO: company

ARMY OF THE WEST (Lyon)

Lyon's Bodyguard (unkn.)

Voerster's Pioneer CO (Voerster)

1ST BDE (Sturgis)

2nd MO (Osterhaus)

BN of Regulars (Plummer)

COS B, C, D, 1st U.S.; Lt. H. C. Wood's CO of recruits

CO D, 1st U.S. Cavalry (Canfield)

KS Rangers, Mounted CO I, 2nd KS (S. Wood)

Mounted Home Guard COS (Switzler and Wright)

Totten's Battery, CO F, 2nd U.S. Artillery (Totten)

2ND BDE (Sigel)

3rd MO (Albert)

5th MO (Salomon)

CO I, 1st U.S. Cavalry (Carr)

CO C, 2nd U.S. Dragoons (Farrand)

Backof's Battery, MO Lt. Artillery (Schaefer)

3RD BDE (Andrews)

BN of Regulars (Steele)

COS B and E, 2nd U.S.; Lothrop's CO of recruits;
    Morine's CO of recruits

1st MO (Andrews)

Du Bois's Battery (Du Bois)

4TH BDE (Deitzler)

1st IA (Merritt)

1st KS (Deitzler)

2nd KS (Mitchell) [minus S. Wood's CO]

13th IL BN (Beardsley)

RESERVES IN SPRINGFIELD

CO B, 1st U.S. Cavalry (unkn.)

CO C, 1st U.S. Cavalry (Stabley)

Green and Christian County Home Guards (Boyd)

Section (two guns), Backof's Battery (unkn.)

Southern Forces   **WESTERN ARMY** (McCulloch)

Reiff's AR Cavalry CO (Reiff)

MCCULLOCH'S CONFEDERATE BDE (McIntosh)

3rd LA (Hébert)

South KS-TX Cavalry (Greer)

1st AR Mounted Rifles (Churchill)

2nd AR Mounted Rifles (McIntosh)

ARKANSAS STATE TROOPS (Pearce)

3rd AR (Gratiot)

4th AR (Walker)

5th AR (Dockery)

Carroll's Cavalry (C. Carroll)

1st AR Cavalry (D. Carroll)

Fort Smith Lt. Battery (Reid)

Pulaski Lt. Battery (Woodruff)

MISSOURI STATE GUARD (Price)

3rd Division (Clark)

Burbrdge's Infantry (Burbridge)

Major's Cavalry (Major)

4th Division (Slack)

Hughes's Infantry (Hughes)

Rives's Cavalry (Rives)

6th Division (Parsons)

Kelly's Infantry (Kelly)

Brown's Cavalry (Brown)

Guibor's Battery (Guibor)

7th Division (McBride)

Wingo's Infantry (Wingo)

Foster's Infantry (Foster)

8th Division (Rains)

Weightman's Infantry (Weightman)

Cawthorn's Cavalry (Cawthorn)

Bledsoe's Battery (Bledsoe)

PEA RIDGE

Union Forces ARMY OF THE SOUTHWEST (Curtis)

> 24th MO (Weston)
>
> 3rd IA Cavalry (Bussey)
>
> Bowen's MO Cavalry BN (Bowen)

1ST AND 2ND DIVISIONS (Sigel)

1st Division (Osterhaus)

1ST BDE (Osterhaus)

> 25th IL (Coler)
>
> 44th IL (Knobelsdorff)
>
> 17th MO (Poten)

2ND BDE (Greusel)

> 36th IL (Greusel)
>
> 12th MO (Wangelin)
>
> 4th Independent Battery, OH Lt. Artillery (Hoffman)
>
> Welfley's Independent Battery, MO Lt. Artillery (Welfley)

2nd Division (Asboth)

1ST BDE (Schaefer)

> 2nd MO (Laiboldt)
>
> 15th MO (Joliat)
>
> 1st MO Flying Battery (Elbert)
>
> 2nd Independent Battery, OH Lt. Artillery (Chapman)

NOT BRIGADED

> 3rd MO (Conrad)
>
> 4th MO Cavalry (Meszaros)
>
> 5th MO Cavalry (Nemett)

3rd Division (Davis)

1ST BDE (Pattison)

> 8th IN (Benton)
>
> 18th IN (Washburn)
>
> 22nd IN (Hendricks)
>
> 1st Battery, IN Lt. Artillery (Klauss)

2ND BDE (White)

> 37th IL (Barnes)
>
> 59th IL (Frederick)
>
> Battery A, 2nd IL Lt. Artillery (Davidson)

NOT BRIGADED

> 1st MO Cavalry (Ellis)

4th Division (Carr)

1ST BDE (Dodge)

  4th IA (Galligan)

  35th IL (Smith)

  1st Independent Battery, IA Lt. Artillery (Jones)

  3rd IL Cavalry (McConnell)

2ND BDE (Vandever)

  9th IA (Herron)

  25th MO (Phelps)

  3rd Independent Battery, IA Lt. Artillery (Hayden)

Confederate Forces   **ARMY OF THE WEST** (Van Dorn)

McCulloch's Division (McCulloch)

HÉBERT'S BDE (Hébert)

  3rd LA (Tunnard)

  4th AR (McNair)

  14th AR (Mitchell)

  15th AR (McRae)

  16th AR (Hill)

  17th AR (Rector)

  1st AR Mounted Rifles (dismounted) (Churchill)

  2nd AR Mounted Rifles (dismounted) (Embry)

  4th TX Cavalry BN (dismounted) (Whitfield)

MCINTOSH'S BDE (McIntosh)

  3rd TX Cavalry (Greer)

  6th TX Cavalry (Stone)

  9th TX Cavalry (Sims)

  11th TX Cavalry (Young)

  1st AR Cavalry BN (Brooks)

  1st TX Cavalry BN (Crump)

PIKE'S INDIAN BDE (Pike)

  1st Cherokee Mounted Rifles (Drew)

  2nd Cherokee Mounted Rifles (Watie)

  1st Choctaw and Chickasaw (Cooper)

  1st Creek Mounted Rifles (McIntosh)

  Welch's Texas Cavalry Squadron (Welch)

ARTILLERY: Hart's AR Battery (Hart), Provence's AR Battery
  (Provence), Gaines's AR Battery (Gaines), Good's TX Battery
  (Good)

UNASSIGNED:

  19th AR (Smith)

  20th AR (King)

Price's Division (Price)

Cearnal's MO Cavalry BN (Cearnal)

1ST MO BDE (Little)

2nd MO (Burbridge)

3rd MO (Rives)

Wade's MO Battery (Wade)

Clark's MO Battery (C. Clark)

1st MO Cavalry (Gates)

2ND MO BDE (Slack)

Hughes's MO BN (Hughes)

Bevier's MO BN (Bevier)

Rosser's MO BN (Rosser)

Landis's MO Battery (Landis)

Jackson's MO Battery (Lucas)

Riggins's MO Cavalry BN (Riggins)

3RD MO BDE (Greene)

Several partially organized BNS and COS

MISSOURI STATE GUARD

2nd Division (Green)

Various infantry and cavalry units

Kneisley's Battery (Kneisley)

3rd Division (Clark)

1st Infantry (Rucker)

2nd Infantry (Jackson)

3rd Infantry (Hutchinson)

4th and 5th Infantry (Poindexter)

6th Infantry (Peacher)

Tull's Battery (Tull)

5th Division (Saunders)

Various infantry and cavalry units

Kelly's Battery (Kelly)

6th Division (Lindsay)

Various infantry and cavalry units

Gorham's Battery (Gorham)

7th and 9th Divisions (Frost)

Various infantry and cavalry units

Guibor's Battery (Guibor)

MacDonald's St. Louis Battery (MacDonald)

8th Division (Rains)

1st Infantry (Erwin)

2nd Infantry (Bowman)

3rd Infantry (Pearcy)

4th Infantry (Stemmons)

Shelby's Cavalry co (Shelby)

Bledsoe's Battery (Higgins)

PRAIRIE GROVE

Union Forces   **ARMY OF THE FRONTIER** (Blunt)

1st Division (Blunt)

1ST BDE (Salomon)

  2nd Indian Home Guard (Wright)

  9th wi (Jacobi)

  6th ks Cavalry (Judson)

  9th ks Cavalry (Lynde)

  3rd wi Cavalry (Calkins)

  25th oh Battery (Stockton)

2ND BDE (Weer)

  3rd Indian Home Guard (Phillips)

  10th ks (Williams)

  13th ks (Bowen)

  1st ks Battery (Tenney)

3RD BDE (Cloud)

  1st Indian Home Guard (Wattles)

  11th ks (Ewing)

  2nd ks Cavalry (Bassett)

  2nd in Battery (Rabb)

  2nd ks Battery (Stover)

  3rd ks Battery (Hopkins)

2nd Division (Huston)

1ST BDE (Clark)

  26th in (Clark)

  Battery A, 2nd il (Borris)

2ND BDE (Dye)

  37th il (Black)

  20th ia (Leake)

  Battery F, 1st mo (Murphy)

3rd Division (Herron)

1ST BDE (Bertram)

  20th wi (Starr)

  Battery L, 1st mo (Backof)

2ND BDE (Orme)

　94th IL (McNulta)

　19th IA (McFarland)

　Battery E, 1st MO (Foust)

PROVISIONAL BDE (Wickersham)

　10th IL Cavalry (Stuart)

　1st IA Cavalry (Gower)

　6th MO Cavalry (Montgomery)

　7th MO Cavalry (Bredett)

　8th MO Cavalry (Geiger)

　2nd WI Cavalry (Miller)

UNATTACHED

　1st AR Cavalry (Harrison)

　1st MO Cavalry (Hubbard)

　14th MO State Militia Cavalry (Richardson)

Confederate Forces　　　　　**ARMY OF THE TRANS-MISSISSIPPI** (Hindman)

Roane's Division (Roane)

ROANE'S BDE (Roane)

　20th TX Cavalry (dismounted) (Bass)

　22nd TX Cavalry (dismounted) (Stone)

　31st TX Cavalry (dismounted) (Guess)

　34th TX Cavalry (dismounted) (Alexander)

　9th MO (Clark)

　Reid's AR Battery (Reid)

　Shoup's AR Battery (J. Shoup)

Shoup's Division (F. Shoup)

FAGAN'S BDE (Fagan)

　34th AR (Brooks)

　35th AR (King)

　37th AR (Pleasants)

　39th AR (Hawthorn)

　Chew's AR BN S.S. (Chew)

　Blocher's AR Battery (Blocher)

MCRAE'S BDE (McRae)

　26th AR (Morgan)

　28th AR (Glenn)

　30th AR (McNeill)

　32nd AR (Young)

　Woodruff's (Pulaski) AR Battery (Marshall)

Frost's Division (Frost)

PARSONS'S BDE (Parsons)

  8th MO (Mitchell)

  10th MO (Steen)

  11th MO (Hunter)

  12th MO (Ponder)

  16th MO (Caldwell)

  Pindall's 9th MO BN S.S. (Pindall)

  Tilden's MO Battery (Tilden)

SHAVER'S BDE (Shaver)

  23rd AR (Adams)

  33rd AR (Grinsted)

  38th AR (Adams)

  Robert's MO Battery (Roberts)

Marmaduke's (Cavalry) Division (Marmaduke)

MONROE'S BDE (Monroe)

  Carroll's AR Cavalry (Thomson)

  Monroe's AR Cavalry (Johnson)

SHELBY'S BDE (Shelby)

  5th MO Cavalry (Gordon)

  6th MO Cavalry (Thompson)

  12th MO Cavalry (Jeans)

  Elliott's 9th MO Cavalry BN (Elliott)

  Quantrill's Band (Gregg)

  Bledsoe's MO Battery (Bledsoe)

MACDONALD'S BDE (MacDonald)

  MacDonald's MO Cavalry (Young)

  1st TX Partisan Rangers (Crump)

  West's AR Battery (West)

Notes

Wilson's Creek

1. "A Boy's Experiences at Wilson's Creek," *Volunteer Wire* 18 (September 1998): 3.

2. "In the Ranks under General Lyon in Missouri, 1861: The Observations of a Private Soldier," *Blue and Gray* 4 (1894): 590; Joseph B. Plummer to James Powell, August 16, 1861, in U.S. War Department, *The War of the Rebellion: A Compilation of the Official Records of the Union and Confederate Armies*, 128 vols. (Washington DC: Government Printing Office, 1880–1901), ser. 1, 3:72 [hereafter cited as *OR*; all references are to series 1]; W. H. Tunnard, *A Southern Record: The History of the Third Regiment of Louisiana Infantry* (Fayetteville: University of Arkansas Press, 1997), 29; William Watson, *Life in the Confederate Army* (Baton Rouge: Louisiana State University Press, 1995), 216.

3. Alonzo Shelton, *Memoir of a Confederate Veteran: Alonzo Shelton, 1839–1930* (Clay County MO: Clay County Historical Museum, 1974), 6, 10.

4. William E. Woodruff Jr. to Father, August 12, 1861, in *Little Rock True Democrat*, August 22, 1861.

5. Tunnard, *Southern Record*, 31.

6. Otto C. B. Lademann, "The Battle of Wilson's Creek, August 10, 1861," *War Papers Read before the Commandery of the State of Wisconsin, Military Order of the Loyal Legion of the United States*, vol. 4 (Milwaukee: Burdick and Allen, 1919), 337.

7. William Garrett Piston and Richard W. Hatcher III, *Wilson's Creek: The Second Battle of the Civil War and the Men Who Fought It* (Chapel Hill: University of North Carolina Press, 2000), 244.

8. John M. Schofield, *Forty-six Years in the Army* (New York: Century, 1897), 44.

9. Christopher Phillips, *Damned Yankee: The Life of General Nathaniel Lyon* (Columbia: University of Missouri Press, 1990), 255–56.

10. Thomas L. Snead, *The Fight for Missouri from the Election of Lincoln to the Death of Lyon* (New York: Charles Scribner's Sons, 1886), 286.

11. Pat Carr, ed., *In Fine Spirits: The Civil War Letters of Ras Stirman* (Fayetteville AR: Washington County Historical Society, 1986), 18–19.

Pea Ridge

1. Thomas W. Knox, *Camp-Fire and Cotton-Field: Southern Adventure in Time of War* (New York: Blelock, 1865), 141; *New York Herald*, March 19, 1862.

2. Victor M. Rose, *The Life and Services of Gen. Ben McCulloch* (Philadelphia: Pictorial Bureau of the Press, 1888), 204.

3. Joseph M. Bailey, "The Death of General McCulloch," *Confederate Veteran* 36 (1928): 175.

4. James F. Harris letter, *New Orleans Commercial Bulletin*, April 16, 1862.

5. William Fithian to wife, March 29, 1862, Black Family Papers, Illinois State Historical Library, Springfield.

6. Nannie M. Tilley, ed., *Federals on the Frontier: The Diary of Benjamin F. McIntyre, 1862–1864* (Austin: University of Texas Press, 1963), 42; Noble L. Prentis, *Kansas Miscellanies* (Topeka: Kansas Publishing House, 1889), 46–47.

7. Tunnard, *Southern Record*, 133.

8. Eugene A. Carr quoted in Sam Black, *A Soldier's Recollections of the Civil War* (Minco OK: Minco Minstrel, 1912), 6.

9. Black, *Soldier's Recollections*, 6–7, 10.

10. James Harding, "Personal Reminiscences of Service with the Missouri State Guard," *St. Louis Missouri Republican*, July 18, 25, 1885.

11. Grenville M. Dodge to brother, March 15, 1862, Dodge Family Papers, Denver Public Library.

12. Grenville M. Dodge to sister, April 2, 1862, Dodge Family Papers.

13. William C. Kennerly, *Persimmon Hill: A Narrative of Old St. Louis and the Far West* (Norman: University of Oklahoma Press, 1948), 242.

14. William H. Kinsman letter, *Council Bluffs (Iowa) Weekly Nonpareil*, April 12, 1862.

15. Asa M. Payne, "Story of the Battle of Pea Ridge," Pea Ridge National Military Park.

16. Grenville M. Dodge, *The Battle of Atlanta and Other Campaigns, Addresses, Etc.* (Council Bluffs IA: Monarch, 1911), 22, 36.

17. Samuel R. Curtis quoted in John D. Crabtree, "Recollections of the Pea Ridge Campaign, and the Army of the Southwest, in 1862," in *Military Essays and Recollections: Papers Read before the Commandery of the State of Illinois, Military Order of the Loyal Legion of the United States*, vol. 3 (Chicago: Dial, 1899), 223; Samuel R. Curtis to Henry W. Halleck, April 1, 1862, *OR*, 8:202.

18. John J. Good to wife, March 23, 1862, in Lester Newton Fitzhugh, ed., *Cannon Smoke: The Letters of Captain John J. Good, Good-Douglas Texas Battery, CSA* (Hillsboro TX: Hill Junior College Press, 1971), 171; W. L. Truman, "The Battle of Elk Horn, or Pea Ridge, Arkansas," *Confederate Veteran* 36 (1928): 170.

19. Dabney H. Maury, "Recollections of the Elkhorn Campaign," *Southern Historical Society Papers* 2 (1876): 191–92.

20. Payne, "Battle of Pea Ridge."

21. Peter J. Osterhaus quoted in William G. Bek, ed., "The Civil War Diary of John T. Buegel," *Missouri Historical Review* 40 (1946): 321.

22. Samuel R. Curtis to brother, March 13, 1862, Samuel R. Curtis Papers, Huntington Library, San Marino CA; Silas Miller letter, *Aurora (Ill.) Beacon*, March 27, 1862; George E. Currie quoted in Norman E. Clarke, ed., *Warfare along the Mississippi: The Letters of Lieutenant Colonel George E. Currie* (Mount Pleasant MI: Central Michigan University Press, 1961), 32.

23. George E. Currie quoted in Clarke, *Warfare along the Mississippi*, 19–20.

24. Harding, "Personal Reminiscences," July 18, 25, 1885.

25. Tunnard, *Southern Record*, 130.

26. B. P. Hollinsworth, "Battle of Elkhorn (Arkansas)," *The New Texas School Reader*, comp., J. R. Hutchison (Houston: E. H. Cushing, 1864), 134–35.

27. Junius Henri Browne in *New York Tribune*, March 20, 1862.

28. Nathaniel Bacon to Franz Sigel, March 25, 1862, Franz Sigel Papers, New-York Historical Society.

29. Samuel R. Curtis to Henry W. Halleck, March 10, 1862, Samuel R. Curtis Papers, State Historical Society of Iowa, Des Moines.

30. Samuel R. Curtis to wife, March 13, 1862, Letters Sent, January–October 1862, Army of the Southwest, Records of the War Department, RG 393, National Archives and Records Administration, Washington DC.

31. Washington L. Gammage, *The Camp, the Bivouac, and the Battle Field* (Selma AL, 1864), 24.

32. Benjamin McCulloch quoted in Watson, *Life in the Confederate Army*, 290.

33. Dodge, *Battle of Atlanta*, 19–20.

34. Robert S. Bevier, *History of the First and Second Missouri Confederate Brigades, 1861–1865* (St. Louis: Bryan, Brand, 1879), 90.

Prairie Grove

1. Thomas C. Hindman to S. S. Anderson, December 25, 1862, *OR*, 22(1): 141.

2. Tilley, *Federals on the Frontier*, 67–68.

3. Donald C. Elder, ed., *A Damned Iowa Greyhound: The Civil War Letters of William Henry Harrison Clayton* (Iowa City: University of Iowa Press, 1998), 38–39.

4. Prentis, *Kansas Miscellanies*, 21–22.

5. Robert F. Braden to Mother, December 12, 1862, Robert F. Braden Papers, Indiana State Library, Indianapolis.

6. Alcander O. Morse Journal, December 7, 1862, Prairie Grove Battlefield State Park.

7. Daniel Huston testimony, John C. Black Court of Inquiry, Records of the War Department, RG 94, National Archives and Records Administration, Washington DC.

8. Lurton D. Ingersoll, *Iowa and the Rebellion* (Philadelphia: J. B. Lippincott, 1866), 327.

9. Theo M. Cook, ed., *Immortal Blue: Co. H, 19th Iowa Volunteer Infantry, 1862–1865* (Bonaparte IA, 1966), 15; Tilley, *Federals on the Frontier*, 72–74.

10. William P. Black to Mother, December 9, 1862, Black Family Papers.

11. Albert R. Greene, "Campaigning in the Army of the Frontier," *Collections of the Kansas State Historical Society, 1915–1918*, vol. 14 (Topeka, 1918), 300.

12. Joyce Farlow and Louise Barry, eds., "Vincent Osborne's Civil War Experiences," *Kansas Historical Quarterly* 20 (1952): 207; Spencer H. Mitchell to parents, January 30, 1863, Spencer H. Mitchell Letters, University of Missouri–Columbia.

13. John W. Rabb to William F. Cloud, December 10, 1862, *OR*, 22(1): 100; Henry E. Palmer, "An Outing in Arkansas, or Forty Days and a Week in the Wilderness," in *Civil War Sketches and Incidents: Papers Read by Companions of the Commandery of the State of Nebraska, Military Order of the Loyal Legion of the United States* (Wilmington NC: Broadfoot, 1992), 222.

14. Edwin C. Bearss, ed., *The Civil War Letters of Major William G. Thompson of the 20th Iowa Infantry* (Fayetteville AR: Washington County Historical Society, 1966), 90–91.

15. Nancy Morton Staples, "Personal Recollections," Arkansas History Commission, Little Rock.

16. Chester Barney, *Recollections of Field Service with the Twentieth Iowa Infantry Volunteers: Or, What I Saw in the Army* (Davenport IA: Gazette, 1865), 130.

17. Greene, "Campaigning in the Army of the Frontier," 297.

Wire Road

1. Hiram S. Rumfield to Frank, June 22, 1860, in Archer Butler Hulbert, ed., *Letters of an Overland Mail Agent in Utah* (Worcester MA: American Antiquarian Society, 1929), 14.

2. Prentis, *Kansas Miscellanies*, 13.

3. Roscoe P. Conkling and Margaret B. Conkling, *The Butterfield Overland Mail, 1857–1869*, 3 vols. (Glendale CA: Arthur H. Clark, 1947), 1:191.

4. "Postmaster-General's Report for 1858," quoted in Conkling and Conkling, *Butterfield Overland Mail*, 1:210; Ormsby in *New York Herald*, October 8, 1858, quoted in Conkling and Conkling, *Butterfield Overland Mail*, 1:210; William Talleck, in *The California Overland Express*, quoted in Conkling and Conkling, *Butterfield Overland Mail*, 1:211.

5. Conkling and Conkling, *Butterfield Overland Mail*, 1:209.

Headquarters in the field. BLCW 1:399

Sources	Shortened titles given here are listed in full in section "For Further Reading."

WILSON'S CREEK

Stop 3	(Gibson Mill) Phillips, *Damned Yankee*, 240–56; Cutrer, *Ben McCulloch*, 219–44.
Stop 5	(Ray House) William Garrett Piston, "'Springfield Is a Vast Hospital': The Dead and Wounded at the Battle of Wilson's Creek," *Missouri Historical Review* 93 (July 1999): 345–66.
Stop 7	(Ray Cornfield) Tunnard, *Southern Record*, 28–53; Watson, *Life in the Confederate Army*, 213–31.
Stop 9	(Edwards Cabin) Castel, *Sterling Price*, 25–47; Alonzo Shelton, *Memoir of a Confederate Veteran: Alonzo Shelton, 1839–1930* (Clay County MO: Clay County Historical Museum, 1974), 1–10.
Stop 12	(Pulaski Light Battery) Woodruff, *With the Light Guns*, 39–52.
Stop 13	(Sigel's Second Position) Engle, *Yankee Dutchman*, 49–79.
Stop 14	(Sigel's Final Position) Franz Sigel, "The Flanking Column at Wilson's Creek," in *Battles and Leaders of the Civil War*, 4 vols., ed. Robert U. Johnson and C. C. Buel (New York: Century, 1887–88), 1:304–6.
Stop 15	(McCulloch's Attack) Otto C. B. Lademann, "The Battle of Wilson's Creek, August 10, 1861," *War Papers Read before the Commandery of the State of Wisconsin, Military Order of the Loyal Legion of the United States*, vol. 4 (Milwaukee: Burdick and Allen, 1919), 33–39; Tunnard, *Southern Record*, 30–32.
Stop 16	(Guibor's Battery) Richard W. Hatcher III and William Garrett Piston, *Kansans at Wilson's Creek: Soldiers' Letters from the Campaign for Southwest Missouri* (Springfield MO: Wilson's Creek National Battlefield Foundation, 1993), 65–92; Piston and Sweeney, "'Don't Yield an Inch!'" 10–26; Bearss, *Battle of Wilson's Creek*, 107–8.
Stop 18	(Bloody Hill) Michael N. Ingrisano Jr., *An Artilleryman's War: Gus Dey and the 2nd United States Artillery* (Shippensburg PA: White Mane, 1998), 68–82.

Stop 19	(Lyon Marker) John M. Schofield, *Forty-six Years in the Army* (New York: Century, 1897), 33–48.
Stop 21	(The Sinkhole) Carr, *In Fine Spirits*, 10–21; Ware, *Lyon Campaign*, 310–35; William Garrett Piston, "The First Iowa Infantry: Honor and Community in a Ninety-Day Regiment," *Civil War History* 44 (Mar. 1998): 5–23.
Stop 22	(Bloody Hill) Max S. Lale, ed., "The Boy-Bugler of the Third Texas Cavalry: The A. B. Blocker Narrative," pt. 2, *Military History of the Southwest* 14, no. 3 (1978): 147–67; Douglas Hale, *Third Texas Cavalry in the Civil War* (Norman: University of Oklahoma Press, 1988), 50–69.
Stop 23	(Historic Overlook) Jared C. Lobdell, ed., "The Civil War Journal and Letters of Colonel John Van Deusen Du Bois, April 12, 1861, to October 16, 1861," pt. 2, *Missouri Historical Review* 61 (Oct. 1966): 22–50.

PEA RIDGE

Stop 4	(Oberson's Field) Shea and Hess, *Pea Ridge*, 103–12.
Stop 6	(Foster's Farm) Brown, "Albert Pike and the Pea Ridge Atrocities," 345–59; Shea and Hess, *Pea Ridge*, 94–103.
Stop 8e	(Clemon's Field) Shea and Hess, *Pea Ridge*, 197–202.
Stop 9	(Ruddick's Field) Shea and Hess, *Pea Ridge*, 202–6.
Stop 10a	(Ruddick's Field) Sigel, "Pea Ridge," 326–31; Shea and Hess, *Pea Ridge*, 236–39, 256–59.
Stop 10c	(Welfley's Knoll) Shea and Hess, *Pea Ridge*, 243–60.
Stop 12	(Skirmish at Little Sugar Creek) Shea and Hess, *Pea Ridge*, 38–44.
Stop 14d	(The Y Junction) Shea and Hess, *Pea Ridge*, 68–78.
Stop 15c	(Bentonville Detour) Shea and Hess, *Pea Ridge*, 78–87.

WIRE ROAD

Section 2	(Springfield to Wilson's Creek) Conkling and Conkling, *Butterfield Overland Mail*, 1:184–86.

Section 3   (Madry to State Line) Conkling and Conkling, *Butterfield Overland Mail*, 1:186–91.

Section 5   (Cross Hollow to Strickler's Station) Conkling and Conkling, *Butterfield Overland Mail*, 1:195–209.

Section 6   (Strickler's Station to Fort Smith) Bearss and Gibson, *Fort Smith*, 320–31; Conkling and Conkling, *Butterfield Overland Mail*, 1:209–15.

Camp gossip. From a photograph. BLCW 1:ix

For Further Reading

Wilson's Creek   *Wilson's Creek: The Second Battle of the Civil War and the Men Who Fought It* (Chapel Hill: University of North Carolina Press, 2000) by William Garrett Piston and Richard W. Hatcher III, is the first history of the campaign and battle to be based on primary source materials. Prior to this the standard account was Edwin C. Bearss, *The Battle of Wilson's Creek* (Bozeman MT: Artcraft, 1975), an excellent brief volume that remains very worthwhile. William Brooksher, *Bloody Hill: The Civil War Battle of Wilson's Creek* (Washington: Brassey's, 1995), provides an excellent overview of events in Missouri during the summer of 1861, but it devotes only half as much space to the battle as Bearss does. Older accounts of interest include Hans Christian Adamson, *Rebellion in Missouri, 1861: Nathaniel Lyon and His Army of the West* (New York: Chilton, 1961); and Return I. Holcombe and W. S. Adams, *An Account of the Battle of Wilson's Creek* (Springfield MO: Dow and Adams, 1883). A brief tour guide accompanies Richard W. Hatcher III and William Garrett Piston, "The Battle of Wilson's Creek," *Blue and Gray* 14, no. 1 (October 1996): 8–18, 48–63.

For Missouri's place in the coming of the war and the larger Trans-Mississippi conflict, see William E. Parrish, *Turbulent Partnership: Missouri and the Union, 1861–1865* (Columbia: University of Missouri Press, 1963); and Jay Monaghan, *The Civil War on the Western Border, 1854–1865* (Boston: Little, Brown, 1955). Although he also served east of the Mississippi, Sterling Price so embodied the war in Missouri that an indispensable source is Albert Castel, *General Sterling Price and the Civil War in the West* (Baton Rouge: Louisiana State University Press, 1968). Wiley Britton, *The Civil War on the Western Border* (New York: G. P. Putnam, 1899), though an older work, remains useful.

Excellent recent biographies exist for three of the leading figures connected with Wilson's Creek: Thomas Cutrer, *Ben McCulloch and the Frontier Military Tradition* (Chapel Hill: University of North Carolina Press, 1993); Stephen D. Engle, *Yankee Dutchman: The Life of Franz Sigel* (Fayetteville: University of Arkansas Press, 1993); and Christopher Phillips, *Damned Yankee: The Life of General Nathaniel Lyon* (Columbia: University of Missouri Press, 1990).

Of the soldiers' memoirs and reminiscences that touch upon Wilson's Creek, three classics are available in reprint editions: W. H. Tunnard, *A Southern Record: The History of the Third Regiment of Louisiana Infantry* (Fayetteville: University of Arkansas Press, 1997); E. F. Ware, *The Lyon Campaign in Missouri; Being a History of the First Iowa Infantry* (Iowa City: Camp Pope, 1991); and William Watson, *Life in the Confederate Army* (Baton Rouge: Louisiana State University Press, 1995). We also highly recommend W. E. Woodruff, *With the Light Guns* (Little Rock: Eagle, n.d.); and Pat Carr, ed., *In Fine Spirits: The Civil War Letters of Ras Stirman* (Fayetteville AR: Washington County Historical Society, 1986). Thomas L. Snead, *The Fight for Missouri from the Election of Lincoln to the Death of Lyon* (New York: Charles Scribner's Sons, 1886), contains many factual errors and is biased against McCulloch, but as Price's adjutant, Snead witnessed many crucial events firsthand.

The Missouri State Guard, clearly Confederate in sympathy but technically the militia guaranteed Missourians by the Second Amendment to the Constitution, was like no other force in the Civil War. For its organization and membership, see Carolyn M. Bartles, *The Forgotten Men: The Missouri State Guard* (Shawnee Mission KS: Two Trails, 1995); and Richard C. Peterson et al., *Sterling Price's Lieutenants: A Guide to the Officers and Organization of the Missouri State Guard* (Shawnee Mission KS: Two Trails, 1995). Scholars owe an incalculable debt to the authors of these indispensable reference works. For a narrative history, see William Garrett Piston and Thomas P. Sweeney, "'Don't Yield an Inch!' The Missouri State Guard," *North and South* 2, no. 5 (June 1999): 10–26.

Pea Ridge   The standard study of the campaign and battle of Pea Ridge is William L. Shea and Earl J. Hess, *Pea Ridge: Civil War Campaign in the West* (Chapel Hill: University of North Carolina Press, 1992). A brief guide to the battlefield is in Michael A. Hughes, "Pea Ridge, or Elkhorn Tavern, Arkansas—March 7–8, 1862," *Blue and Gray Magazine* 5, no. 3 (January 1988): 8–36, 48–60. A very useful pamphlet to one segment of the March 7 battlefield north of Elkhorn Tavern is Steven R. Hayes, *A Headquarters Creek Trail: A Self-Guiding Nature and Historical Trail* (Pea Ridge National Military Park Pamphlet).

Useful, though dated, information on the historic markers that relate to the battle can be found in *Reports on the Historic Marker Program, March 10, 1963* (Rogers AR: Pea Ridge Memorial Association, 1963).

Among the participants, Franz Sigel was alone in publishing an extended description of the battle. His account is "The Pea Ridge Campaign," *Battles and Leaders of the Civil War*, vol. 1, ed. Robert U. Johnson and C. C. Buel (reprint; New York: Thomas Yoseloff, 1956), 314–34.

Finally, the most controversial episode of the battle was the scalpings that took place on Foster's farm on March 7. For a thorough discussion of this unusual incident, see Walter L. Brown, "Albert Pike and the Pea Ridge Atrocities," *Arkansas Historical Quarterly* 38 (1979): 345–59.

Prairie Grove

Prairie Grove is one of the least-studied campaigns of the Civil War. William L. Shea is preparing a full-length history, but at present the only account based on primary sources is Michael E. Banasik, *Embattled Arkansas: The Prairie Grove Campaign of 1862* (Wilmington NC: Broadfoot, 1996). It is rich in detail but lacks analysis and is not always reliable. Readable overviews are Don Montgomery, *The Battle of Prairie Grove* (Prairie Grove AR, 1996); and William L. Shea, *War in the West: Pea Ridge and Prairie Grove* (Fort Worth TX: Ryan Place, 1995). A brief tour guide to the battlefield accompanies Dave Roth, Scott Sallee, and Don Montgomery, "The Civil War in the Ozarks, April '62–January '63," *Blue and Gray* 21, no. 5 (Fall 2004): 6–25, 45–66.

The only biography of a major Prairie Grove participant is Diane Neal and Thomas W. Kremm, *Lion of the South: General Thomas C. Hindman* (Macon GA: Mercer University Press, 1993). But while biographies are rare, excellent first-person accounts are not. Among the best are Chester Barney, *Recollections of Field Service with the Twentieth Iowa Infantry Volunteers: Or, What I Saw in the War* (Davenport IA: Gazette, 1865); and J. Irvine Dungan, *History of the Nineteenth Iowa Volunteer Infantry* (Albany MO: Century Reprints, 2000). Both were written before memoirs became stylized and provide vivid accounts of the campaign. Also worthwhile is Nannie M. Tilley, ed., *Federals on the Frontier: The Diary of Benjamin F. McIntyre, 1862–1864* (Austin: University of Texas Press, 1963). An interesting tale of a Union veteran's return to Prairie Grove many years after the battle is Noble L. Prentis, *Kansas Miscellanies* (Topeka: Kansas Publishing, 1889).

Wire Road

Anyone interested in learning more about the route of Wire Road must begin with Roscoe P. Conkling and Margaret B. Conkling, *The Butterfield Overland Mail, 1857–1869*, 3 vols. (Glendale CA: Arthur H. Clark, 1947). Researching and writing the series of three books was a labor of love for the Conklings. It involved extensive travel along the historic route of the entire Overland Mail line, including Wire Road. The Conklings were pioneers in the use of onsite visits to enhance their historic study, and they made many comments on the route of Wire Road as it appeared in the 1920s and 1930s.

Interesting comments by people who had personal experience with Wire Road before and during the Civil War can be found in Hiram S. Rumfield, *Letters of an Overland Mail Agent in Utah*, ed. Archer Butler Hulbert (Worcester MA: American Antiquarian Society, 1929); and in Prentis, *Kansas Miscellanies*.

Information on Civil War soldiers buried in Fayetteville can be found in W. J. Lemke, "Pea Ridge Dead in the National Cemetery at Fayetteville," *Flashback* 12 (March 1962): 27–30. (*Flashback* is the publication of the Washington County Historical Society in Arkansas.) Van Buren's Civil War memorial is described in "Monument at Van Buren, Ark.," *Confederate Veteran* 7 (1899): 155.

The standard history of Fort Smith, at the southern end of Wire Road, is Edwin C. Bearss and Arrell M. Gibson, *Fort Smith: Little Gibraltar on the Arkansas* (Norman: University of Oklahoma Press, 1969). A brief tour of both Van Buren and Fort Smith is in Roth, Sallee, and Montgomery, "Civil War in the Ozarks," 6–25, 45–66.

Finally, the primary route south from Fort Smith is detailed in Amelia Martin, "Texas Road," *Fort Smith Historical Society Journal* 2, no. 1 (April 1978): 5–7.

In This Hallowed Ground: Guides to the Civil War Battlefields series

Chickamauga: A Battlefield Guide
with a Section on Chattanooga
Steven E. Woodworth

Gettysburg: A Battlefield Guide
Mark Grimsley and Brooks D. Simpson

Shiloh: A Battlefield Guide
Mark Grimsley and Steven E. Woodworth

Wilson's Creek, Pea Ridge, and Prairie Grove: A Battlefield Guide
with a Section on Wire Road
Earl J. Hess, Richard W. Hatcher III, William Garrett Piston, and William L. Shea

Route step. BLCW 2:530